W9-ANQ-103

About This Book

The best Webs on the Internet display stunning multimedia and provide functionality that is rapidly approaching the functionality of desktop programs. Several technologies are driving the revolution in Web content and functionality, including scripting, software components, and additions to the Web's foundation—HTML. The new Microsoft FrontPage provides you with all the tools to publish full-blown Webs rapidly that take complete advantage of the latest technologies. This book puts you in control of these tools from Day One.

The first day you use *Teach Yourself Microsoft FrontPage 97 in a Week* you build and publish a complete Web. By the end of the week you use FrontPage to build and maintain Webs that include tables, forms, scripts, Java applets, ActiveX controls, Netscape plug-ins, and many other exciting technologies.

Who Should Read This Book

Teach Yourself Microsoft FrontPage 97 in a Week is written for anyone who is familiar with Windows and who has surfed the Web. If you create documents using a word processor, you can create Web documents using FrontPage. This book is for you if

- ☐ You always wanted a Web, but you thought it would be to difficult or time-consuming to build one.
- ☐ You have your own Web that you built manually, but you want a way to maintain, edit, and expand it.
- ☐ You want to add the latest technologies to your Web.
- ☐ You want to learn about FrontPage and the capabilities of state-of-the-art Webs.

Conventions

The following sidebars will help you throughout the week:

	A Note box presents interesting pieces of information related to the surrounding discussion.

	A Tip box offers advice or teaches an easier way to do something.

	A Warning box alerts you to impending disaster and how to steer clear.

Teach
Yourself
MICROSOFT®
FRONTPAGE™
97

in a Week

Teach Yourself
MICROSOFT®
FRONTPAGE 97™
in a Week

Donald Doherty

201 West 103rd Street
Indianapolis, Indiana 46290

Copyright © 1997 by Sams.net Publishing

FIRST EDITION

All rights reserved. No part of this book shall be reproduced, stored in a retrieval system, or transmitted by any means, electronic, mechanical, photocopying, recording, or otherwise, without written permission from the publisher. No patent liability is assumed with respect to the use of the information contained herein. Although every precaution has been taken in the preparation of this book, the publisher and author assume no responsibility for errors or omissions. Neither is any liability assumed for damages resulting from the use of the information contained herein. For information, address Sams.net Publishing, 201 W. 103rd St., Indianapolis, IN 46290.

International Standard Book Number: 1-57521-225-0

Library of Congress Catalog Card Number: 96-72229

2000   99   98   97   4   3   2

Interpretation of the printing code: the rightmost double-digit number is the year of the book's printing; the rightmost single-digit, the number of the book's printing. For example, a printing code of 97-1 shows that the first printing of the book occurred in 1997.

Composed in AGaramond and MCPdigital by Macmillan Computer Publishing

Printed in the United States of America

All terms mentioned in this book that are known to be trademarks or service marks have been appropriately capitalized. Sams.net Publishing cannot attest to the accuracy of this information. Use of a term in this book should not be regarded as affecting the validity of any trademark or service mark.

Trademarks

FrontPage is a trademark of Microsoft Corporation. Microsoft is a registered trademark of Microsoft Corporation.

Publisher and President   Richard K. Swadley

Publishing Manager   Mark Taber

Director of Editorial Services   Cindy Morrow

Assistant Marketing Managers   Kristina Perry
Rachel Wolfe

Acquisitions Editor
Beverly Eppink

Development Editor
Scott Meyers

Software Development Specialist
Bob Correll

Production Editor
Nancy Albright

Indexer
Johnna VanHoose

Technical Reviewer
Ramesh Chandak

Editorial Coordinator
Katie Wise

Technical Edit Coordinator
Lorraine Schaffer

Resource Coordinator
Deborah Frisby

Editorial Assistants
Carol Ackerman
Andi Richter
Rhonda Tinch-Mize

Cover Designer
Alyssa Yesh

Book Designer
Alyssa Yesh

Copy Writer
Peter Fuller

Production Team Supervisors
Brad Chinn
Charlotte Clapp

Production
Cyndi Davis
Sonja Hart
Chris Livengood
Gene Redding

Overview

Contents

Appendixes

Acknowledgments

No author is an island. In fact, in this age an author is a part of an electronic web of coordinators, editors, designers, and other people who work hard to bring you the best book possible.

Thanks go out to all the people at Sams, especially to Beverly Eppink, whose support and encouragement kept me writing. Thanks also to Nancy Albright for her excellent editing. And finally, thanks to John Jung and Jerry Ablan for their contributions to this book.

Don Doherty

About the Authors

Lead Author

Dr. Donald Doherty

Dr. Donald Doherty is a neuroscientist and a computer expert. He received his Ph.D. from the Department of Psychobiology at University of California, Irvine. Don's computer experience includes programming large-scale computer models of brain systems. He has written on a wide range of computer topics. You can reach him by e-mail at Brainstage@sprintmail.com or visit his Web site (created using FrontPage) at http://ourworld.compuserve.com/homepages/Brainstage/ddoherty.htm.

Contributing Authors

Jerry Ablan

Jerry Ablan (munster@mcs.net) has been involved in computers since 1982 and actually remembers life before the Internet. He has worked on and owned a variety of microcomputers, and has programmed in many languages, including several that are not cool (RPG II, for example). Jerry is the author of *Developing Intranet Applications with Java* and co-author of the *Web Site Administrator's Survival Guide*. When not playing multiplayer games on the Internet with his friends, working, writing, or otherwise cavorting, Jerry and his brother Dan operate NetGeeks (http://www.netgeeks.com), an Internet presence consulting firm. As for his real job, Jerry is the Manager of Internet/Intranet Software Development at the Chicago Board Options Exchange.

John Jung

John Jung (jjung@netcom.com) is a professional systems administrator with a worldwide information services company. He graduated from the University of Southern California with a degree in Computer Science. He has been on the Internet for over eight years and spends entirely too much time online. He has worked on almost a dozen books and is the co-author of *Special Edition: Using HTML, Second Edition*.

Tell Us What You Think!

As a reader, you are the most important critic and commentator of our books. We value your opinion and want to know what we're doing right, what we could do better, what areas you'd like to see us publish in, and any other words of wisdom you're willing to pass our way. You can help us make strong books that meet your needs and give you the computer guidance you require.

Do you have access to CompuServe or the World Wide Web? Then check out our CompuServe forum by typing **GO SAMS** at any prompt. If you prefer the World Wide Web, check out our site at http://www.mcp.com.

NOTE

> If you have a technical question about this book, call the technical support line at (800) 571-5840, ext. 3668.

As the publishing manager of the group that created this book, I welcome your comments. You can fax, e-mail, or write me directly to let me know what you did or didn't like about this book—as well as what we can do to make our books stronger. Here's the information:

Fax: 317/581-4669

E-mail: newtech_mgr@sams.mcp.com

Mail: Mark Taber
Sams.net Publishing
201 W. 103rd Street
Indianapolis, IN 46290

Introduction

The best Webs on the Internet display stunning multimedia and provide functionality that is rapidly approaching the functionality of desktop programs. Several technologies are driving the revolution in Web content and functionality, including scripting, software components, and additions to the Web's foundation—HTML. The new Microsoft FrontPage provides you with all the tools to rapidly publish full-blown Webs that take complete advantage of the latest technologies. This book puts you in control of these tools from Day One.

The first day you use *Teach Yourself Microsoft FrontPage 97 in a Week,* you build and publish a complete Web. By the end of the week, you use FrontPage to build and maintain Webs that include tables, forms, scripts, Java applets, ActiveX controls, Netscape plug-ins, and many other exciting technologies.

What This Book Contains

This book is written to teach you Microsoft FrontPage in one week of two chapters per day. Nevertheless, the pace you keep is up to you. The book is designed as a course. You start with the basics and progress to increasingly advanced topics through the week. In addition to instruction, each chapter provides examples as well as exercises for you to try. *Teach Yourself Microsoft FrontPage 97 in a Week* is written with the philosophy of "learning by doing." You create and publish a Web on your first day and then expand on your initial effort by carrying out various projects throughout the rest of the week. The following sections outline what to expect.

Day 1

During Day 1, you're introduced to the FrontPage Web authoring and publishing environment while you create and publish your first Web.

Chapter 1, Building Your First Web

Chapter 1 introduces you to Microsoft FrontPage 97 while you create your first personal Web. In this chapter, you use three major FrontPage components: FrontPage Explorer, the FrontPage Editor, and the Personal Web Server. You're introduced to the FrontPage Web-authoring system while you create a Web using the Personal Web template, edit text, edit hyperlinks, use WebBots, and use the Import Wizard.

Chapter 2, Publishing Your Web

In Chapter 2, you learn how to publish your Web using FrontPage Explorer's built-in publishing tools or the Web Publishing Wizard. You can publish your Web to servers that run the FrontPage Server Extensions or those that don't, including online services such as CompuServe and America Online.

Day 2

During Day 2, you learn all the Web basics and how to dress up your Web pages with decorative elements, including graphics.

Chapter 3, Web Publishing Basics: Text, Lists, and Links

In Chapter 3, you learn how to enter, edit, and format text and how the FrontPage Editor translates your work into HTML code. You manipulate font types, sizes, and colors. You create bookmarks and hyperlinks: hyperlinks between Web pages, to bookmarks inside the same Web page, and to bookmarks on different pages. You even expand your Web by adding pages and linking them. In fact, you create an entire Web from scratch.

Chapter 4, Decorating and Expanding Your Web

In Chapter 4, you make your Web more attractive and professional-looking by adding FrontPage clip-art to your Web.

Day 3

During Day 3, you go the extra mile to make your Web pages look professional by using graphics and tables.

Chapter 5, Adding Graphics to Your Web Page

In Chapter 5, you learn how to add interesting graphics to your Web pages and how to use those graphics as navigation tools. In particular, you add an image map to your Web.

Chapter 6, Adding Tables to Your Web Page

In Chapter 6, you learn how to insert tables into your Web pages and how to use tables to create page layouts.

Day 4

During Day 4, you create sophisticated page layouts that incorporate advanced navigation methods using frames. Then you add multimedia to your Web.

Chapter 7, Including Frames in Your Web

In Chapter 7, you create frames and learn how they can enhance your Web.

Chapter 8, Adding Multimedia to Your Web Page

In Chapter 8, you add sound, animation, and video to your Web pages.

Day 5

During Day 5, you add interactive elements—forms—to your Web pages and you learn how to build scripts that tie the elements together into interactive Web pages.

Chapter 9, Adding Forms and Other Interactive Elements

In Chapter 9, you add forms to your Web and you add form fields to your forms.

Chapter 10, Tying It Together with Scripts

In Chapter 10, you explore the Internet Explorer Object Model, VBScript, and JavaScript. You learn how to enter scripts using FrontPage Editor's scripting tools, including Script Wizard.

Day 6

During Day 6, you explore how to add nearly any capability to your Web pages by adding Java applets and ActiveX controls. Then you learn to manage your growing Web using FrontPage Explorer.

Chapter 11, Adding Java Applets and ActiveX Controls

In Chapter 11, you learn how Java applets and ActiveX controls work. You add them and a Netscape plug-in to your Web.

Chapter 12, Managing Your Web

In Chapter 12, you learn how to carry out Web-wide procedures from FrontPage Explorer. Specifically, you delete a Web, import and export files, spell check your Web, and perform a find-and-replace procedure on your Web.

Day 7

During Day 7, the final day, you learn how to use FrontPage features that require your Web to be published on a server with the FrontPage Extended Server.

Chapter 13, Connecting Your Web to a Database

In Chapter 13, you learn how to add database connectivity to your Web.

Chapter 14, Using WebBots with an Extended Server

In Chapter 14, you explore WebBots and learn how to use a wide variety of WebBots in your Webs.

In addition to the week of lessons, there are eight appendixes. The first six provide ready references for FrontPage installation, wizards and templates, VBScript, JavaScript, HTML, and sites and resources. Appendix G provides answers to the Quizzes you'll find at the end of each chapter. Appendix H tells you What's on the CD-ROM.

Teach Yourself Microsoft FrontPage 97 in a Week is written for anyone who is familiar with Windows and who has surfed the Web. If you create documents using a word processor, you can create Web documents using FrontPage. Whether you're a beginner or an expert, publish and maintain state-of-the-art Webs today!

DAY

1

Chapter 1

Building Your First Web

Create a Web in minutes with Microsoft FrontPage. The FrontPage Web authoring and publishing software does all the drudgery work for you, enabling you to focus on creating the Web's content: the creative text, graphics, and other materials that you want in your Web. FrontPage gives you the power to create content that uses all the most up-to-date Web technologies, such as frames and ActiveX controls, while making the task relatively easy—even fun.

In this chapter, you're introduced to Microsoft FrontPage 97 while you create your first personal Web. The three major FrontPage components that you use in this chapter are

- ☐ FrontPage Explorer
- ☐ FrontPage Editor
- ☐ Personal Web Server

You're introduced to the FrontPage Web-authoring system while

☐ Creating a Web using the Personal Web template

☐ Editing text

☐ Editing hyperlinks

☐ Using WebBots

☐ Using the Import Wizard

FrontPage creates a Web for you and then you edit the Web's content to your liking.

NOTE

You need to install the FrontPage Web authoring and publishing software before you continue. Step-by-step installation instructions are provided in Appendix A, "Installing FrontPage." Instructions on how to set up FrontPage's Personal Web Server are also included in Appendix A.

FrontPage Explorer

FrontPage Explorer is the hub for all you do in FrontPage. You almost always begin creating a new Web or working with an existing Web by opening FrontPage Explorer.

Open FrontPage Explorer by clicking on the Start button located on the Windows Taskbar. Select the FrontPage Explorer command from the Programs, Microsoft FrontPage menu. FrontPage Explorer opens with the Getting Started with Microsoft FrontPage dialog box displayed, as shown in Figure 1.1.

Figure 1.1.

FrontPage Explorer displays the Getting Started with Microsoft FrontPage dialog box on startup.

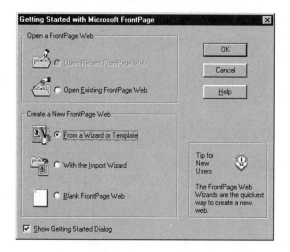

Creating a Web

The Getting Started with Microsoft FrontPage dialog box gives you easy access to Web creation tools and to any existing Webs that you might have. There is also an area in the lower right of the dialog box that displays helpful tips. Because you're building your first Web, you use the tools available in the Create a New FrontPage Web area. Select the From a Wizard or Template radio button and then click on the OK button. The New FrontPage Web dialog box opens, as shown in Figure 1.2.

Figure 1.2.

Select a wizard or template from the New FrontPage Web dialog box.

Several wizards and templates are listed in the New FrontPage Web dialog box. Select Personal Web from the list and click on the OK button. The Personal Web Template dialog box appears, as shown in Figure 1.3.

 NOTE

Descriptions of all the Web wizards and templates are provided in Appendix B, "Wizards and Templates."

Figure 1.3.

Type a Web location and give your Web a name in the Personal Web Template dialog box.

You must select either a Web location or a server in the Personal Web Template dialog box's Web Server or File Location combobox and then type a name for your Web in the Name of the New FrontPage Web textbox.

 A computer *server* is similar to a server in a restaurant. You tell the server what you want and the server brings it to you. You learn more about why you need a server with FrontPage later in this chapter in the section The FrontPage Personal Server.

Create your Web page without using a server by typing the path of a folder in the Web Server or File Location combobox. You should create an empty folder set aside exclusively to hold your Webs. Create a folder named Webs, for instance, by typing C:\Webs into the Web Server or File Location combobox, as shown in Figure 1.3. You see in a moment that FrontPage creates the folder for you if it doesn't already exist.

 NOTE

> If you installed the Personal Web Server, your drive contains a folder named FrontPage Webs. You cannot select this folder for the Webs you create without the server. You must create a new folder that is not inside the FrontPage Webs folder.

Type the name of your Web in the Name of New FrontPage Web textbox. Because this is your personal Web, give it your last name. Click on the OK button. A FrontPage Explorer dialog box appears asking you if you want to create the C:\Webs folder, as shown in Figure 1.4.

Figure 1.4.

FrontPage can create a new folder for you.

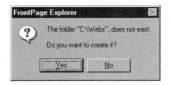

Click on the Yes button. FrontPage creates the Webs folder and places several folders and files in the Webs folder, including a folder with the name of your Web. This folder contains all the pages of your new personal Web that are displayed in FrontPage Explorer, as shown in Figure 1.5. You've built your first Web!

Figure 1.5.
FrontPage Explorer displays your new personal Web.

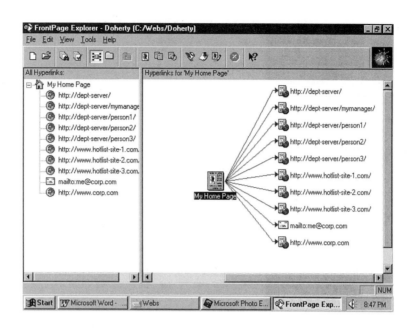

Understanding the Interface

At first glance, the FrontPage Explorer window looks like the Windows 95 Explorer (or Windows NT Explorer). In fact, their organization is nearly identical, except that with FrontPage Explorer you're looking at Web pages, hyperlinked objects, and the hyperlinks themselves rather than files, folders, and directories. In Table 1.1, objects that fill similar roles between the two Explorers are listed across columns.

Table 1.1. Similar objects between two Explorers.

FrontPage Explorer	Windows Explorer
Hyperlinked objects	Folders
Objects	Files
Hyperlinks	Directories

NOTE

Like files in Windows Explorer, objects in FrontPage Explorer are diverse. However, there isn't a catch-all word, such as "file," for them yet. Objects in the FrontPage Explorer list include HTML documents, URLs, images, e-mail addresses, and so forth.

You can see the similarities between these objects by looking at their organization in FrontPage Explorer. First, change the FrontPage Explorer window to Folder View by selecting the Folder View command from the View menu or by clicking on the toolbar's Folder View button. The FrontPage Explorer window should change to look something like the one in Figure 1.6.

Figure 1.6.

The FrontPage Explorer window displayed in Folder View.

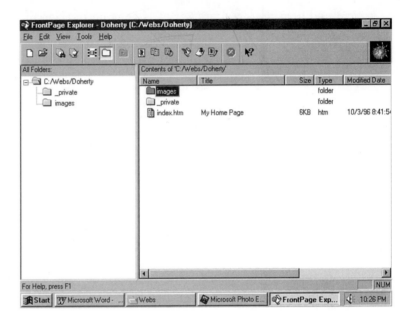

FrontPage Explorer in Folder View is nearly identical to the Windows Explorer. Folders display in the left pane, the All Folders pane, in a hierarchy that shows their directory relationships. The top folder, C:/Webs/Doherty, is the root folder for this Web. You see two folders arrayed under the top folder and moved to the right. There is a line from C:/Webs/ Doherty to _private and one to images. These lines trace the connection from the top of the folder hierarchy, from C:/Webs/Doherty, to the next lower level—that is, to the two folders found inside the top folder.

You can see the same two folders, _private and images, in the right pane, the Contents pane, when the C:/Webs/Doherty folder is selected in the All Folders pane. In addition, you can see the file index.htm. These are the contents of the C:/Webs/Doherty folder.

NOTE

FrontPage Explorer displays directory names using the Internet standard slash (/) rather than the MS DOS and Windows standard backslash (\).

Just as in Windows Explorer, you can expand and collapse the hierarchy in the left pane by clicking on the plus or minus sign displayed to the left of a folder. You can double-click on folders in the right pane to move down in the folder hierarchy, or you can double-click on the files to open them.

Now return to FrontPage Explorer's Hyperlink View by selecting the Hyperlink View command from the View menu or by clicking on the Hyperlink View toolbar button. FrontPage Explorer should look something like Figure 1.5.

The FrontPage Explorer window's left pane is the All Hyperlinks pane. This is something of a misnomer, because the left pane actually shows all the Web's objects. These objects include Web pages, URLs, images, e-mail addresses, and a wide array of other things. It's true that the relationships between these objects, their hyperlinks, are shown in the same way that the directory relationships are shown between folders in Folder View. If your Web has an unlinked HTML document, image, or other object, however, it appears in the All Hyperlinks pane.

The right pane is the Hyperlinks for pane. The object selected in the left pane is displayed, as an icon, in the center of the Hyperlinks for pane. All the hyperlinks contained by that object are displayed as lines sweeping to the right and pointing to icons representing the objects that they link to. For instance, in Figure 1.5, the My Home Page object, an HTML page, is selected in the All Hyperlinks pane. An icon for the My Home Page object displays in the center of the Hyperlinks for pane, and several lines with arrowheads point right to icons representing the objects that My Home Page is linked to, including several URLs and a single e-mail address.

NOTE

> The Web page and e-mail addresses currently part of your personal Web are dummy addresses. They are there as placeholders until you replace them with real addresses. You do this soon, in the FrontPage Editor section.

The left pane in Hyperlinks View displays the contents of the object selected in the right pane in a similar way to how a folder's contents is displayed in the left pane in Folder View. Rather than files and other folders, hyperlinks and Web objects are displayed.

Select the second URL from the top of the All Hyperlinks pane list named http://dept-server/mymanager/. The FrontPage Explorer window should look something like Figure 1.7.

 NEW TERM A *Uniform Resource Locator (URL)* is an address on the World Wide Web (WWW). The address represents a resource on the Web. Resources include HTML documents, images, sound files, video files, Internet e-mail addresses, and nearly everything else available over the Web.

Figure 1.7.

A line with an arrowhead pointing from the left represents a hyperlink to an object.

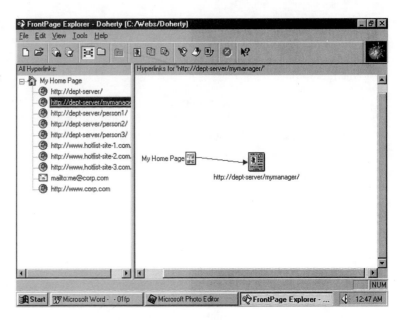

The hyperlink to the URL displays as a line sweeping from the left to the icon in the center of the window representing the URL. The hyperlink doesn't connect to the URL itself, of course, but to the resource at the address represented by the URL.

You can expand and collapse the hierarchy in the left pane by clicking on the plus or minus sign displayed to the left of a Web object. You can double-click on Web objects in the right pane to open them. For instance, a double-click on a URL in the Hyperlinks for pane results in your Web browser launching and loading the resource found at that URL.

The FrontPage Editor

You've built your first Web, but it isn't very personal. The Personal Web template set up a Web page named My Home Page, with generic text, several hyperlinks using phony URLs, and a fake e-mail address. In this section, you replace all the placeholder text, URLs, and the e-mail address with your own real information. You transform My Home Page into your personal home page with the FrontPage Editor.

The FrontPage Web authoring environment is completely integrated. Open the FrontPage Editor from FrontPage Explorer. Select My Home Page in FrontPage Explorer's All Hyperlinks pane, then double-click on the My Home Page icon in the Hyperlinks for pane. The FrontPage Editor launches and loads the My Home Page HTML document, as shown in Figure 1.8. You're ready to edit My Home Page.

Figure 1.8.

*The FrontPage Editor
loaded with My
Home Page.*

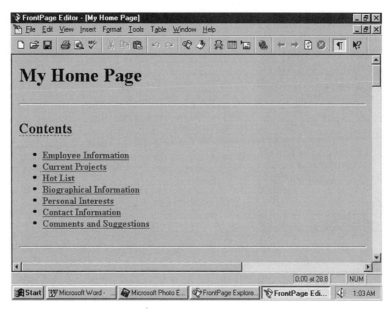

Editing Text

Start turning My Home Page into your personal Web page by editing the title. Double-click on My in the title at the top of the FrontPage Editor window. My should be highlighted with white letters and a black background. Now simply type your last name (like Doherty's shown in Figure 1.9).

You enter and edit text in the FrontPage Editor in the same way that you enter and edit text in most word processors today. In fact, if you're familiar with Microsoft Word, you're familiar with many of the text editing features of the FrontPage Editor.

You decide that using your last name in the title of your Web page is too formal and you want to reverse the previous change. Select Edit, Undo Typing or click on the Undo toolbar button. The title reads My Home Page again.

Type your first name, possessive—Don's, for example. Now the title reads Don's Home Page. This is better, except you notice that the title bar still says My Home Page. This is the title that people will see in their browsers' title bars and in their Favorites lists.

You want to edit the title displayed in the title bar so that it's the same as the title at the top of the Web page. Right-click on the Web page in your FrontPage Editor and select Page Properties from the shortcut menu. The Page Properties dialog box appears, as shown in Figure 1.10.

Figure 1.9.

Use the FrontPage Editor like any WYSIWYG word processor.

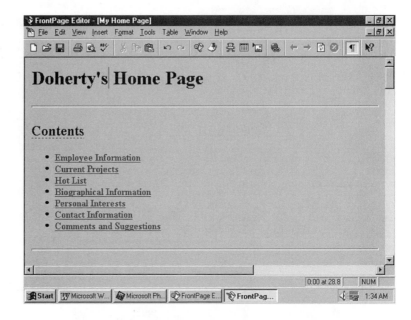

Figure 1.10.

Use the Page Properties dialog box to change your Web page's title.

Select the General tab if the General page isn't already open. Change My Home Page in the Title textbox to Don's Home Page (or your equivalent). Click on the OK button. Your home page should look similar to the one in Figure 1.11 (except your name should be used instead of mine).

Figure 1.11.

Don's Home Page is displayed at the top of the page and in the title bar.

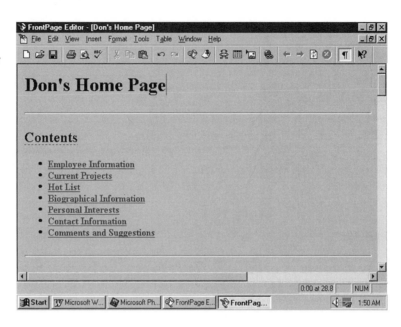

Hyperlinks to Bookmarks

Below the title and a horizontal line you should see the word Contents with a blue dashed underline. The blue dashed underline indicates that the word has been set up as a bookmark. A bookmark is an anchor that you can place anywhere on a Web page. You can create hyperlinks from the same page or from other pages to the bookmark. In this case, a table of contents is titled Contents, followed by several hyperlinks in a bulleted list to bookmarks throughout the Web page. The title, Contents, is itself a bookmark so that you can easily return to the page's table of contents by clicking on a hyperlink to the Contents bookmark.

Right-click on Contents and select Bookmark Properties from the shortcut menu. The Bookmark dialog box appears, as shown in Figure 1.12.

The word in the Bookmark Name textbox—top—is the Content bookmark's name. All other bookmarks defined on the page are listed in the Other Bookmarks on this Page list. You can select a bookmark name in the Other Bookmarks on this Page list and then click on the **G**oto button to jump to the bookmark. Click on the Cancel button to close the Bookmark dialog box.

Below Contents is a bulleted list of the page's contents. Each entry in the bulleted list is blue with a solid blue underline. This means that each entry is a hyperlink. Right-click on

Employee Information and select Hyperlink Properties from the shortcut menu. The Edit
Hyperlink dialog box appears, as shown in Figure 1.13.

Figure 1.12.

*Use the Bookmark
dialog box to navigate
a page's bookmarks.*

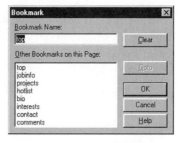

Figure 1.13.

*Use the Edit
Hyperlink dialog box
to edit and create
hyperlinks to book-
marks.*

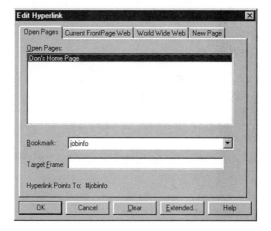

The Edit Hyperlink dialog box's Open Pages page has a handy Bookmark drop-down list.
Select the Web page that you want to create a hyperlink to in the Open Pages list. Only pages
opened in the FrontPage Editor are in this list. Once you select the page you want, select the
bookmark you want to link to in the Bookmark drop-down list. Employee Information is
currently linked to jobinfo, a bookmark to Employee Information just below the Content
bulleted list. Leave the hyperlink as it is by clicking on the Cancel button to close the Edit
Hyperlink dialog box.

All the bookmarks and bookmark hyperlinks on your personal Web page work well without
modification. However, the hyperlinks to the World Wide Web contain dummy URLs,
placeholders, which must be modified.

Hyperlinks to the World Wide Web

Move down the Web page to the Employee Information section shown in Figure 1.14.

Figure 1.14.

Modify the various placeholders in the Employee Information section.

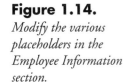

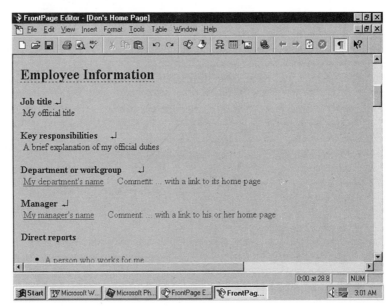

Modify the various placeholders, such as Job title and My official title, using the FrontPage Editor's text editing capabilities. Edit up through Department or workgroup. Under this heading is the hyperlinked text (blue text with a solid blue underline) My department's name.

Modifying hyperlinked text takes special care or the hyperlink is wiped out. Select the text, My department's name, starting from the second letter y through the second to the last letter m and type in your own text: Sams, for instance. Now you can delete the first and last letters. If you type over either the first or last letter of hyperlinked text, it will cease to be hyperlinked. Your page should look something like Figure 1.15.

Right-click on what is now the hyperlinked Sams text (or your own text) and select Hyperlink Properties from the shortcut menu. The Edit Hyperlink dialog box appears. Select the World Wide Web tab if it isn't selected already. The Edit Hyperlink dialog box's World Wide Web page is shown in Figure 1.16.

Figure 1.15.

The Employee Information section after editing.

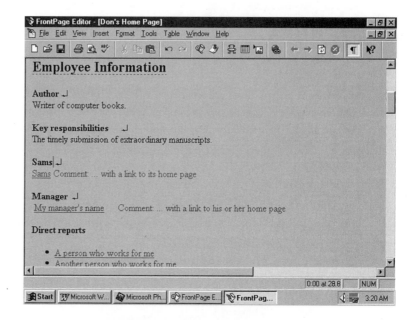

Figure 1.16.

Use the Edit Hyperlink dialog box's World Wide Web page to create hyperlinks to the Web.

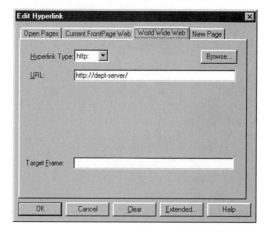

You can see the dummy URL, http://dept-server/, in the URL textbox. Notice that http: is selected in the Hyperlink Type drop-down list. HTTP stands for HyperText Transfer Protocol and is the protocol used by Web servers to transfer Web pages to your browser. Set the Hyperlink Type drop-down list to http: whenever you want to create a hyperlink to a Web page. There are several other kinds of hyperlinks you can make (see Table 1.2).

Table 1.2. Hyperlink types.

Protocol	Description
file	Use local disk access.
ftp	Use a File Transfer Protocol site.
gopher	Use a Gopher menu system.
http	Use a standard Web server.
https	Use a Windows NT Web server.
mailto	Send e-mail.
news	Connect with a news server.
telnet	Start a Telnet session.
wais	Use a Wide Area Information System.

To find the URL you're looking for, the Sams Web page (or another page of your choosing), click on the Browse button. The Microsoft Internet Explorer or your current Web browser appears, as in Figure 1.17.

Figure 1.17.

Browse the Web for the page you want.

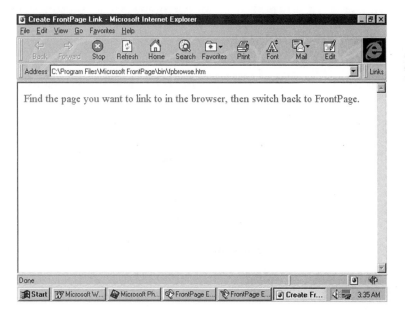

Be sure that you're connected with the Internet, then browse the Web for the page you want. When you find the page, switch back to the FrontPage Editor. The URL of the current page in your browser is in the Edit Hyperlink dialog box's URL text field. Click on the OK button to close the Edit Hyperlink dialog box. You created your own hyperlink to the Internet.

NOTE   Remember to save your document periodically by selecting the Save command from the File menu or by clicking on the Save toolbar button.

Hyperlinks to E-Mail

There is one last type of hyperlink to look at on your personal Web page: the hyperlink to an e-mail address. When a person clicks on a hyperlink to an e-mail address, a new e-mail message form opens with the hyperlink's e-mail address placed in the To field. This makes sending mail a snap, because people visiting your page simply click on the hyperlink, type in their messages, then click on the Send button.

Your personal Web page has a placeholder for a hyperlink to e-mail in the Contact Information section, as shown in Figure 1.18.

Figure 1.18.

Text hyperlinked to an e-mail address displays in blue with a solid blue underline.

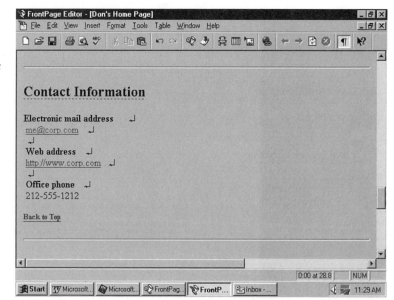

The hyperlink to an e-mail address is indicated by the blue text with a solid blue underline under the heading Electronic mail address that reads me@corp.com. Edit me@corp.com to reflect your own e-mail address. Use the same editing method as before when you edited a hyperlink to a page on the World Wide Web. That is, highlight all but the first and last letters of the hyperlinked text. Type your new text. Then delete the first and last letters, which are the remnants of the old text. This preserves the hyperlink.

Right-click on the hyperlink to an e-mail address and select the Hyperlink Properties command from the shortcut menu. The Edit Hyperlink dialog box appears. Select the World Wide Web tab if it isn't selected already so that the World Wide Web sheet displays as in Figure 1.19.

Figure 1.19.

Create a hyperlink to an e-mail address in the Edit Hyperlink dialog box.

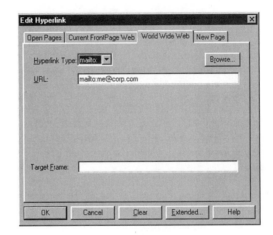

Notice that mailto: is selected in the Hyperlink Type drop-down list. MAILTO is the hyperlink protocol for e-mail listed in Table 1.2.

Edit the text following the protocol name (me@corp.com) by typing in your own e-mail address. Then click on the OK button to close the Edit Hyperlink dialog box. Now when someone clicks on this hyperlink, a new message form opens with your e-mail address already placed in the To field.

Comment and Timestamp WebBots

You may have noticed some of the areas with purple text in your Web page. When your cursor moves over these areas, it turns into a robot with an arrow (see Figure 1.20). These areas are occupied by Comment WebBots, one of several WebBots available in FrontPage.

Figure 1.20.

The cursor is turned into a robot when pointing at the Comment WebBot.

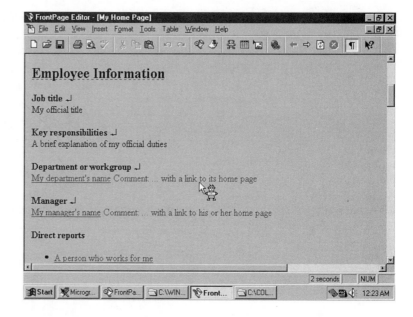

WebBots are automated entities that you place in your Web page to do your chores for you. Some WebBots require special server extensions, but many, including the Comments WebBot, don't.

 NOTE

You learn more about servers and the server extensions later in this chapter, in the Personal Web Server section.

Double-click on the Comments WebBot to open the Comment dialog box, as shown in Figure 1.21.

Type your comments in the Comment dialog box. Your comments should document your Web page for when you or someone else is editing it. Comments in the Comment WebBot show up only during editing; they don't appear on a Web page in a browser.

Another useful WebBot is on your personal Web page, the Timestamp Bot. You find the Timestamp Bot at the bottom of your page, displaying a date (see Figure 1.22). The Timestamp Bot displays the date the page was last edited.

Figure 1.21.

Edit comments in the Comment dialog box.

Figure 1.22.

The Timestamp Bot displays the date when the page was last edited.

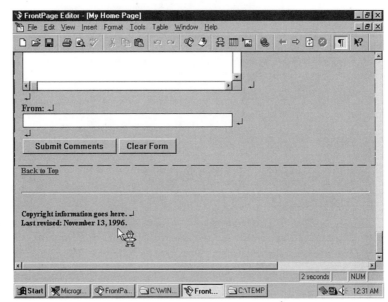

Double-click on the Timestamp Bot to open the Timestamp Bot Properties dialog box, as shown in Figure 1.23. Timestamp Bot can display the time in addition to the date. Select the time format in the Time Format drop-down list to display the time.

Timestamp Bot is also capable of displaying the date of the last automatic update. Automatic updates and Timestamp Bot's notice of an automatic update require the use of server extensions, discussed later in this chapter in the section The Personal Web Server.

Figure 1.23.

Change Timestamp
Bot's display properties
in the Timestamp Bot
Properties dialog box.

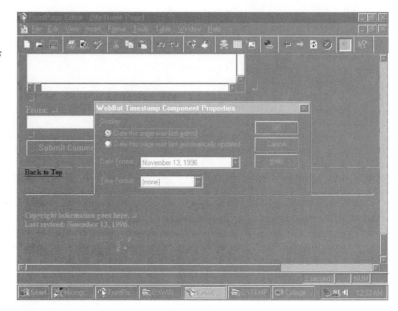

Forms and WebBots

The final feature to look at on your new personal Web page is forms. In the page's Comments and Suggestions section, you see a Comments text area and a From textbox, as shown in Figure 1.24. You also see two buttons below the From textbox. All these elements are surrounded by a rectangle composed of dashed lines. The rectangle outlines a form, and each of the elements—textboxes and buttons—is a form field.

At the top of the form is a comment field created using a Comment Bot. It says that when the contents typed into the form are stored, they are stored in a text database file named HOMERESP.TXT. You click on the Submit Comments button to store the contents of the form.

Test out the form. To test it, you need to load the Web page into a browser. Select the Preview in Browser command from the File menu and the Preview in Browser dialog box opens, as shown in Figure 1.25.

Select the browser you want to use for previewing your Web page. You can add browsers that are installed on your computer but are not listed in the Browser list by clicking on the Add button. The Add Browser dialog box appears, as shown in Figure 1.26.

Figure 1.24.

The text area and textbox are forms.

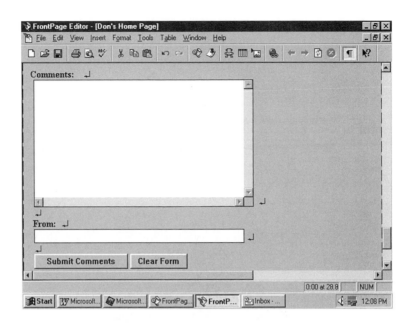

Figure 1.25.

Select a browser in the Preview in Browser dialog box.

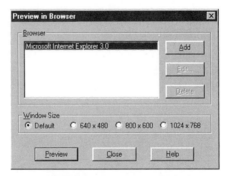

Figure 1.26.

Add browsers through the Add Browser dialog box.

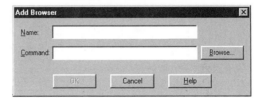

Type the name of the browser in the Name textbox. Then type its path and program filename. Alternatively, click on the Browse button and find and select the program file. Click on the Add Browser dialog box's OK button.

If you want, you can select a particular window size to open your browser with in the Window Size area.

Once you select the browser you want, click on the Preview button and the browser opens with your Web page loaded.

NOTE

> The Microsoft Internet Explorer is the default preview browser. If you want to preview your Web page using the Internet Explorer, you can click on the Preview in Browser toolbar button and bypass the Preview in Browser dialog box.

Click on the Comments and Suggestions hyperlink in your Web page's Contents section. This hyperlink takes you to the form under the Comments and Suggestions bookmark.

Type some text in the scrolling textbox titled Comments and the textbox titled From, as shown in Figure 1.27.

Figure 1.27.

Type some text in the form's text fields.

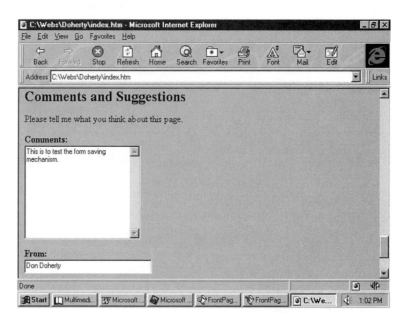

Click on the Submit Comments button. The Security Information dialog box appears, as shown in Figure 1.28.

Figure 1.28.
The Internet Explorer Security Information dialog box.

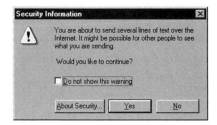

Click on the Yes button. Nothing seems to happen.

Check for the file, HOMERESP.TXT. Activate FrontPage Explorer through Window's taskbar and change to folder view by clicking on the Folder View toolbar button. Update the screen with any new files that may have been added by selecting the Refresh command from the View menu. You should see something similar to Figure 1.29. HOMERESP.TXT is not listed.

Figure 1.29.
HOMERESP.TXT was not created.

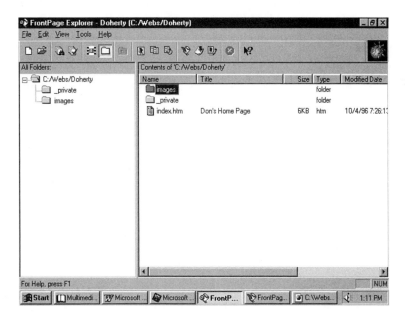

Personal Web template's form content is saved using the Save Results WebBot Component, which must have the FrontPage Server Extensions available to work. If the server you're using doesn't have the FrontPage Server Extensions available—and most don't—you cannot use some WebBots. There are some features that you're unable to use, but there are so many available to you that FrontPage's usefulness remains undiminished. In fact, most of what you learn this week assumes that your server doesn't give you access to any special features.

It's recommended that you continue to create Webs without using the FrontPage Personal Server if the server that you publish on doesn't supply you with FrontPage Server Extensions. That way, when you test your Webs, you know to remove WebBots that don't work. On the other hand, if the server you publish on does supply you with the FrontPage Server Extensions, use the Personal Web Server.

The Personal Web Server

FrontPage provides you with a personal Web server so that you can build and test Webs that use server extensions "offline." In other words, you can build the Web and then publish it on a server later—if your server provides the FrontPage Server Extensions, you want to use the Personal Web Server.

The Personal Web Server is tightly integrated with the rest of FrontPage, so there is little that you need to do that is different from the previous sections. You create a Web starting with FrontPage Explorer's Getting Started with Microsoft FrontPage dialog box. As in earlier sections, you can create a personal Web using the Personal Web template, described in the next section, Creating a Personal Web Server Web. You will find the section redundant, however, if you've followed along and built a personal Web without the Personal Web Server. You can import the Web you've already completed to a Web supported by the Personal Web Server by using the Import Wizard, described in the section Import a Web with Import Wizard.

Creating a Personal Web Server Web

Creating a Web supported by the Personal Web Server is nearly identical to creating one without server support. Open FrontPage Explorer by clicking on the Taskbar Start button and select the FrontPage Explorer command from the Programs, Microsoft FrontPage menu. FrontPage Explorer opens, displaying its Getting Started with Microsoft FrontPage dialog box.

In the Create a New FrontPage Web area, select the From a Wizard or Template radio button and then click on the OK button. The New FrontPage Web dialog box opens. Select Personal Web from the Templates or Wizard list and click on the OK button. The Personal Web

Template dialog box appears. Select or type a server name into the Web Server or File Location combobox and type the name of your personal Web in the Name of New FrontPage Web textbox, as shown in Figure 1.30.

NOTE

> The FrontPage Personal Web Server is referred to as localhost by default.

Figure 1.30.

Create a Web while using a Web server.

Click on the OK button. The various folders and files for your new personal Web are generated and the FrontPage Personal Web Server is started. After a few moments, the Name and Password Required dialog box appears, as shown in Figure 1.31.

Figure 1.31.

Enter your name and password.

Enter your name and password as you entered them when you installed the FrontPage Personal Web Server, then click on the OK button.

NOTE

> For information on installing the FrontPage Personal Web Server, see the section Personal Web Server in Appendix A, "Installing FrontPage."

Your new personal Web is displayed in FrontPage Explorer, as shown in Figure 1.32.

Figure 1.32.

FrontPage Explorer displays your new personal Web.

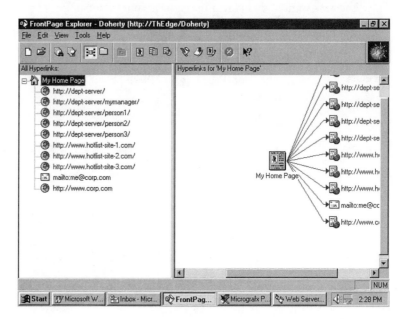

Importing a Web with Import Wizard

You can import existing Webs into the FrontPage development environment. Import the personal Web that you created earlier without the Personal Web Server.

Open FrontPage Explorer by clicking on the Taskbar Start button and select the FrontPage Explorer command from the Programs, Microsoft FrontPage menu. FrontPage Explorer opens, displaying its Getting Started with Microsoft FrontPage dialog box.

In the Create a New FrontPage Web area, select the With the Import Wizard radio button and then click on the OK button. The Import Web Wizard dialog box opens. Select or type a server name in the Web Server or File Location combobox and type the name of your personal Web in the Name of New FrontPage Web textbox, as shown in Figure 1.33.

Figure 1.33.

*Select a server and
type the new name for
an existing Web in the
Import Web Wizard
dialog box.*

Click on the OK button. Import Web Wizard's Choose Directory page opens, as shown in
Figure 1.34. Type in the full directory of the folder where the Web that you want to import
is found, or find it through the browse feature by clicking on the Browse button. If some of
the Web's files are in subdirectories, select the Include subdirectories checkbox. Click on the
Next button.

Figure 1.34.

*Enter the existing
Web's directory in
Import Web Wizard's
Choose Directory
page.*

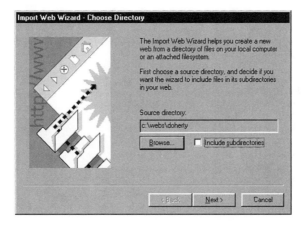

Import Web Wizard's Edit File List page opens, as shown in Figure 1.35. All the files that
will be imported are listed in the Files list. If there is a file that you don't want in the new Web,
exclude it by selecting the file in the Files list and clicking on the Exclude button. Once you're
satisfied with the Files list, click on the Next button.

Import Web Wizard's Finish page opens, as shown in Figure 1.36. The Finish page gives you
a pat on the back for a job well done. Click on the Finish button.

Figure 1.35.

Exclude any files that you wish to exclude from the Edit File List page's Files list.

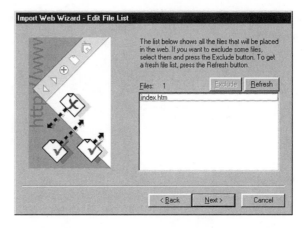

Figure 1.36.

Import Web Wizard's Finish page gives you a pat on the back.

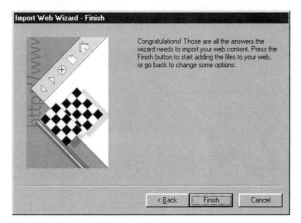

Your newly imported Web now appears in FrontPage Explorer.

Forms and WebBots

Everything in your personal Web works without the FrontPage Server Extensions except for the Comments and Suggestions form. Now that you've created or imported a personal Web that uses server extensions, take another look at the Comments and Suggestions form.

Open your personal Web's home page in the FrontPage Editor. Preview the page in a browser by clicking on the Preview in Browser toolbar button or by selecting the Preview in Browser command on the File menu. Go to the page's Comments and Suggestions section and type some sample text in the Comments scrolling textbox. Type your name in the From textbox, as shown in Figure 1.37.

Figure 1.37.

Type some text in the form's text fields.

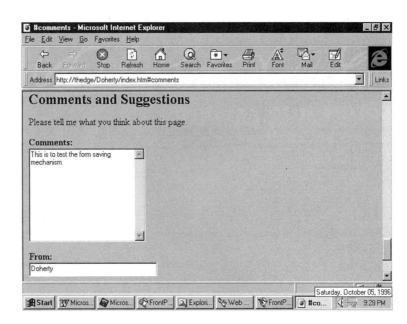

Click on the Submit Comments button. The Security Information dialog box appears. Click on the Yes button. Something happens and a confirmation page appears, as shown in Figure 1.38.

Figure 1.38.

The Form Confirmation page appears after submitting a form.

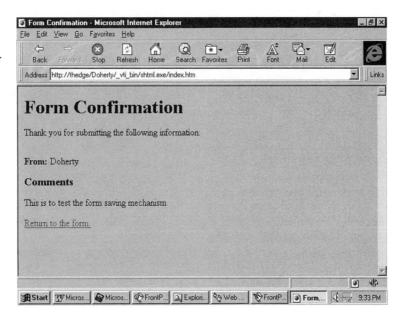

Check for the file HOMERESP.TXT. Activate FrontPage Explorer through Window's taskbar and change to Folder View by clicking on the Folder View toolbar button. Update the screen with any new files that may have been added by selecting the Refresh command from the View menu. You should see something similar to Figure 1.39. HOMERESP.TXT is listed.

Figure 1.39.
HOMERESP.TXT
was created.

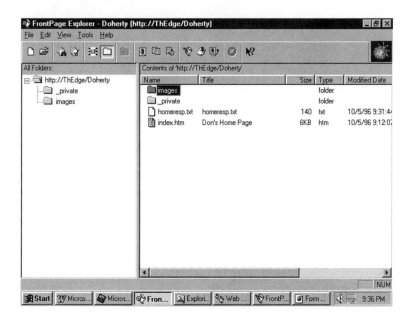

Text typed into the forms created by Personal Web Template is saved using the Save Results WebBot Component, a WebBot that works only if the FrontPage Server Extensions are available. The Personal Web Server provides the server extensions. Build Webs that you'll publish to servers with the FrontPage Server Extensions with your Personal Web Server.

Summary

Congratulations! It's your first day using FrontPage and you already built yourself a Web. You are acquainted with the FrontPage Web authoring environment and the Personal Web Server. You also know how to enter and edit text, edit hyperlinks, and work with some of the WebBots. Continue to edit your personal Web until you've personalized all the generic text and placeholder links the way you want them. In the next chapter, you publish your Web. The rest of this book shows you how to improve on your first Web by displaying splashy graphics, using multimedia, and by using cutting edge technologies such as Java applets and ActiveX controls.

Q&A

Q What does it mean to publish my Web to a server?

A You must put your Web onto a computer that is accessible to other people on the Internet. Most of the time you don't want people on the Internet to access your personal computer, because of security reasons and also because it's very likely to be a slow connection. There are companies that provide space on a computer for your Webs so that they can be accessed from the Internet. Chapter 2, "Publishing Your Web," goes into detail on Web publishing.

Q How do I know that the server I publish supports the FrontPage Server Extensions?

A The short answer is that you need to ask your Web server provider. Chapter 2 goes into detail on Web publishing.

Q How do I update the date in the Timestamp WebBot?

A The date is automatically updated whenever you open the page containing the Timestamp WebBot in the FrontPage Editor. You do nothing.

Workshop

You created a Web using the Personal Web Template. Experiment with some of the other templates and wizards available in FrontPage Explorer (they're listed and described briefly in Appendix B). You get a sense of the wide range of possible Webs as you work with them.

Quiz

1. What are the three major parts of the FrontPage Web-authoring system?

2. The FrontPage Web-authoring system is tightly integrated. Can you figure out the fastest way to get from the FrontPage Editor to FrontPage Explorer? (*Hint:* Look at the FrontPage Editor's toolbar buttons.)

3. How do you enter and edit text in the FrontPage Editor?

Chapter 2

Publishing Your Web

You can publish Webs developed by using FrontPage to nearly any server. You can even build your Webs directly on servers that run the FrontPage Server Extensions. Doing so can make a separate publishing stage unnecessary. However, it's generally a good idea to keep Web development and Web publishing separate so that you can always have a working Web available even while you revise it. That's why the Microsoft Personal Web Server, included with FrontPage, is useful.

FrontPage Explorer provides built-in tools for publishing your Web. However, the built-in FrontPage Explorer Web publishing tools require that you publish to a server that runs the FrontPage Server Extensions. There are many servers that don't run the FrontPage Server Extensions—in fact, most don't. The FrontPage Web authoring and publishing package includes the Web Publishing Wizard to fill the gap. The Web Publishing Wizard publishes your Webs to servers that aren't running the FrontPage Server Extensions, including online services such as CompuServe and America Online.

In this chapter, you

- [ ] Learn basic terminology
- [ ] Look at traditional forms of publishing
- [ ] Publish your Web from FrontPage Explorer
- [ ] Publish your Web using the Web Publishing Wizard

Basic Terminology

FrontPage uses a number of terms and phrases that might be new to you. Some of these terms relate only to FrontPage and how it's structured. Other terms are in relatively wide use and refer to a generally accepted concept.

Publishing a Web

One of the most common terms used in Intranets, and some Internet Service Providers (ISPs), is *publishing a Web*. In these environments, there are usually multiple Web servers. Only one of these Web servers is the *real* Web server—"real" in the sense that it's the one that everyone on the Internet will try to access. All the other servers are either Intranet servers, or *staging area servers,* or both. The staging area servers are used to allow Web authors to create and debug their Web pages. That is, all new contents, new CGI-BIN scripts, or whatever, are created and tested out on that system.

The staging area serves two important functions. The first is to allow Web authors to create, edit, and fine-tune their content; for example, if they're creating new Web pages, they can see how certain backgrounds will look. The staging area can also be a place where content is screened out before it's made public (so that the wording or images for a Web page can be screened out). Another important function of a staging area server is to test out scripts and programs. Many people like to add some pizzazz to their Web pages with JavaScript or CGI-BIN scripts. The staging area allows these scripts to be tested before being put on the real server. The network administrator can look over any new such programs and make sure they're safe to use. Additionally, by putting these programs on a staging area, they can be easier to debug.

So what does all this mean to the word "publish"? It simply means that you want your Web page to be copied over from the staging area to the real Web server. Because FrontPage comes with its own Web server, you can use it as your own personal staging area. You can see how your Java applets look under your personal Web server before you publish it.

FrontPage's Web Structure

Many people think that a company's home page is its one and only Web. There may be a lot of Web pages underneath the main home page, but it's all one big structure. Because FrontPage is intended to be used by a lot of people, it has to break this misconception. In particular, FrontPage creates two new terms, which make it easier to understand a large Web site. The two new terms are the *root Web* and the *child Web*.

The best way to understand these new terms is to think of a disk directory structure. When you first access a drive, you're usually taken to the *root directory*—that is, the top-level directory from which all files and subdirectories are based. Similarly, the *root Web* is the main Web for the company, or ISP, from which all other Web pages are based. It can have its own Web pages just as a root directory can hold its own files. Child Webs are, therefore, similar to subdirectories. They are all based off of the root Web and contain files of their own. If there is a need, a child Web can also contain other child Webs.

Traditional Forms of Publishing

Most traditional Web servers are programs that run off of workstation machines. Typically, these systems are running some form of UNIX, intended mainly for engineers. Consequently, there's never been a Web development platform for these systems. This also means that there is little uniformity in how Web pages are published. There are, however, two basic approaches that most Web sites employ.

Immediate Publish

The immediate publish approach is perhaps the most common form of Web publishing available. In this model, the Web pages are stored on the same machine as the Web server so that when you create a new Web page, it's immediately available. If you change an existing Web page, the changes are immediately implemented. The obvious drawback with this approach is that any incorrect links or bad CGI-BIN scripts will also be immediately available. There is no ability for the Webmaster to preemptively screen out malicious CGI-BIN scripts. This form of publishing is most often seen with ISPs and the Web server they provide to their customers. For the sake of security, some ISPs prevent users from using their personal CGI-BIN scripts.

Requested Publish

The requested publish approach is typically seen in places that have a staging area but aren't using FrontPage. In this model, all Web pages are created, modified, and updated on the staging area. When authors want a page made publicly available, they e-mail the Webmaster. Often, they will ask their Webmaster to publish their Web pages from the staging area to the actual Web server. This method gives the Web authors the chance to fine-tune their Web pages. It also allows the Webmaster to check for possibly harmful CGI-BIN scripts or inappropriate material. The Webmaster might have to inform Web authors where their Web pages will be stored. This is to minimize breaking hypertext links when the pages are moved to the actual server.

Publishing from FrontPage Explorer

You publish your Web while working in FrontPage Explorer. First, the Web that you want to publish must be opened in FrontPage Explorer. Then select the **P**ublish FrontPage Web command from the **F**ile menu. The Publish FrontPage Web dialog box appears, as shown in Figure 2.1.

Figure 2.1.

Specify the server to publish your Web on in the Publish FrontPage Web dialog box.

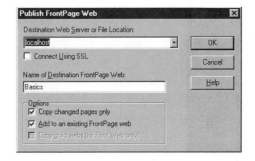

Select the server you want to publish your Web on in the Destination Web **S**erver or File Location drop-down list. If the server isn't listed, type the name. Check the Connect **U**sing SSL checkbox if the server supports Secure Sockets Layer (SSL).

NOTE

Secure Sockets Layer (SSL) gives a secure, encrypted connection between FrontPage and the server. This is particularly useful for companies or Intranets that span multiple sites. SSL makes it possible to publish possibly sensitive information without worrying about who will see it. The server must support SSL for you to be able to take advantage of it.

Type the folder that the Web will reside in on the server in the Name of **D**estination FrontPage Web textbox. Servers are set up to have a root directory where all files, programs, and folders (or directories) are placed. If you type a name in the Name of **D**estination FrontPage Web textbox, a folder is created in the server's root directory by that name. You can also leave the textbox blank. If you do, your Web is placed in the server's root directory.

There are three options in the O**p**tions area of the Publish FrontPage Web dialog box. Check the Copy changed pages **o**nly checkbox if you've published this Web to the same server before and you only want the changed files to be updated. Check the **A**dd to an existing FrontPage Web checkbox if you want to add the current Web to an already existing Web. The current Web is added in a subfolder of the existing Web. The third checkbox is available if you're publishing FrontPage's root Web. Check the Copy **c**hild webs (for Root Web only) checkbox if you want to publish the child Web in addition to the root Web. Click on the OK button.

Using the Web Publishing Wizard

Most people use the Web Publishing Wizard to publish FrontPage Webs. The Web Publishing Wizard publishes Webs to servers that aren't running the FrontPage Server Extensions. The FrontPage Server Extensions are programs and scripts for systems that aren't running FrontPage. You can read more about the extensions in Chapter 14, "Using WebBots with an Extended Server." The Web Publishing Wizard also works well with most online services, such as CompuServe.

Sometimes, FrontPage automatically starts the Web Publishing Wizard while you're trying to publish a Web through its built-in facilities, and it detects that the server you're publishing to doesn't support the FrontPage Server Extensions. You can also start the Web Publishing Wizard from the Start menu. The Web Publishing Wizard is in the Internet Tools menu in the Accessories menu.

Launch the Web Publishing Wizard. The opening sheet, as shown in Figure 2.2, simply tells you that you're using the Web Publishing Wizard and that it helps you copy Web pages to a Web server.

Figure 2.2.
The Web Publishing Wizard's opening sheet tells you a bit about itself.

Click on the **N**ext button. The Web Publishing Wizard's second sheet appears, as shown in Figure 2.3.

Figure 2.3.

Select the folder with the Web you want to publish to in Web Publishing Wizard's second sheet.

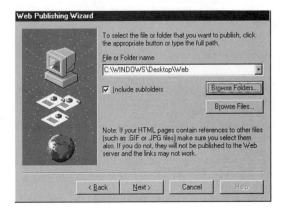

Select or type in the location of the folder containing the Web in the **F**ile or Folder name drop-down list. If you're not sure about the location of the folder you want to publish, click on the Br**o**wse Folders button. Select the folder containing the Web you want to publish in the Browse for Folder dialog box. Click on the OK button. Check the **I**nclude subfolders checkbox if you want to include folders inside the folder you just selected or typed. You can also publish a single Web page by clicking on the B**r**owse Files button. Use the file selection dialog box to locate the file you want to publish and click on the **O**pen button. Click on the **N**ext button. The Web Publishing Wizard's third sheet appears, as shown in Figure 2.4.

Figure 2.4.

Select the Web server that you want to publish to in Web Publishing Wizard's third sheet.

Select the name of the Web server that you want to publish to from the drop-down list. Click on the **N**ext button.

Adding New Servers

If the server isn't listed, click on the New button. Another sheet appears, as shown in Figure 2.5, that's used for adding new servers to the list.

Figure 2.5.

*Start adding a new
server to the server list
from this sheet.*

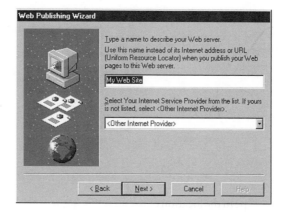

Type a name for your Web server in the textbox and select your Internet Service Provider from the drop-down list. If your service provider isn't listed, select <Other Internet Provider> from the drop-down list. Click on the **N**ext button. A sheet appears asking you to type the URL of the location where your Web pages will be, as shown in Figure 2.6. Once you've entered the URL, click on the **N**ext button.

Figure 2.6.

*Type the URL of
your Web pages in
this page.*

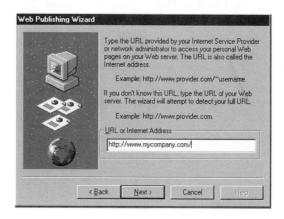

Entering Personal Information

The next step varies according to the type of service you use. Most online services ask you to enter personal information at this stage. CompuServe's Personal Information sheet, for example, is shown in Figure 2.7.

Figure 2.7.

Many online services use a Personal Information sheet similar to CompuServe's Personal Information sheet.

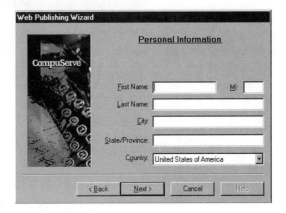

Enter your personal information into the Personal Information sheet, then click on the **N**ext button. CompuServe follows the Personal Information sheet with the Directory Information sheet, as shown in Figure 2.8.

Figure 2.8.

The Directory Information sheet asks for occupation and hobby information to use in a member directory.

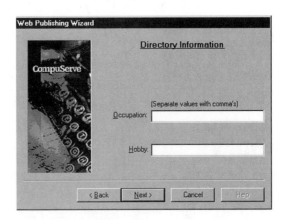

You can optionally type your occupation in the **O**ccupation textbox and type your hobbies in the **H**obby textbox. Click on the **N**ext button. The Account Information sheet appears, as shown in Figure 2.9.

Figure 2.9.

Enter your user ID and your password in the Account Information sheet.

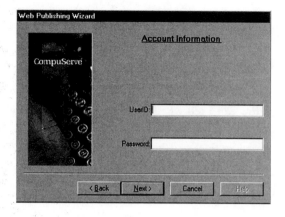

Type your user ID in the UserID textbox, and type your password in the Password textbox. Click on the **Next** button. The final sheet appears, as shown in Figure 2.10. Click on the Finish button to publish your Web.

Figure 2.10.

The last sheet asks you to click on the Finish button.

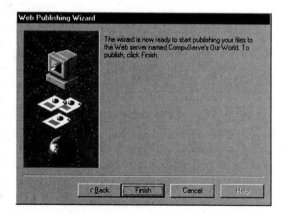

Summary

You just published your first Web. Now you know how to author and publish Webs. The rest of the book builds on the skills you learned today. By the end of a week, you'll be building and publishing exciting professional Webs.

Q&A

Q My service provider isn't listed in the Web Publishing Wizard. What should I do?

A Select <Other Internet Provider> from the drop-down list of Internet providers.

Q How can I tell whether my server provides the FrontPage Server Extensions?

A Ask the server administrator or your Internet service provider whether the server provides the FrontPage Server Extensions.

Workshop

Find out from your Webmaster what type of publishing environment you are working under. Plan ahead to see what possible hurdles you may encounter when you publish your Web page.

Quiz

1. Why do most sites using the immediate publish model prevent custom CGI-BIN scripts?
2. Can you publish an individual Web page, using the Web Publishing Wizard?
3. What is the top level of the FrontPage Web structure called?

DAY

2

Chapter **3**

Web Publishing Basics: Text, Lists, and Links

Now that you've created and published your first Web, take a more leisurely look at the fundamental steps in building a Web page. FrontPage wizards and templates usually perform these steps for you. Nevertheless, your grasp of Web publishing and your ability to build outstanding Web pages will benefit when you understand how to do these steps on your own. In this chapter, you learn how to create a Web, starting with a blank Web page.

In this chapter, you

- ☐ Create a Web with a blank page
- ☐ Modify the background color
- ☐ Work with fonts and text
- ☐ Create lists
- ☐ Add space to a page

Creating a Web with a Blank Page

You begin learning Web publishing basics by creating a Web with a single blank Web page. The Normal Web template, available in FrontPage Explorer's New FrontPage Web dialog box, creates a Web with a single blank Web page.

The Normal Web Template

Most people use the Normal Web template as the starting point for their Web site. The most direct method of accessing the Normal Web page is by first starting up the FrontPage Explorer. If it isn't already running, FrontPage Explorer presents you with a dialog box. Click on the **F**rom a Wizard or Template radio button. If you already have the FrontPage Explorer up and running, you can easily create a new Normal Web. This can be done by clicking on the **F**ile menu heading, then the **N**ew menu item, followed by the FrontPage **W**eb submenu option.

Select Normal Web from the New FrontPage Web dialog box's **T**emplate or Wizard list. Click on the OK button. The Normal Web Template dialog box appears. Enter server information in the Web **S**erver or File Location listbox, and enter your new Web's name—Basics, for example—in the **N**ame of the New FrontPage Web textbox. Click on the OK button. FontPage creates your new Web, containing a single blank Web page, similar to Figure 3.1.

Figure 3.1.

Create a Web containing a single blank Web page with the Normal Web template.

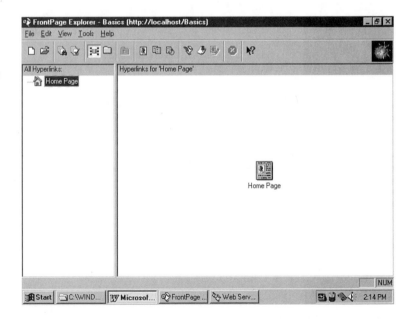

Double-click on the Home Page icon in the Hyperlinks for pane, or right-click on the Home Page icon and select the Open command from the shortcut menu. The blank Home Page opens in the FrontPage Editor.

Understanding HTML

A special markup language, known as the Hypertext Markup Language (HTML), defines a Web page's format and layout. Markup languages in general are as old as the printing press. With the advent of printers attached to computers, markup languages such as PostScript were designed. Finally, someone came up with the great idea of providing a markup language that anyone connected on the Internet could use. The markup language would define text format and layout and provide a means to link text in one page to text in another page. HTML was born.

HTML consists of tags that are like commands. A tag tells a Web browser what to do. There are tags that tell your browser to display bold text, to format lines of text as a list, and to show a hyperlink. The FrontPage Web development environment makes it unnecessary for you to deal directly with these tags. Nevertheless, the tags exist behind the scenes, and FrontPage provides the tools to work with them directly if you want. Look at the HTML source code to your blank Web page by selecting the **H**TML command from the **V**iew menu. The View or Edit HTML dialog box opens, as shown in Figure 3.2.

Figure 3.2.

View a blank page's HTML source code in the View or Edit HTML dialog box.

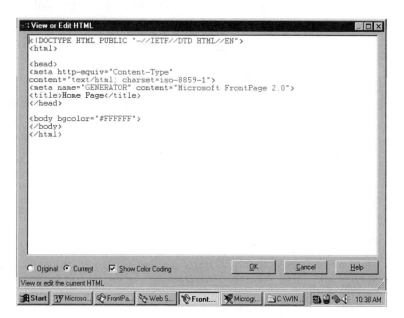

FrontPage's default blank Web page already contains a variety of tags. These tags are mostly to indicate the type of document, the version of the language, and the organization of the page.

At the top of your Web page's source file you see a <!DOCTYPE> tag. The <!DOCTYPE> tag tells browsers the version of HTML used in the document. The latest HTML specification, version 3.2, requires that the <!DOCTYPE> tag be included in every HTML document.

The next element in your Web page's source file is the <HTML> tag, which informs browsers that the code that follows, up to the </HTML> end-tag, is HTML code.

The <HEAD> tag marks the beginning of the Web page's heading. Browsers load and evaluate all code in a heading, the code between <HEAD> and </HEAD>, before displaying any of the Web page's content. The heading is a particularly useful place to enter script procedures that might be called by a user's action. Procedures must be loaded into a browser and be ready to work before a user is able to click on buttons or other interface elements that call the procedures. You learn about scripts on Day 5. Other things go in the heading as well and are included in the HTML source of your blank Web page.

<META> tags are placed in the heading, for example. The <META> tag provides information about an HTML document to browsers, servers, and other applications. FrontPage automatically includes two <META> tags: one gives information about the character set that the document uses, and the other reveals that the document was generated by Microsoft FrontPage, including the version of the program—version 2.0 in this case.

A Web page's title, the one displayed in a browser's title bar and used by the Favorites menu, is also defined in the heading section. Text set between the <TITLE> tag and </TITLE> end-tag is the page's title. Home Page is the default title of the page created by FrontPage Explorer's Normal Web template.

Following your blank Web page's heading is its body. The page's body is everything between the <BODY> tag and the </BODY> end-tag. Unlike the <HEAD> tag, the <BODY> tag can take several arguments, one of which is BGCOLOR. The value of the BGCOLOR argument set to the hexadecimal number #FFFFFF by the Normal Web template defines the background color of the Web page.

NOTE

> The hexadecimal number #FFFFFF represents the color white.

Because your Web page is blank, its body is empty. Most of the content you add to your Web page is added to its body. Close the View or Edit HTML dialog box by clicking on the OK button.

Modifying the Background Color

You saw how HTML defines a page's background color. The FrontPage Editor makes it easy for you to change it. Select the Page Properties command from the **F**ile menu, or right-click anywhere on the page loaded in the FrontPage Editor and select Page Properties from the shortcut menu. The Page Properties dialog box appears. Select the Background tab if the Background sheet isn't already displayed. On the Background sheet, as shown in Figure 3.3, select a color—Teal, for example—in the Ba**c**kground drop-down list. You can also change the color of the text in the body by clicking on the **T**ext drop-down list and selecting a color. Click on the OK button.

Figure 3.3.

Select a teal background for your Home Page.

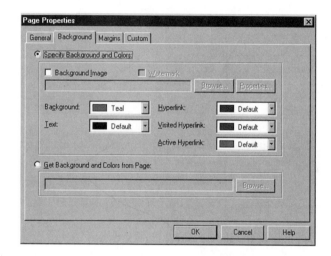

The background color of your Home Page is now teal. The source code is changed from this:

```
<BODY BGCOLOR="#FFFFFF">
```

to the following:

```
<BODY BGCOLOR="#008080">
```

Entering Text

Start creating content for your new Web. Make it your Cool Company Page. This page is where you tell the world about your Cool Company. Type the title Cool Company Page at the top of your Home Page, as displayed in the FrontPage Editor in Figure 3.4.

Figure 3.4.

Type a title at the top of your blank Web page.

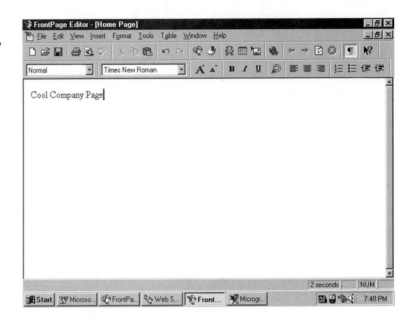

You probably won't find the text format appropriate for a company Web page title—or any title for that matter. For one thing, the font is small.

Formatting Text

Look at the FrontPage Editor's Format toolbar, as shown in Figure 3.5. The Format toolbar should be right above the editing window and right under the Standard toolbar.

Figure 3.5.

The Format toolbar allows easy access to styles, fonts, and more.

There is a Change Style drop-down list at the far left of the Format toolbar. It should read Normal. The Normal style is equivalent to adding raw text to the HTML source without any formatting tags except one: the paragraph tag or <P> and </P>.

Each new paragraph in the Normal style starts with <P> to signify the beginning of a paragraph. When browsers interpret <P>, they create space between the new paragraph and anything that is shown above it. Everything you type is added to the paragraph until you press the Enter key. Then `</P>` is placed at the end of the text you entered, indicating the end, or close, of the paragraph. You can see the tags and text that form the source code of the Normal style paragraph that you just created by selecting the **H**TML command from the **V**iew menu. The View or Edit HTML dialog box opens, as shown in Figure 3.6.

NOTE

The `</P>` tag used to be a requirement whenever you used the `<P>` tag. With the evolution of HTML, however, it has become optional.

Figure 3.6.

The Normal style consists of unformatted text.

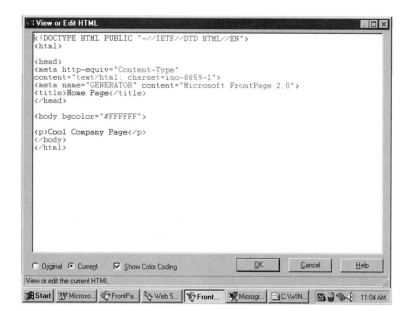

You can change the format of your title by selecting another style. Close the View or Edit HTML dialog box by clicking on either the **O**K or the **C**ancel button. Click on the down arrow to the right of the Change Style drop-down list on the FrontPage Editor's Format toolbar. A list of styles should appear, as shown in Figure 3.7. Each style is associated with a different set of formatting tags.

Figure 3.7.

Several styles are available from the Change Style drop-down list.

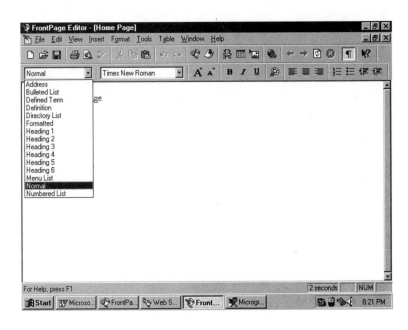

Select Heading 1 from the list. Now your text looks more impressive, like that in Figure 3.8.

Figure 3.8.

The Heading 1 style results in large letters.

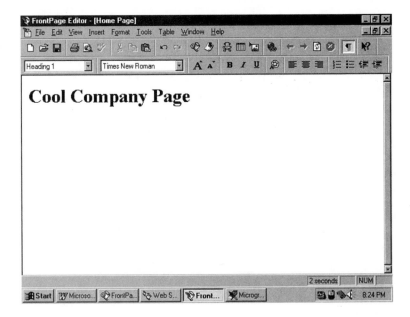

You changed your paragraph into a section level 1 heading. Open the View or Edit HTML dialog box by selecting the **H**TML command from the **V**iew menu. Your text remains unchanged, but the tags surrounding the text have changed in the source code, as shown in Figure 3.9.

NOTE

You can always open the View or Edit HTML dialog box to view your Web page's source code. From here on, the relevant code is reproduced on the page rather than having you open the dialog box or reproducing a figure of the dialog box.

Figure 3.9.

The HTML source code for text displayed in the Heading 1 style.

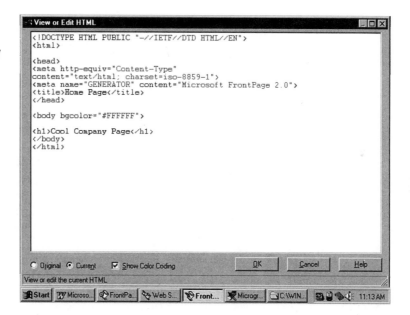

You see `<H1>` in place of `<P>` at the beginning of the text and `</H1>` in place of `</P>` at the end of the text. These are the heading section level 1 tag and end-tag, respectively. They tell the browser that the text between them forms a top-level section heading, like a section heading in a book. Top-level section headings have the largest font size of all the section headings. As the section heading number increases, the level of the section heading decreases. So, for example, if you apply a Heading 2 style, the section heading font size is smaller than when you applied a Heading 1 style.

The <Hn> tag (n represents any section heading level) can accept one argument, the ALIGN argument. Your text, Cool Company Page, is aligned left even after applying the Heading 1 style. That's because the <Hn> tag's default alignment is set to LEFT. Try changing the title's alignment so that it's centered rather than aligned left. At the center-right of the Format toolbar are three alignment buttons: Align Left, Center, and Align Right. Click on the Center button. Your Web page should look similar to the one in Figure 3.10. The alignment buttons also work for a number of other HTML tags, not just the <Hn> ones.

Figure 3.10.

Center text by clicking on the Format toolbar's Center button.

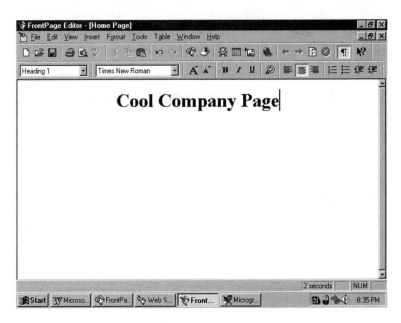

If you look at the source of your Web page, you see that the <H1> tag now includes the ALIGN argument and that the ALIGN argument is set equal to CENTER. Here is the code:

```
<H1 ALIGN="center">Cool Company Page</H1>
```

You can do the same formatting tasks that you've performed through the Format toolbar by clicking your right mouse button while pointing to the text you want to format and selecting the Paragraph Properties command from the shortcut menu. The Paragraph Properties dialog box appears, as shown in Figure 3.11.

Figure 3.11.

*Use the Paragraph
Properties dialog box
to apply text styles and
alignment.*

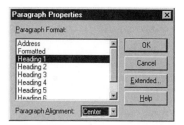

Select a style, such as Heading 1, from the Paragraph Format list and select alignment from the Paragraph Alignment drop-down list. When you're finished, click on the OK button and the selected style and alignment are applied.

The Format toolbar's Style List is somewhat different than the Paragraph Format list in the Paragraph Properties dialog box. There are more styles in the Format toolbar's Style List, because it includes more than paragraph styles. It also includes styles for lists. You learn about the list styles later in this chapter in the Creating Lists section.

Changing Fonts

So far, you haven't used any tags that specify fonts or font sizes. Your browser determines the exact font and font size used for headings. In fact, you can usually set your own preferences for heading fonts and font sizes in your browser. The heading tags specify a certain general result. The headings use relatively large fonts, and top headings use larger fonts than headings below them. However, headings do not guarantee that any specific font or font size is used.

You can specify fonts and font sizes by using the FrontPage Editor. Keep in mind that viewers of your Web page may not have access to all the fonts that you can access. Otherwise, manipulating fonts in the FrontPage Editor is the same as with any word processor.

Specify the font type for your Web page's title. Highlight Cool Company Page, then click on the down arrow to the right of the Format toolbar's Change Font drop-down list. A list of available fonts appears, as shown in Figure 3.12.

Select a font from the list and it is applied to the selected text. When Matura MT Script Capitals, for example, is selected, the typeface looks like the text shown in Figure 3.13.

Figure 3.12.

The list of available fonts may vary from system to system.

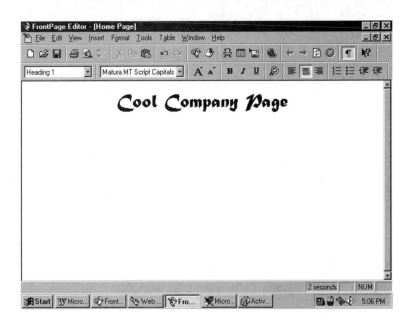

Figure 3.13.

The Matura MT Script Capitals font is applied to Cool Company Page.

The <FONT> tag and </FONT> end-tag are now placed inside the heading tags in the Home Page source code. The <FONT> tag includes an argument, the FACE argument. Here is the relevant source code:

```
<H1 ALIGN="center"><FONT FACE=" Matura MT Script Capitals">Cool Company Page</
➥FONT></H1>
```

The <FONT> tag's FACE argument specifies the font you want used. FACE is set equal to Matura MT Script Capitals because this was the font selected in the Format toolbar's Change Font drop-down list.

In addition to using the Format toolbar, you can change fonts through the Font dialog box. In fact, you can manipulate several font attributes through the Font dialog box, and it's the best place to control font size.

Manipulating Font Size

You can also set the title's font size. Open the Font dialog box by highlighting the text you want to manipulate; then select the Font Properties command from the Edit menu. Another approach is to highlight the text, and then select the Font command from the Format menu. Once you have the text highlighted, you also can click on the highlighted text with your right mouse button and select the Font Properties command from the shortcut menu. The FrontPage Editor gives you several ways to do common chores so that you can do them in the way that you like best. Whichever way you choose, the Font dialog box appears, as shown in Figure 3.14.

Figure 3.14.
Manipulate fonts through the Font dialog box.

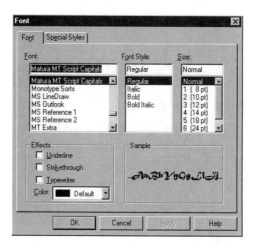

Select 7 (36 pt) from the Size list on the right side of the Font dialog box and click on the OK button. Now the title, shown in Figure 3.15, looks like you're in business!

Figure 3.15.

The new Cool Company Page title has an expressive font and large font size.

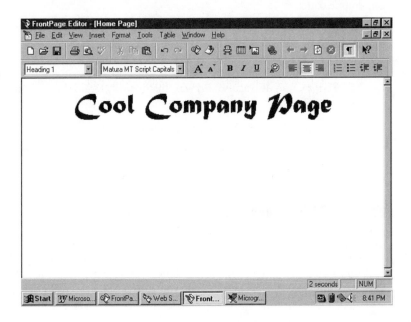

When you look at your Web page's source code, you see that the FrontPage Editor added the SIZE argument to your title's <FONT> tag. The <FONT> tag's SIZE argument specifies the size of the font applied to text up to the </FONT> end-tag. The following is the relevant line of source code:

```
<h1 align="center"><font size="7" face="Matura MT Script Capitals">Cool Company
➥Page</font></h1>
```

Creating Lists

It's time to add content to your Web page, and one of the best ways to start is by creating a list. Most people find a brief list—as opposed to a long and ponderous one—useful when they first encounter a Web page. Think of a list as a table of contents; it gives a road map to your Web page or even to your Web site.

The Cool Company Page will provide information about your cool company, the company's product, and the company's employees. The list looks something like the following:

- ☐ The Cool Company
- ☐ The Cool Product
- ☐ Cool Company Employees

Bulleted Lists

Toward the right side of the Format toolbar, there are two buttons related to building lists: the Numbered List button and the Bulleted List button. Enter the previous list in the Cool Company Page as a bulleted list. Click on the line just beneath the page's title and then click on the Format toolbar's Bulleted List button. A bullet should appear next to your cursor. Begin typing the list. When you reach the end of the first list item, press the Enter key. Your cursor moves to the next line and a new bullet appears. When you're finished, your Web page should look similar to the one in Figure 3.16.

Figure 3.16.

A bulleted list is added to the Cool Company Page.

Your source code now contains two new tags: the <UL> and <LI> tags (and their end-tags). The <UL> tag tells a browser that the following block of text, up to the </UL> end-tag, is a bulleted list. The <LI> tag is set in front of each item in the bulleted list.

```
<UL>
    <LI>The Cool Company</LI>
    <LI>The Cool Product</LI>
    <LI>Cool Company Employees</LI>
</UL>
```

You can apply paragraph properties and font properties to text in lists just as with any other text. In addition to these properties, you can also apply list properties and list item properties.

List properties apply to the whole list. Maybe you'd like hollow bullets rather than solid bullets, for example. Click your right button while pointing to the list, then select the List Properties command from the shortcut menu. Alternatively, click on the list, then select the Bullets and **N**umbering command from the F**o**rmat menu. Either method opens the List Properties dialog box, as shown in Figure 3.17. You can also use this dialog box if you want to use a numbered list rather than a bulleted list. This is done by clicking on the Numbered tab and selecting the number scheme of your choice. If you want to create a list other than a numbered or bulleted list, click on the Other tab. This sheet lets you select from the various lists available in HTML, such as a Definition, Directory, or Menu list.

Figure 3.17.

Modify your list's properties through the List Properties dialog box.

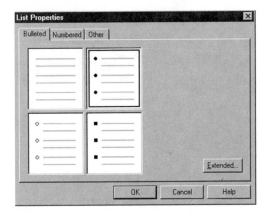

Click on the box at the lower-left on the List Properties dialog box's Bulleted sheet, the one displaying the hollow bullets. Click on the OK button. Your list should have hollow bullets like the ones in Figure 3.18. The FrontPage Editor added the TYPE argument to the list's <UL> tag and set it equal to circle:

```
<UL TYPE="circle">
```

List item properties apply to individual items in a list. To highlight your cool product, for example, you decide to change the bullet next to The Cool Product to a solid square. Right-click on The Cool Product and select the List Item Properties command from the shortcut menu. The List Item Properties dialog box appears, as shown in Figure 3.19.

Figure 3.18.

The list on the Cool Company Page has hollow bullets.

Figure 3.19.

Change individual items in a list through the List Item Properties dialog box.

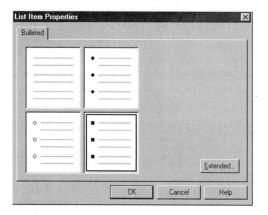

Select the lower right box displaying the filled squares, then click on the OK button. The bullet next to The Cool Product should now be a solid square like the one in Figure 3.20. The FrontPage Editor added a TYPE argument to The Cool Product <LI> tag and set it equal to square:

```
<LI TYPE="square">The Cool Product</LI>
```

Figure 3.20.

The bullet of an individual list item, The Cool Product line, is changed to a solid square.

Adding Space to a Page

As a final touch to this page, add space between the title and the list until it's aesthetically pleasing to you. Click your mouse cursor before the T at the beginning of the first list item and press Enter. A new blank list line with a bullet should be created at the top of the list. Move the cursor back to the blank list line by pressing the up arrow once or clicking with your mouse cursor. Press Enter again. The blank list line automatically disappears and is replaced by a blank line.

Press Enter about three more times or until the layout is how you like it. The page should look something like the one in Figure 3.21.

Figure 3.21.

Make the page layout aesthetically pleasing.

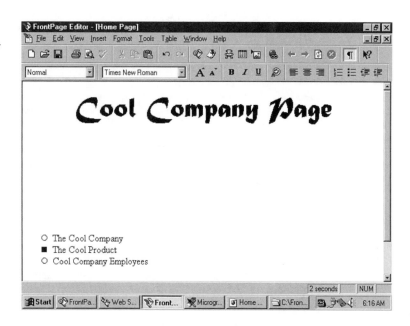

Each blank line is created by a <P> tag and </P> end-tag pair surrounding the HTML equivalent for a space character: .

Be sure to save your Home Page!

Adding New Pages

Add a new Web page for each item on your Home Page's list. In the FrontPage Editor, click on the Standard toolbar's New button and a new blank Web page is created. Alternatively, select the **N**ew command from the **F**ile menu. The New Page dialog box appears. Select Normal Page from the Template or Wizard list and click on the OK button to create a blank Web page.

Type The Cool Company and then format it with the Heading 1 style. Either select the Heading 1 style from the Format toolbar's Change Style drop-down list, or select the **P**aragraph command from the F**o**rmat menu and then select Heading 1 from the Paragraph Properties dialog box's Paragraph Format list and click the OK button.

Save the new Web page by clicking on the Standard toolbar's Save button or by selecting the **S**ave command from the **F**ile menu. The Save As dialog box appears, as shown in Figure 3.22.

Figure 3.22.

The Save As dialog box suggests a page title and filename.

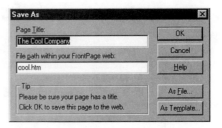

The heading that you just entered, The Cool Company, is automatically entered as the new page's title in the Save As dialog box's Page **T**itle textbox. Accept this and the suggested file name by clicking on the OK button. Your new page should look similar to the one in Figure 3.23.

Figure 3.23.

The new Web page with heading and title.

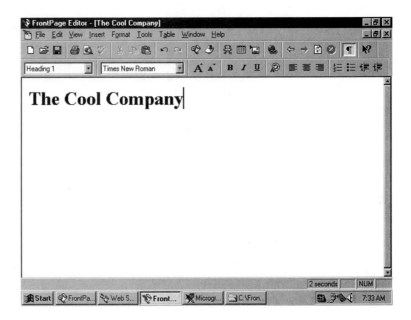

Move to FrontPage Explorer either by clicking on the Show FrontPage Explorer button in the FrontPage Editor's Standard toolbar or by clicking on the FrontPage Explorer button in Window's Taskbar. The new Web page, The Cool Company, is listed under Home Page in FrontPage Explorer's All Hyperlinks pane, as shown in Figure 3.24. You've added a new page to your Web.

Add two more Web pages—one titled The Cool Product and the other titled Cool Company Employees—using the same methods. When you're finished, all three pages plus your Home Page should be listed in FrontPage Explorer, as shown in Figure 3.25.

Figure 3.24.

The new Web page appears in FrontPage Explorer immediately after you save it.

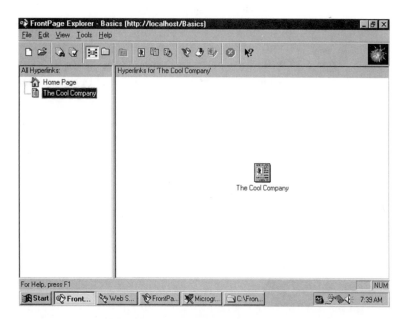

Figure 3.25.

All four Web pages appear in FrontPage Explorer, but none of them has a hyperlink.

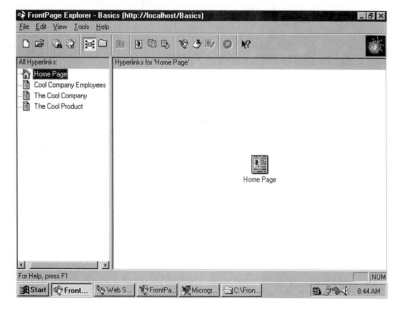

NOTE

All three new pages present COOL.HTM as the default filename. No two filenames can be the same, so type a variation on the default name. For instance, type `COOLEMPL.HTM` for your Cool Company Employees page and `COOLPROD.HTM` for The Cool Product page.

Creating Hyperlinks

Your Web contains four pages, but none of them has a hyperlink. From your Home Page, you want people to glance at a list and decide rapidly what they're interested in. When they decide, you want them to click on the list item they decided on so that they go right to the relevant information. You want a hyperlink from the list item to the page or location with the information. In this section, you create a hyperlink between list items on your Home Page and their appropriate Web pages.

All four Web pages in the current Web should be open in the FrontPage Editor. View your Home Page by selecting Home Page from the **W**indow menu if it's not already displayed.

Highlight The Cool Company, the first item in the list on your Home Page. Click on the Create or Edit Hyperlink button on the Standard toolbar, or select the Hyperlin**k** command from the **E**dit menu, or select the Hyperlin**k** command from the **I**nsert menu. The Create Hyperlink dialog box appears, as shown in Figure 3.26.

Figure 3.26.

Create hyperlinks through the Create Hyperlink dialog box.

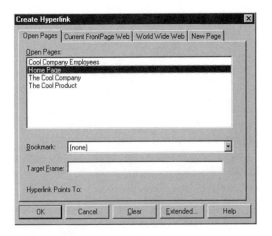

Select the Open Pages tab if the Open Pages sheet isn't already displayed. The Open Pages sheet lists all Web pages currently opened in the FrontPage Editor. Select the appropriate Web page to link with the highlighted text in the Home Page list—in this case, The Cool Company page. Click on the OK button. The list item you just added a hyperlink to on

Home Page is underlined and blue. Save the page and then look at the FrontPage Explorer window, as shown in Figure 3.27. You should see a hyperlink from Home Page to The Cool Company.

Figure 3.27.

FrontPage Explorer graphically shows the hyperlink you created between Home Page and The Cool Company.

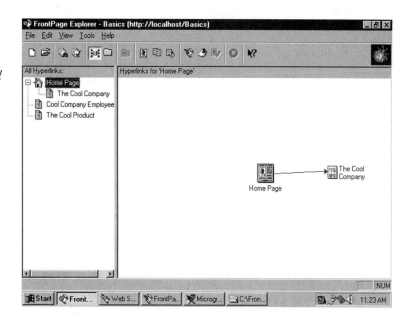

If you look at the source code for The Cool Company page, you see that the FrontPage Editor added an <A> tag, an anchor tag, and an </A> end-tag between the <LI> tag and </LI> end-tag for The Cool Company list item. The <A> tag creates an anchor for a hyperlink to a place specified by the <A> tag's HREF argument. In this case, HREF is specified as COOL.HTM. When you select this hyperlink, the COOL.HTM Web page loads. The following is the line of modified code:

```
<LI><A HREF="cool.htm">The Cool Company</A></LI>
```

Create hyperlinks between the other two list items on Home Page to their appropriate Web pages. When you're finished, the graphic representation of your Web's hyperlinks should look similar to the one in Figure 3.28.

TIP

When you're typing an e-mail address or URL, you don't need to create a hyperlink for it. FrontPage will automatically create the appropriate link for the text you type.

Figure 3.28.

Your Web has three hyperlinks and a total of four pages at this point.

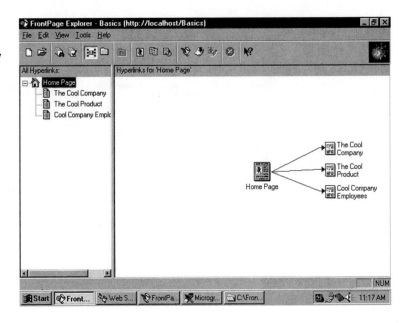

Following Links

You can move through Web pages in the FrontPage Editor by following links. Open the FrontPage Editor to Home Page and follow The Cool Company hyperlink to The Cool Company Web page. Click on The Cool Company list item and select the Follow **H**yperlink command from the **T**ools menu, or right-click on The Cool Company list item and select the Follow Hyperlink command from the shortcut menu. The appropriate Web page, The Cool Company page, is loaded and displayed. The follow hyperlink feature is particularly useful as the size of your Web grows.

Adding Symbols

You have a wide range of symbols you can add graphically to your Web pages. For example, your cool company has trademarked the word Cool, so you want to display the fact with a TM mark. Click your cursor at the end of Cool in The Cool Company title. Select the **S**ymbol command from the **I**nsert menu. The Symbol dialog box appears, as shown in Figure 3.29.

Figure 3.29.

The currently selected symbol displays next to the Symbol dialog box's Insert button.

Select the TM symbol by clicking on it in the Symbol dialog box. The currently selected symbol displays to the right of the Symbol dialog box's **I**nsert button. Click on the **I**nsert button and then close the Symbol dialog box by clicking on the **C**lose button. The result should look similar to Figure 3.30. If you look at the source code, you notice that the HTML character code for TM (™) was added to the heading:

```
<H1>The Cool&trade; Company</H1>
```

Figure 3.30.

Cool is trademarked in The Cool Company Web page.

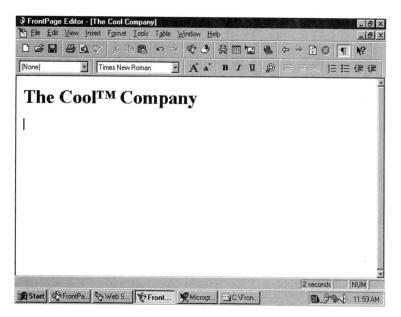

Use the same method to add any symbols, such as the copyright symbol, to your Web pages.

Adding a Horizontal Line

Section off The Cool Company heading from the content you will add below with a horizontal line. Click your cursor on the line below The Cool Company heading. Select the Horizontal Line command from the Insert menu. A horizontal line is added, as shown in Figure 3.31.

Figure 3.31.

A horizontal line separates a Web page into sections.

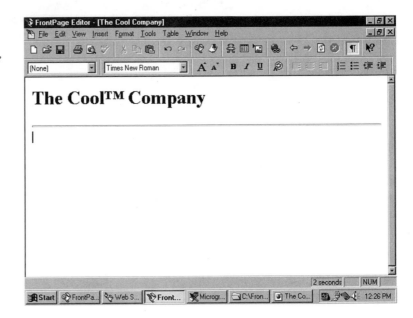

The <HR> tag creates horizontal lines. If you look at the source code of The Cool Company page, you see the <HR> tag added below the heading.

Adding More Lists: Numbered Lists

You now tell the viewers why your company is cool. You start with a short blurb on its own line that says We're cool because.... On the next line you start a numbered list giving three reasons why your company is cool.

Start the numbered list by clicking on Format toolbar's Numbered List button or by selecting Numbered List from the Format toolbar's Change Style drop-down list. The Arabic number 1 displays at the beginning of the line by default.

Alternatively, you can select the Bullets and **N**umbering command from the F**o**rmat menu to open the List Properties dialog box. Select the Numbered tab if the Numbered sheet isn't already open. From the Numbered sheet, as shown in Figure 3.32, you can select from a variety of numbering styles and which number you want to start the list. If you use this method, accept the default. That is, the Arabic number format at top center should be selected, and the number in the Start At spin box should be 1.

Figure 3.32.

Select different numbering styles from the List Properties dialog box's Numbered page.

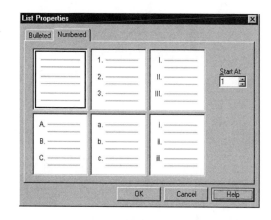

The three reasons that your company is cool are

☐ We sell ice cubes

☐ We wear shades in the fog

☐ We are located in Berkeley

Type each of these reasons, or something like them, into your list so that there are three numbered list items. The result should look something like the one in Figure 3.33.

If you look at The Cool Company page source code, you see that the FrontPage Editor added the <OL> tag and </OL> end-tag. The <OL> tag tells browsers that the items contained between the tags are an ordered list. The <LI> tag and </LI> end-tag surround each list item. Here is the code:

```
<OL>
    <LI>We sell ice cubes</LI>
    <LI>We wear shades in the fog</LI>
    <LI>We are located in Berkeley</LI>
</OL>
```

Figure 3.33.

The Cool Company page now has a numbered list.

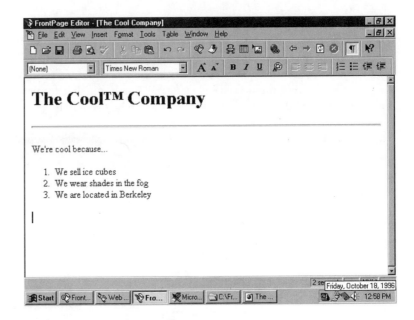

Using the Address Style

You often want to include your address at the bottom of a Web page. The FrontPage Editor makes it easy for you to use the address style. Place your cool company's address at the bottom of The Cool Company page.

First, insert another horizontal line to separate the list from the address below. Click your cursor on the line below the list you just created. Select the Horizontal Line command from the Insert menu. A horizontal line appears.

With the cursor insertion point below the newly created horizontal line, select the Address style from the Format toolbar's Change Style drop-down list. Type the address:

```
The Cool Company
Number One on Telegraph Ave.
Berkeley, CA 94709
```

If you simply press Enter after typing each line, a large space is left between each line. When this happens and you want the lines to be closely spaced, you want a line break.

Line Breaks

When you get to the end of a line that you want close to the next line, enter a line break by selecting the **B**reak command from the **I**nsert menu. The Break Properties dialog box opens, as shown in Figure 3.34. Select the Normal Line Break radio button and click on the OK button. Alternatively, hold down the Shift key when you press Enter.

Figure 3.34.
Select special formatting options from the Break Properties dialog box.

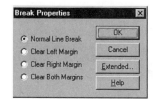

Line breaks display under the FrontPage Editor as arrows bent to the left, as shown in the completed Web page in Figure 3.35.

Figure 3.35.
The completed Web page displayed in the FrontPage Editor.

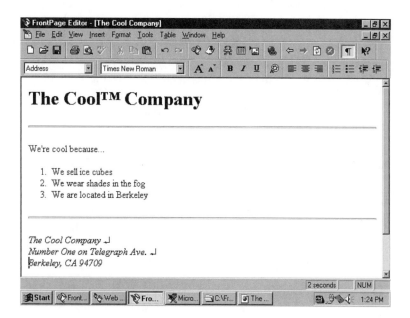

If you look at the source code, you see that the FrontPage Editor used the <ADDRESS> tag and </ADDRESS> end-tag to mark a block of text for the address format. The <BR> tag also is placed at the end of each line where a line break was entered. Here is the source code:

```
<ADDRESS>
    The Cool Company<BR>
    Number One on Telegraph Ave.<BR>
    Berkeley, CA  94709
</ADDRESS>
```

Remember to save your work!

More on Fonts

There are more things you can do with fonts, including applying color to them, adding effects, and applying different styles. Add some content to The Cool Product page while taking some of the font features for a spin.

Open the FrontPage Editor to The Cool Product page. Click your mouse cursor on the line under the page's heading and enter Sale!. Press Enter. On the new line, enter Buy Now!!.

Make the sale notice stand out by giving it a large font size and by making it red. Highlight the Sale! text and open the Font dialog box by clicking your right mouse button while pointing to the highlighted text and selecting the Font Properties command from the shortcut menu. Select the Font tab in the Font dialog box if the Font sheet isn't already showing. Select 5 (18 pt) from the Size list and select Red from the Color drop-down list, as shown in Figure 3.36. Click on the OK button.

Figure 3.36.

*The Font dialog box
with 18 point red
fonts selected.*

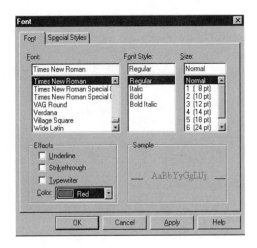

Make the Buy Now!! text stand out, but make it look different than the sale notice. Highlight the Buy Now!! text. Change the text's font size by clicking once on the Format toolbar's Increase Text Size button. Change the text's color by clicking on the Format toolbar's Text Color button. The Color dialog box appears, as shown in Figure 3.37. Select a color—perhaps a bright blue—and then click on the OK button.

Figure 3.37.

Select ready-made colors or create your own custom colors through the Color dialog box.

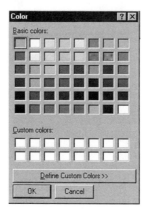

Finally, apply the special style blinking font to Buy Now!! in an attempt to hypnotize your customers. Right-click on the highlighted Buy Now!! text, and select the Font Properties command from the shortcut menu. The Font dialog box appears. Select the Special Styles tab so that the Font dialog box displays its Special Styles sheet, as shown in Figure 3.38. Check the box next to Blink (<blink>) and click on the OK button. You can make the selected text subscript or superscript by clicking on the Vertical Position drop-down list and selecting the appropriate value. You also can control how much the highlighted text is raised or lowered by adjusting the By value.

Figure 3.38.

Select special font styles from the Font dialog box's Special Styles sheet.

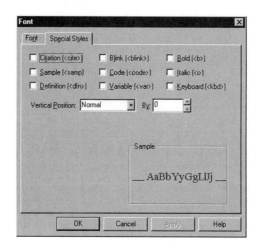

A light green dashed line surrounds the text formatted with a special style. Not all browsers recognize the special style tags. Everyone should see the blue Buy Now!!, but not everyone will see it blinking. The page should look like the one in Figure 3.39.

Figure 3.39.

The Cool Product Web page displayed in the FrontPage Editor.

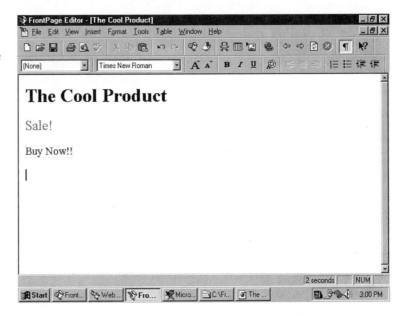

The source code for The Cool Product Web page is similar to code you've seen before, except that the <FONT> tag uses its COLOR argument. The <BLINK> tag and </BLINK> end-tag are also added around Buy Now!!. The <BLINK> tag is recognized only in Netscape's browsers. Here is the source code:

```
<P><FONT COLOR="#FF0000" SIZE="5">Sale!</FONT></P>
<P><FONT COLOR="#0000FF" SIZE="4"><BLINK>Buy Now!!</BLINK></FONT></P>
```

Adding More Lists: Menu Lists

Add content to the Cool Company Employees Web page. First, create a menu list of the employees.

Place your cursor on the line under the Cool Company Employees heading and add a horizontal line by selecting Horizontal Line from the Insert menu.

With the cursor placed on the new line after the horizontal line, select Menu List from the
Format toolbar's Change Style drop-down list. Type the names of the Cool Company
employees:

☐ Jan

☐ John

☐ Jack

☐ Don

The result should be similar to Figure 3.40.

Figure 3.40.

*The Cool Company
Employees Web page
displayed in the
FrontPage Editor.*

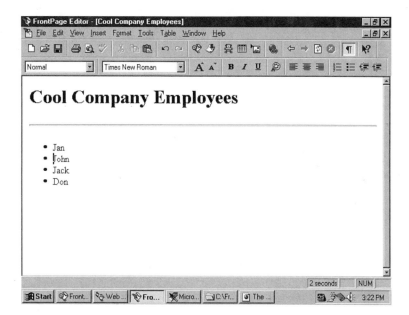

The FrontPage Editor added the `<MENU>` tag and the `</MENU>` end-tag that indicate that the
items contained between them are menu items. Each item, as in bulleted and numbered lists,
is prefaced with the `<LI>` tag and followed by the `</LI>` end-tag. Here is the source code:

```
<MENU>
    <LI>Jan</LI>
    <LI>John</LI>
    <LI>Jack</LI>
    <LI>Don</LI>
</MENU>
```

Bookmarks and Links to Bookmarks

The menu list on the Cool Company Employees page isn't very useful, but you make it useful by creating bookmarks on the page and setting hyperlinks from the menu list to the bookmarks.

Enter about five blank spaces after the menu list and then insert a horizontal line. After the horizontal line, type Jan and select Heading 2 from the Format toolbar's Change Style drop-down list. Highlight Jan, then select the **B**ookmark command from the **E**dit menu. The Bookmark dialog box opens with a suggested bookmark name in the **B**ookmark Name textbox, as shown in Figure 3.41. The suggested name, Jan, is good, so accept it by clicking on the OK button. A dashed line displays under Jan in the FrontPage Editor to let you know that there is a bookmark set to Jan. You should use bookmarks when you have a lot of related information and want it kept on one Web page. Rather than have multiple pages that define various terms, you can have a single definition page and use bookmarks for each definition.

Figure 3.41.

Enter the bookmark name in the Book-mark dialog box.

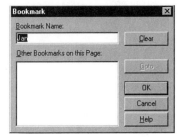

When you created the Jan bookmark, the FrontPage Editor inserted an <A> tag with the NAME argument set equal to Jan. The following line displays the source code:

```
<H2><A NAME="Jan">Jan</A></H2>
```

Enter about seven blank lines, then insert a horizontal line. Type John and select Heading 2 from the Format toolbar's Change Style drop-down list. Highlight John, then select the **B**ookmark command from the **E**dit menu. The Bookmark dialog box opens, with John as the suggested bookmark name in the **B**ookmark Name textbox. Accept the suggested bookmark name by clicking on the OK button.

Repeat this procedure for Jack and Don.

Go back to the menu list at the top of the Cool Company Employees page and create hyperlinks between the names in the list and the appropriate bookmarks. Content specific to each person can be added to the areas under the bookmarks.

Highlight the first menu list item, Jan. Click on the Standard toolbar's Create or Edit Hyperlink button. The Create Hyperlink dialog box appears. Click on the Open Pages tab if the Open Pages sheet isn't already displayed, such as the one in Figure 3.42.

Figure 3.42.

Create hyperlinks to bookmarks through the Create Hyperlink dialog box.

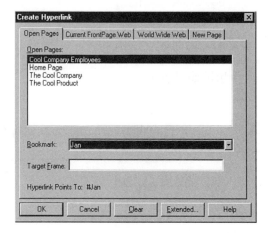

Select the Jan bookmark from the **B**ookmark drop-down list and click on the OK button. Jan turns blue and is underlined, indicating it's a hyperlink. If you leave the cursor on Jan and select the Follow **H**yperlink command from the **T**ools menu, you are taken to the Jan heading further down the current Web page.

When you created a hyperlink between the Jan menu list item and the Jan bookmark, the FrontPage Editor inserted an <A> tag with the HREF argument set equal to #Jan, the Jan bookmark. The following line displays the source code:

```
<LI><A HREF="#Jan">Jan</A></LI>
```

Create the rest of the hyperlinks to bookmarks in the same way.

Editing the Source Code

The Home Page heading, Cool Company Page, is something of a misnomer. The Home Page is really the front door to the company's Web. Change Page to Web in the heading, but don't do it the easy way this time.

You can do nearly everything without dealing directly with HTML. However, there are times when working directly with HTML can be helpful. For example, suppose you're looking at the HTML source for a Web page on the Internet. You could simply highlight and copy the code you want and paste it into the HTML view. The FrontPage Editor enables you to edit any Web page's HTML source code directly through the View or Edit HTML dialog box.

Open the View or Edit HTML dialog box by selecting the **H**TML command from the **V**iew menu. Find the heading code with Cool Company Page. The code you're looking for is this:

```
<H1 ALIGN="center"><FONT SIZE="7" FACE="Matura MT Script Capitals">Cool Company
➡Page</FONT></H1>
```

Change Page to Web so that the line now looks like this:

```
<H1 ALIGN="center"><FONT SIZE="7" FACE="Matura MT Script Capitals">Cool Company
➡Web</FONT></H1>
```

Click on the OK button. Now your Home Page should look similar to the one in Figure 3.43.

Figure 3.43.

You changed the Home Page heading by editing the HTML source code.

Links to Bookmarks on Other Web Pages

While you're modifying your Cool Company's Home Page, you decide that you'd like a hyperlink from the Home Page directly to information on the company's president, Don. It can be done. Hyperlinks to bookmarks on other Web pages are powerful and should probably be used more often than they are.

Click at the end of the last list item in the Home Page list and then press Enter. A new bulleted list item is created. Type in The Cool Company President and then highlight the list item. Click on the Standard toolbar's Create or Edit Hyperlink button. The Create Hyperlink dialog box appears.

3

Select the Open Pages tab if the Open Pages sheet isn't already displayed. Select Cool Company Employees in the **O**pen Pages list. In the **B**ookmark drop-down list, select Don. Click on the OK button.

Select the Follow **H**yperlink command from the **T**ools menu. You go directly to the Don section of the Cool Company Employees Web page. Select the **B**ack command from the **T**ools menu. You go back to Home Page.

The FrontPage Editor set the `<A>` tag's HREF argument equal to both a file and its anchor. A filename is followed by a pound sign that is followed by an anchor name. The source code looks like the following line:

```
<LI><A HREF="coolempl.htm#Don">The Cool Company President</A></LI>
```

Summary

In this chapter, you learned how to enter, edit, and format text, and you learned how the FrontPage Editor translates your work into HTML code. You manipulated font types, sizes, and colors. You created bookmarks and you also created hyperlinks—hyperlinks between Web pages, to bookmarks inside the same Web page, and to bookmarks on different pages. You even expanded your Web by adding pages and linking them. In fact, you created an entire Web from scratch. Now that you know the core skills for building Webs, it's time to decorate. In the next chapter, you add graphics to your Webs.

Q&A

Q What's with all these tags and arguments? Do I really need to hurt my brain with HTML code?

A A sprinkling of HTML code is presented in this chapter to give you an idea of what the FrontPage Editor is doing behind the scenes when you carry out a task. Sometimes the knowledge is helpful. However, with the FrontPage Web authoring system, you don't need to know anything about HTML to produce excellent Webs.

Q Where can I learn more about HTML? I can't get enough!

A A masochist among us? An excellent reference for the HTML code is included in the Microsoft ActiveX SDK provided on this book's CD-ROM. After installing the ActiveX SDK, look in Programs, ActiveX SDK from the Windows Start menu for the ActiveX SDK Help InfoViewer command. You'll find the HTML Reference inside the Microsoft ActiveX SDK book.

Q **When there is a hyperlink to a Web page or a bookmark, shouldn't there be a hyperlink back?**

A You're absolutely right. The hyperlinks from Home Page to the three other Web pages should be reciprocated with Home Page links. Also, when there are links from the top of a Web page to various bookmarks, there should be links back from each of the sections to the top of the page. Adding hyperlinks and bookmarks is a good exercise.

Workshop

Complete your Cool Company's Web. Add more bookmarks and hyperlinks. Fill in the contents. You have all the skills to make a full-scale and robust Web site. Most importantly, make it a Web that you actually can use.

Quiz

1. With FrontPage, you can create Webs without programming. Nevertheless, FrontPage creates a source code behind the scenes. What is the name of the code?

2. How many kinds of lists can you create using the FrontPage Editor?

3. What's the difference between creating a hyperlink to another Web page and to a bookmark?

3

Chapter 4

Decorating and Expanding Your Web

You created a Web from scratch in the last chapter and expanded it into rich textual documents that included bookmarks and hyperlinks. In this chapter, you decorate your Web with graphics and special effects, including animation.

In this chapter, you

☐ Use the FrontPage To Do List

☐ Insert a marquee into your Web page

☐ Decorate your pages with clip-art

Open the Basics Web you created in Chapter 3, "Web Publishing Basics: Text, Lists, and Links," in FrontPage Explorer and transform each of its pages into a work of art!

Using the To Do List

You can keep track of a list of things you want to do with your Web in the FrontPage Web authoring and publishing system's To Do List. Both FrontPage Explorer and the FrontPage Editor have identical commands available for working with the To Do List, so no matter where you are when you're working on a Web you have the same list at your fingertips.

Create a To Do List for this chapter. Your FrontPage Explorer should be open to the Basics Web you created in Chapter 3. Show the To Do List either by clicking on the Show To Do List toolbar button or by selecting the Show To Do List command from the Tools menu. The FrontPage To Do List dialog box opens, as shown in Figure 4.1.

Figure 4.1.

The Basics Web's FrontPage To Do List is empty.

Although the FrontPage To Do List is a dialog box, it acts a lot like a typical window. You can resize it, maximize it, or minimize it. You also can keep the FrontPage To Do List dialog box open while you're performing tasks by checking the **K**eep window open checkbox at the top left of the dialog box. You use this checkbox when you're using the To Do List dialog box to work on Web pages. If you don't enable the checkbox when you click the Do **T**ask button on a selected task, the To Do List dialog box disappears. However, if the checkbox *is* enabled, the To Do dialog box will still be available, regardless of what task you're working on.

Add a task to the Basics Web's To Do List. Click on the **A**dd button at the bottom of the FrontPage To Do List dialog box. The Add To Do Task dialog box appears, as shown in Figure 4.2. Your name, or whatever name you used to log on to your Personal Web Server, displays in the **A**ssign To textbox.

Today your cool company is starting a hot sale on ice cubes, so it's a high priority that you set up a scrolling marquee with the news on your home page. Add this as a high-priority task. Type Add Marquee to Home Page in the Add To Do Task dialog box's **T**ask Name textbox. In the Priority area, select the **H**igh radio button. Keep your name in the **A**ssign To textbox.

Figure 4.2.

Enter tasks into your
FrontPage To Do List
through the Add To
Do Task dialog box.

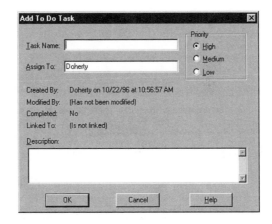

Finally, add a description of the task in the **D**escription scrolling textbox. For example, type
`Include text announcing our hot sale on ice cubes.` Click on the OK button. Your task
is added to the FrontPage To Do List, as in Figure 4.3.

Figure 4.3.

The Add Marquee to
Home Page task is
added to the
FrontPage To Do List
dialog box.

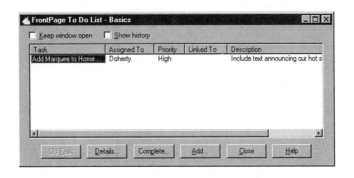

Using the same technique, add these tasks:

- ☐ `Add animation clip-art` at low priority.
- ☐ `Add background clip-art` at medium priority.
- ☐ `Add bullet clip-art` at medium priority.
- ☐ `Add button clip-art` at medium priority.
- ☐ `Add icon clip-art` at low priority.
- ☐ `Add line clip-art` at medium priority.

You should have seven tasks in your Basics Web's FrontPage To Do List. Notice that the tasks
are listed in the order that you entered them. You can sort the tasks according to the various

categories in the labels listed across the column above the list of tasks. For example, click on the Priority label. The tasks are sorted from highest to lowest priority, as in Figure 4.4. Click on the **C**lose button to close the FrontPage To Do List dialog box.

Figure 4.4.

Tasks are listed from highest to lowest priority after clicking on the Priority label.

Oops! There is one more task item that you want on the Basics Web's To Do List. First, make sure that Home Page is selected in FrontPage Explorer's All Hyperlinks pane. You want to add a logo to Basic Web's Home Page. Select the **A**dd To Do Task command from the **E**dit menu. The Add To Do Task dialog box appears. Notice that INDEX.HTM is listed in the dialog box's Linked To field. INDEX.HTM is the Home Page filename. You link a task in the To Do List to a particular file by highlighting the file in FrontPage Explorer before adding the task. In the FrontPage Editor, the active Web page is linked to the task you create. You can link files or pages to a task only when you add it through the **E**dit menu.

Type the following item:

☐ `Add logo clip-art` at low priority.

Click on the OK button. You added another task to the To Do List without actually opening the list. Furthermore, you linked the task with the actual page on which you want to do the task. Look at Basics Web's To Do List again, as shown in Figure 4.5, by clicking on the Show To Do List toolbar button.

Figure 4.5.

Include a link to tasks created using the Add To Do Task command from the Edit menu.

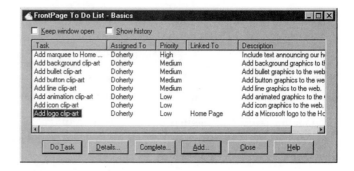

Home Page appears in the Linked To column of the Add logo clip-art task you just added. You see later that links in your To Do List are useful. You select a task with a link in the To Do List and click on the Do **T**ask button and you're taken directly to the Web page or other file that is linked to the task.

Adding a Marquee to Your Web Page

There is only one high-priority task on the Basics Web's To Do List: adding a marquee to Home Page. Do this task first.

Add a scrolling marquee about two lines below the Home Page heading. Open Home Page in the FrontPage Editor and click on the page about two lines down from the heading. Select the Marqu**e**e command from the **I**nsert menu. The Marquee Properties dialog box appears, as shown in Figure 4.6.

Figure 4.6.

Set up your marquee through the Marquee Properties dialog box.

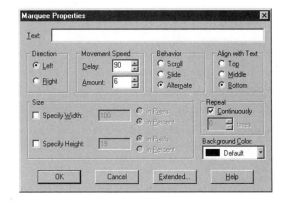

Enter the text used by a marquee into the Marquee Properties dialog box's **T**ext textbox. Type something like `Today only...a red hot sale on ice cubes!` into the **T**ext textbox.

There are several properties that you can manipulate in the Marquee Properties dialog box. You set the direction that the text scrolls set in the Direction area. You select either the **L**eft or the **R**ight radio button.

You adjust how quickly the text moves in the Movement Speed area. The **D**elay value sets the number of milliseconds that the marquee text waits, from when the Web page is loaded, before it moves.

Set the manner in which the text moves in the Behavior area. Select the Scr**o**ll radio button if you want the text to scroll across the screen continuously. Select the **S**lide radio button if you want the text to slide across the page and then stop and remain on the screen. Select the Alternate radio button if you want the text to move from one side of the page to the other while remaining visible at all times.

Set the marquee text alignment with normal text in the Align with Text area. You align the marquee text to either the top middle or bottom of normal text by selecting the To**p**, **M**iddle, or **B**ottom radio button.

You specify the exact width and height of the marquee region in the Size area. The width of the marquee area is set to the width of the page by default. You change the default by selecting the Specify **W**idth checkbox and filling in the width size either in the percentage of the page's width by selecting the in **P**ercent radio button or in number of pixels by selecting the in Pi**x**els radio button. By default, the height of the marquee region is set relative to the font size. You change the default by selecting the Specify Hei**g**ht checkbox and filling in the height size either in the percentage of the page's height by selecting the in **P**ercent radio button or in number of pixels by selecting the in Pi**x**els radio button.

Specify whether you want the marquee text to scroll continuously or only a set number of times in Marquee Properties dialog box's Repeat area. Select the **C**ontinuously checkbox if you want the text to scroll continuously. Otherwise, make sure the **C**ontinuously checkbox isn't checked and set the value in times to the number of times that you want the scroll to be repeated.

Finally, you set a marquee's background color in the Background **C**olor drop-down list. Either select a color or leave it on Default. Default sets the marquee's background color to the same color as the Web page on which it is located.

Once you have all the marquee's properties set the way you want, click on the OK button. Your marquee is added to your Web page. Figure 4.7 shows the marquee with all its properties kept at their default settings. A dashed line surrounds the marquee region.

Open the Basics Web's To Do List by clicking on the Show To Do List toolbar button. Highlight the Add Marquee to Home Page task in the FrontPage To Do List dialog box and click on the Com**p**lete button. The Complete Task dialog box appears, as shown in Figure 4.8.

You can either mark the task as completed or delete the task completely. If you choose to delete this task, all traces of its existence will be removed. However, you should select the Mark this task as completed radio button. This is more useful than deleting the task completely because you're able to track what you've done, in addition to what you want to do, as you see in a moment. When you mark a task as completed, the current date and time also are used to record the completed task. Click on the OK button to close the Complete Task dialog box.

Figure 4.7.

The FrontPage Editor displays the Home Page marquee.

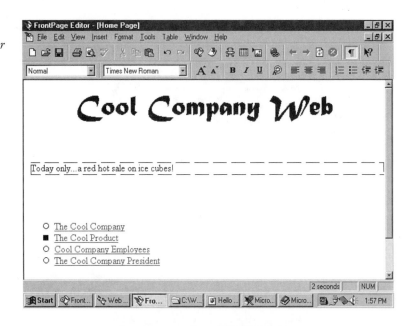

Figure 4.8.

Mark a task as completed in the Complete Task dialog box.

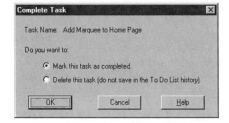

The Add Marquee to Home Page task is no longer listed in the Basics Web's To Do List. However, you see it if you view the To Do List's history. Select the **S**how History checkbox at the top left of the FrontPage To Do List dialog box. The Add Marquee to Home Page task displays in the list with the date completed in the Completed column, as shown in Figure 4.9.

You completed your first task in this chapter. Load Home Page into your Web browser to see the scrolling marquee text.

WARNING

The scrolling marquee is accomplished by using a proposed HTML extension. Microsoft proposed the <MARQUEE> tag, which allows text to scroll around the Web page. Currently, only Microsoft's Web browser supports this HTML tag. That means that if you use the <MARQUEE> tag, most users won't see the special effects.

Figure 4.9.

Completed tasks appear with their date of completion while the Show History checkbox is checked.

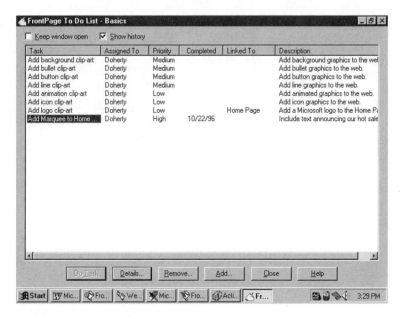

Adding Clip-Art to Your Web

You decorate your Web with FrontPage's clip-art in the following sections. Your To Do List has four medium priority items: adding background, bullet, button, and line clip-art. You use these items to decorate your Web, then you add the low priority items: animation, icon, and logo clip-art.

Bullets

FrontPage provides a variety of bullet clip-art. Unfortunately, there is no way to apply the bullet clip-art to bulleted lists. You need to add bullets to items individually and format the lines manually.

You highlighted The Cool Product hyperlink in Home Page by giving it a solid square bullet, unlike the rest of the bullets that are hollow circles. Make the hyperlink even more prominent, in conjunction with the marquee announcing the sale, by placing a red arrow bullet between the marquee and the bulleted list and then moving The Cool Product hyperlink next to the red arrow bullet.

Open Basics Web's Home Page in the FrontPage Editor and click midway between the marquee you added recently and the bulleted list. Select the **I**mage command from the **I**nsert menu to open the Image dialog box. Select the Clip Art tag in the Image dialog box, then select Bullets from the **C**ategory drop-down list. The Image dialog box's Clip Art sheet displays a selection of bullets, as shown in Figure 4.10.

Figure 4.10.

Select from an array of bullets in the Image dialog box's Clip Art sheet.

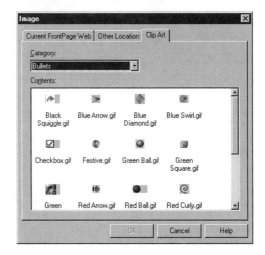

Select the RedArrow.gif from the Co**n**tents area and click on the OK button. A red arrow bullet is added to Home Page, as shown in Figure 4.11.

Figure 4.11.

The red arrow bullet is inserted between the marquee and the bulleted list.

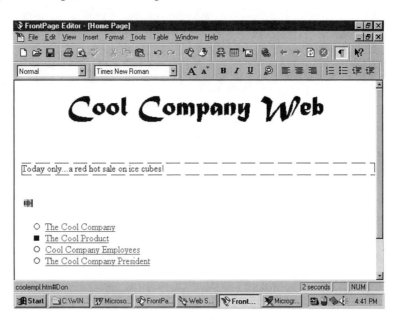

Highlight The Cool Web hyperlink and move it using drag-and-drop next to the red arrow bullet. The result should look something like Figure 4.12.

Figure 4.12.

Edit in the FrontPage Editor using the drag-and-drop technique.

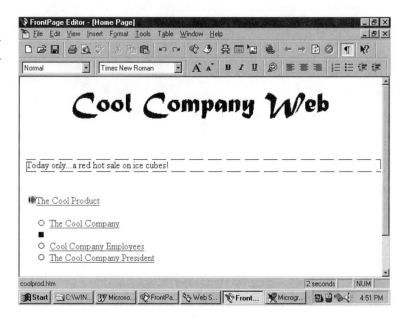

Delete the line in the bulleted list where The Cool Web hyperlink was located. Click on the line next to the solid box bullet. Press the Delete key. The solid box bullet list item is gone and there is one continuous bulleted list with three items.

Add a blank line between the new line with the red arrow bullet and the bulleted list and then save the page by clicking on the Save toolbar button. The Save Image to FrontPage Web dialog box appears, as shown in Figure 4.13.

Figure 4.13.

Save images to your Web through the Save Image to FrontPage Web dialog box.

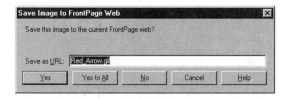

You are asked by the Save Image to FrontPage Web dialog box whether you want to save the RedArrow.gif to your Web. You do want to, so click on the **Y**es button. You can see that RedArrow.gif is now part of your Web by looking at the files in FrontPage Explorer while in Folder View.

Change the spacing around the red arrow bullet by right-clicking on the image and selecting the Image Properties command from the shortcut menu. The Image Properties dialog box appears. Click on the Image Properties dialog box's Appearance tab if the Appearance sheet isn't already displayed. Your Image Properties dialog box should look like Figure 4.14.

Figure 4.14.

Change the horizontal spacing around the red arrow bullet through the Image Properties dialog box's Appearance sheet.

Change the value in the Horizontal Spacing field in the Layout area of the Image Properties dialog box's Appearance sheet to 10 pixels. Several other properties are available, but leave them at their default values. You can set **V**ertical Spacing, **B**order Thickness, **A**lignment, and even the precise size of the image itself. Changing the size of the image can drastically affect how it looks, because it may be stretched or shrunk. Click on the Image Properties dialog box's General tab to display the General sheet, as shown in Figure 4.15.

You see the image's filename in the Image **S**ource textbox. In the Type area are two radio buttons, **G**IF and **J**PEG. The **G**IF radio button should already be selected because you're using a GIF file. If it isn't, select the **G**IF radio button. The two checkboxes next to the **G**IF radio button, **T**ransparent and **I**nterlaced, should be checked already. If they aren't, check them. The **T**ransparent option is particularly important. When you check the **T**ransparent checkbox, you can make one image color transparent. The clip-art's background color is made transparent by default. You see how to set transparent colors manually tomorrow, in Chapter 5, "Adding Graphics to Your Web Page." You should also give a short description of the graphic in the Te**xt** field, under the Alternative Representations section. This text will be shown to people who are using either a text-based Web browser or disabled automatic loading of images. Click on the OK button. The red arrow bullet should be nicely aligned on the page now, as shown in Figure 4.16.

Figure 4.15.

Enable image transparency through the Image Properties dialog box's General sheet.

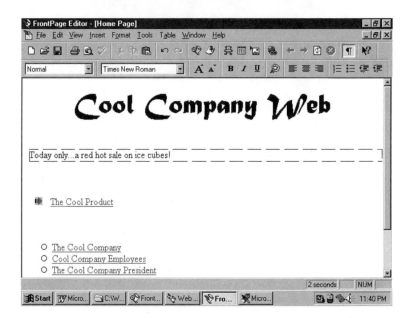

Figure 4.16.

The Cool Product hyperlink is highly visible with the red arrow bullet.

Mark the Add bullet clip-art task in Basics Web's To Do List as completed. Another task completed. Then check out the Home Page in your browser. It's looking cool!

Lines

Turn your decorator's eye to The Cool Company page. You added horizontal lines to this page in Chapter 3. Although they make the page look good, you can make it look even better and more unique by adding line clip-art.

Open The Cool Company page in the FrontPage Editor. Click on the horizontal line just under The Cool Company heading. The horizontal line is highlighted. Select the **I**mage command from the **I**nsert menu. The Image dialog box appears. Click on the Clip Art tab if the Clip Art sheet isn't already displayed. Select Lines from the **C**ategory drop-down list. The Image dialog box should look like Figure 4.17.

Figure 4.17.

Select a line clip-art image from the Image dialog box's Clip Art sheet.

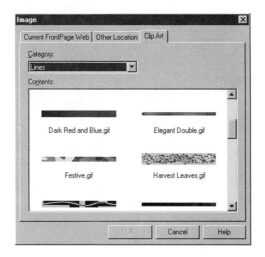

Select a line image. Try HarvestLeaves.gif by selecting it in the Image dialog box's Contents list. Then click on the OK button.

Change the other horizontal line also. Right-click on the HarvestLeaves.gif that you just added to The Cool Company page and select the Copy command from the shortcut menu. Right-click on the horizontal line below the numbered list and select the Paste command from the shortcut menu. Save the page by clicking on the Save toolbar button. The Save Image to FrontPage Web dialog box appears asking whether you want to save the new image file to your Web. Click on the **Y**es button. The Cool Company Web page should look like Figure 4.18.

Figure 4.18.

The Cool Company Web page with its two new line clip-art images.

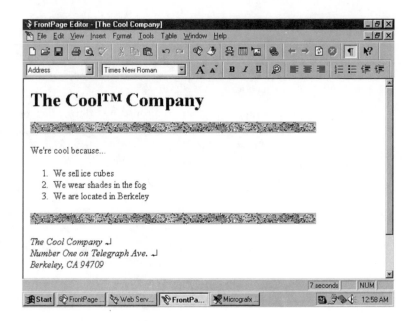

View The Cool Company Web page in your Web browser. The background color is transparent in the line images, making the leaves look particularly good. You're finished with the Add line clip-art task, so mark it as completed in Basics Web's To Do List.

Backgrounds

You dressed up The Cool Company Web page with line clip-art, but it still looks somewhat incomplete. Try adding a background to the page.

Find a subtle background image to apply to The Cool Company page. Select the Page Properties command from the **F**ile menu. The Page Properties dialog box appears. Select the Background tab if the Background sheet, as shown in Figure 4.19, isn't displayed already.

Add a check to the Background **I**mage checkbox, then click on the **B**rowse button to browse for a background image. The Select Background Image dialog box appears. Click on the Clip Art tab if the Clip Art sheet isn't displayed already. Select Backgrounds from the **C**ategory drop-down list. Various background clip-art images are displayed, as shown in Figure 4.20.

The GreenSpeckled.gif looks as if it will complement the leaves you added in the previous section. Select GreenSpeckled.gif in the Select Background Image dialog box's Co**n**tents area and click on the OK button. Add a check to the **W**atermark checkbox on the Page Properties dialog box's Background sheet. When **W**atermark is checked, the background image doesn't scroll; it stays stationary. Click on the OK button.

Figure 4.19.

Apply background clip-art to your Web page through the Page Properties dialog box.

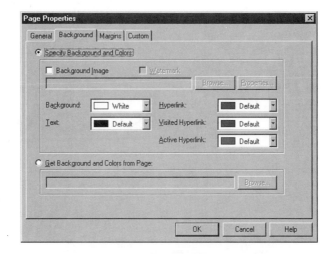

Figure 4.20.

Select background clip-art in Select Background Image dialog box's Clip Art sheet.

Save your work by clicking on the Save toolbar button. The Save Image to FrontPage Web dialog box appears asking whether you want to save the new image file to your Web. Click on the **Y**es button. The Cool Company Web page looks cool loaded in a Web browser, as shown in Figure 4.21.

You're finished with the Add background clip-art task, so mark it as completed in Basics Web's To Do List.

Figure 4.21.

The completely redecorated The Cool Company Web page displayed by a Web browser.

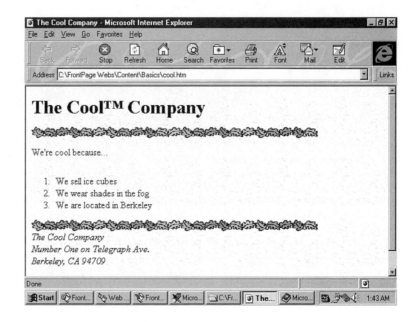

Buttons

Turning your attention to The Cool Company Employees Web page, you realize that the page needs improvements in both aesthetics and navigability. Start by setting a bookmark at the top of the page and then adding a button to each section of the page that, when clicked, moves you back to the top of the page.

Set a bookmark on the Cool Company Employees heading. Highlight Cool Company Employees, then select the **B**ookmark command from the **E**dit menu. The Bookmark dialog box appears. Type top in the **B**ookmark Name textbox and click on the OK button. You set the top bookmark at the top of the Cool Company Employees Web page.

Add a button to each page section devoted to a particular employee and marked off by a level 2 heading. Follow the hyperlinks from the bulleted list at the top of Cool Company Employees to each page section. Start with Jan, for instance. Click on the Jan hyperlink, then select the Follow **H**yperlink command from the **T**ools menu. You are taken to the Jan section where you set the Jan bookmark in Chapter 3.

Insert the up arrow button to the left of the Jan heading, but on the same line. Click your cursor on the left side of Jan. Select the **I**mage command from the **I**nsert menu. The Image dialog box appears. Click on the Clip Art tab if the Clip Art sheet isn't displayed already. Select Buttons from the **C**ategory drop-down list. A variety of buttons display in the Contents area, as shown in Figure 4.22.

Figure 4.22.

Select button clip-art in Image dialog box's Clip Art sheet.

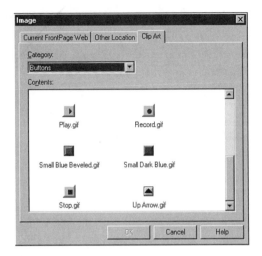

Select Up_Arrow.gif from the Image dialog box's Contents area, then click on the OK button. The up arrow button is inserted to the left of the Jan heading.

Set the horizontal spacing around the up arrow button. Right-click on the arrow button and select the Image Properties command from the shortcut menu. The Image Properties dialog box appears. Click on the Appearance tab if the Appearance sheet isn't displayed already. In the Layout area, change the value of the Horizontal Spacing field to 10 pixels. Click on the OK button. Save your work by clicking on the Save toolbar button. The Save Image to FrontPage Web dialog box asks you whether you want to save Up_Arrow.gif to your Web. Click on the **Y**es button. The up arrow button is inserted and formatted as shown in Figure 4.23.

Create a hyperlink between the up arrow button that you just added and the top bookmark at the top of the Cool Company Employees Web page. Highlight the up arrow and then click on the Create or Edit Hyperlink toolbar button. The Create Hyperlink dialog box appears. Click on the Open Pages tab if the Open Pages sheet isn't displayed already. Select Cool Company Employees in the **O**pen Pages list. Select top from the **B**ookmark drop-down list. Click on the OK button. When people click on the up button, they go back to the top of the Cool Company Employees Web page. Load the page into your Web browser and try it out.

Add the same up arrow button next to each name heading on the Cool Company Employees Web page. You don't need to go through everything again. Highlight the up arrow button that you just entered, formatted, and created a hyperlink on, and click on the Copy toolbar button. Go back up to the bulleted list of employees by following the up arrow button's hyperlink. Select the Follow **H**yperlink command from the **T**ools menu.

Figure 4.23.

The up arrow button is next to the Jan heading.

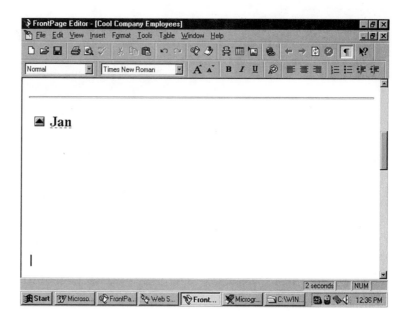

Click on the next name in the employee bulleted list (John) and follow the hyperlink to the employee's section of the page in the usual way. Click on the left side of the employee's name, then click on the Paste toolbar button. The up arrow button is inserted with the formatting and hyperlink intact! Do this for all the employees, then save your work.

You added buttons to your Web and they're even useful. The buttons make navigating the Web intuitive. Mark the Add button clip-art task completed in Basics Web's To Do List. You've finished all but your low-priority tasks. Of course, just because they're low-priority doesn't mean that they aren't decorative. You use some of the best clip-art in the following few sections—animated clip-art, for instance.

Animations

Make the Cool Company Employees Web page more attractive and more functional by adding an animated clip-art that, when clicked on, takes the user to Basics Web's Home Page. Click on a line somewhere toward the bottom of your FrontPage Editor's window, while the Cool Company Employees heading is still visible, and select the Image command from the Insert menu. The Image dialog box appears. Click on the Clip Art tab if the Clip Art sheet isn't displayed already. Select Animations from the Category drop-down list. Several animations are available in the Contents area of the Image dialog box, as shown in Figure 4.24.

Figure 4.24.

Select an animation clip-art from the Image dialog box's Clip Art sheet.

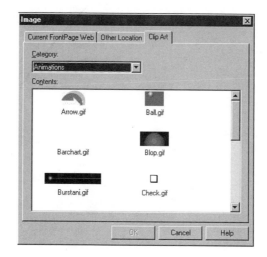

Select House.gif from the Contents area and click on the OK button. The house animation is inserted into the Web page.

Create a hyperlink between the house animation and Basics Web's Home Page. Highlight the house animation, then click on the Create or Edit Hyperlink toolbar button. The Create Hyperlink dialog box appears. Click on the Current FrontPage Web tab if the Current FrontPage Web sheet isn't displayed already. Click on the Browse button. The Current Web dialog box appears, as shown in Figure 4.25.

Figure 4.25.

Select a Web page or file from the Current Web dialog box.

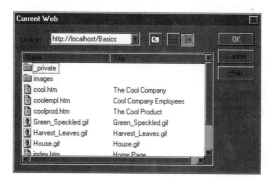

Look for Home Page under Title in the list. When you find it, select its associated filename under Name, INDEX.HTM. Click on the OK button, then click on the OK button in the Create Hyperlink dialog box.

Change the house animation's alignment relative to the page displayed in a browser. Right-click on the house image and select Image Properties from the shortcut menu. The Image Properties dialog box appears. Click on the Appearance tab if the Appearance sheet isn't displayed already. In the Layout area, select "right" in the **A**lignment drop-down list. Click on the OK button. Save your work.

When you load the Cool Company Employees Web page in a Web browser, the house animation runs in the lower right corner of the browser window, as shown in Figure 4.26. Click on the house animation and the Home Page loads into your browser.

Figure 4.26.

The complete Cool Company Employees Web page displayed in a Web browser.

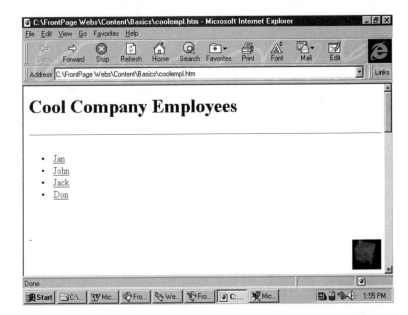

Mark the Add animation clip-art as completed in Basics Web's To Do List. You add a logo to Home Page next. Select Add logo clip-art in the To Do List, then click on the Do **T**ask button. The FrontPage To Do List loads the appropriate file, Basics Web's Home Page, and takes you directly to it, ready for you to perform the task.

Logos

Logos add a professional polish to a Web page. FrontPage provides you with several logos, including one that says that the Web was created using Microsoft FrontPage. Add this logo to Basics Web's Home Page.

You are already looking at Home Page in the FrontPage Editor if you followed along with the last section. If not, open it up. Then click on the line after the list of hyperlinks at the bottom of the page. Select the **I**mage command from the **I**nsert menu. The Image dialog box appears. Click on the Clip Art tab if the Clip Art sheet isn't displayed already. Select Logos from the **C**ategories drop-down list to display a selection of logos in the Co**n**tents area, as shown in Figure 4.27.

Figure 4.27.

Select a logo from the
Image dialog box's
Clip Art sheet.

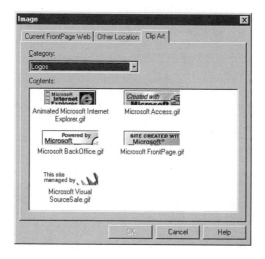

Select Microsoft_FrontPage.gif in the Contents area. Then click on the OK button. The Site Created With Microsoft FrontPage logo is added to Home Page.

Format the logo's location on the Web page. Right-click on the logo, then select the Image Properties command from the shortcut menu. The Image Properties dialog box appears. Click on the Appearance tab if the Appearance sheet isn't displayed already. In the Layout area, select right from the **A**lignment drop-down listbox. Click on the OK button. Save your work by clicking on the Save toolbar button. The FrontPage Editor dialog box appears and asks whether you want to mark the task that opened the page completed, as shown in Figure 4.28. Click on the **Y**es button.

Figure 4.28.

The FrontPage Editor
dialog box asks
whether you want to
mark the task
completed.

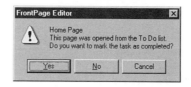

When the Save Image to FrontPage Web dialog box asks whether you want to save Microsoft_FrontPage.gif to the Basics Web, click on the **Y**es button.

Icons

This is your last task! Add some icons to Basics Web's Home Page. The icons make the page look more interesting and give alternate means of navigation to the textual hyperlinks.

Add the icons next to each item in the list of hyperlinks towards the bottom of the page. Right-click on the bulleted list of hyperlinks and select List Properties from the shortcut menu. The List Properties dialog box appears with the Bulleted sheet displayed. Select the non-list format at the top left of the List Properties dialog box and click on the OK button.

The hyperlinks are no longer in a bulleted list and they're widely spaced. Bring them together. Place your cursor at the end of the first item, The Cool Company. Press the Delete key, then press the Enter key while pressing the Shift key. You entered a line break, so now The Cool Company and the Cool Company Employees hyperlinks are spaced closely together. Repeat this procedure once more by placing the cursor after the Cool Company Employees hyperlink and pressing the Delete key. Again, press the Delete key, then press the Enter key while pressing the Shift key. All three hyperlinks should now be close vertically.

Insert an icon next to each of the hyperlinks. Click on the left of The Cool Company hyperlink. Then select the **I**mage command from the **I**nsert menu. The Image dialog box appears. Click on the Clip Art tab if the Clip Art sheet isn't displayed already. Select Icons from the **C**ategory drop-down list to display icons in the Co**n**tents area. Select Handshake.gif in the Contents area and click on the OK button. Repeat this procedure two more times, insert People.gif to the left of the Cool Company Employees hyperlink, and insert Globe.gif to the left of The Cool Company President.

Finally, format the horizontal spacing around the icons. Right-click on each icon and select the Image Properties command from the shortcut menu. The Image dialog box appears. Click on the Appearance tab if the Appearance sheet isn't displayed already. In the Layout area, change the Horizontal Spacing value to 10 pixels. Click on the OK button. When you're finished, save your work by clicking on the Save toolbar button. The Save Image to FrontPage Web dialog box opens and asks whether you'd like to save one of the GIF files to the Basics Web. Click on the Yes to **A**ll button because you want to save all three GIF files to the Web.

You finished the last task. Mark the Add icon clip-art task complete in Basics Web's To Do List. Basics Web's Home Page should look like Figure 4.29.

Figure 4.29.

The completed Home Page below the Cool Company Web title.

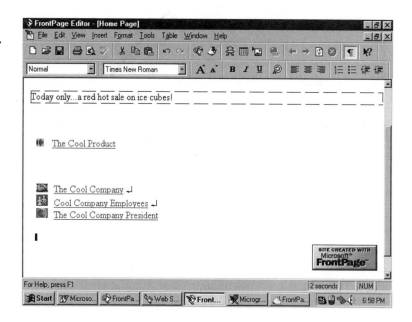

Summary

In this chapter, you added every type of clip-art offered by FrontPage to your Web, which makes your Web more attractive and professional looking. Hyperlinking clip-art or simply using icons next to hyperlinks also makes Web navigation more intuitive. In the next chapter, you learn how to import or create your own graphics and images and you learn how to build image maps to make navigating your Web more exciting and intuitive.

Q&A

Q Do I need a special server to run the clip-art animations?

A No. The animation clip-art runs in your Web browser. No server is required.

Q Arranging clip-art and other items on the page seems cumbersome. Am I missing something?

A You're not missing anything. HTML is notoriously poor for designing page layouts. You overcome this problem somewhat by using tables. You learn about tables tomorrow in Chapter 6, "Adding Tables to Your Web Page."

Q You mentioned transparent colors in GIF files. What are you talking about?

A Don't worry—I only pointed the feature out to you briefly in this chapter. Tomorrow, in Chapter 5, you learn about graphic images in detail, including setting transparent colors.

Workshop

Keep building on what you have. Finish decorating the Basics Web, especially the Cool Company Employees page, where there is a lot of room for your improvement.

Quiz

1. What are the types of clip-art available in FrontPage?
2. Why do icons and other clip-art help make Web navigation easier and more intuitive?
3. What does the FrontPage To Do List's link feature provide you?

DAY

3

Chapter 5

Adding Graphics to Your Web Page

You want unique and dazzling graphics on your Web. Adding clip-art to your pages makes them look good, but you have creative juices that want to flow out onto the Web. Anyone can compose stunning images using Microsoft Image Composer, a tool that comes with the FrontPage Web authoring and publishing package. In this chapter, you focus on a central Web page feature, the graphic image. You learn how to create and manipulate images, and you learn advanced ways of incorporating images in your Webs.

In this chapter, you

- ☐ Use Image Composer
- ☐ Insert an image into your composition
- ☐ Create graphics for your composition
- ☐ Create an image map

Using Image Composer

Compose images in Image Composer by manipulating graphics objects known as *sprites*. Think of a sprite as the digital equivalent of a picture or a piece of a picture cut out of a magazine. One magazine clipping might be a picture of Princess Diana, another might be of the Princess's white hat. Each picture was cut out of magazine pages, and each is treated as a single entity or object—even though one contains the picture of a whole person and the other just the picture of an article of clothing. Image Composer treats pictures as objects.

You compose images with sprites in Image Composer. Each picture you import into an Image Composer composition is a sprite. An imported picture of a person is a sprite. An imported picture of an article of clothing is also a sprite. You can create new graphic objects in Image Composer—also sprites—and incorporate them into your compositions. In fact, every graphic entity in an Image Composer composition is a sprite that you can move, copy, delete, or transform.

Composing an Image

There are two ways to add graphics to your composition; you either import existing images or create graphic objects with Image Composer itself. In this section, you use both methods to compose an image for the top of your personal Web page. You will create an image map for navigating your personal Web with this image.

Open the personal Web you created in Chapter 1, "Building Your First Web," in FrontPage Explorer. FrontPage is a fully integrated environment. You can add images to Webs while you work. You launch Image Composer while your personal Web is open, because you use the image in this Web.

Launching Image Composer

Click on the FrontPage Explorer Show Image Editor toolbar button or select the Show Image Editor command from the Tools menu to launch Image Composer, as shown in Figure 5.1. You can also launch Image Composer, if you are working in the FrontPage Editor, by selecting the Show Image Editor command from the Tools menu.

NOTE

You might not have installed Image Composer on your computer. If you try to launch Image Composer and Microsoft Paint launches instead, you didn't install it. Look at Appendix A, "Installing FrontPage," for more information on installing the Microsoft Image Composer.

Figure 5.1.

Launch Image Composer from inside the FrontPage Web authoring and publishing environment.

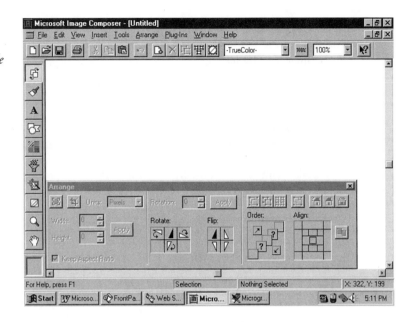

Importing Images

The image you're composing will include graphics that relate to locations in your personal Web. Recall that there are seven hyperlink items on the list at the top of your personal Web page:

☐ Employee Information

☐ Current Projects

☐ Hot List

☐ Biographical Information

☐ Personal Interests

☐ Contact Information

☐ Comments and Suggestions

You want to include a graphic equivalent in your composition for each item on this list, or at least a graphic equivalent to what you consider to be the most important items in the list. You learn the principles of using Image Composer in this chapter while you start to compose this image. It is left for you to complete the image with graphics of your choice.

You can add graphics objects to your image by importing graphics files. In this section, you import a teddy bear graphic. The teddy bear represents your dancing teddy bear page that you will add on Day 6 in Chapter 11, "Adding Java Applets and ActiveX Controls." The dancing teddy bear page will be an item on the Current Projects list of your personal Web page. For now, you use the opportunity to learn how to import images and then how to manipulate imported images.

 The following discussion assumes that you've placed TEDDY0.GIF in the Multimedia Files\My Media folder. This is the default location where Image Composer looks for your media files, including graphics.

When Image Composer launches, a blank, unnamed composition opens. Insert an external image into the composition by clicking on the Insert Image File toolbar button or by selecting the From File command from the Insert menu. The Insert From File dialog box appears, as shown in Figure 5.2.

Figure 5.2.

The Insert From File dialog box opens in the My Media folder by default.

Select JPEG (*.jpg) from the Files of type drop-down list if the JPEG file type isn't already selected. Click on the TEDDY0.JPG file and then click on the OK button. The TEDDY0.JPG file is inserted into your composition, as shown in Figure 5.3.

An outline surrounds the teddy bear image that is now a sprite in your Image Composer composition. Arrows in boxes point out of each corner and midpoint along each side of the sprite. You can resize the sprite with your mouse in the directions indicated by the arrows. In fact, these icons change, depending on the types of manipulations you choose in the Toolbox that, by default, lays along the left side of the Image Composition window. The Arrange button on the Toolbox toolbar is selected by default. A dialog box related to the selected Toolbox toolbar button also displays by default. For now, don't manipulate the teddy bear sprite. First, you set all the sprites on the composition sheet. Then you rearrange and manipulate them.

Figure 5.3.

The teddy bear is a sprite in your composition.

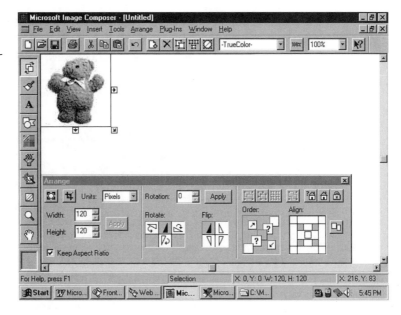

Creating Graphics

You can create graphic objects for your composition, using Image Composer without importing graphics files. There are two ways to create new sprites in your composition. You can either add text or add shapes. Start with adding a textual sprite. Click on the Toolbox toolbar's Text button. The Text dialog box appears, as shown in Figure 5.4.

Figure 5.4.

Add textual sprites to your composition through the Text dialog box.

Type Projects in the Text dialog box's Text textbox. Click on the Select Font button to open the Font dialog box, as shown in Figure 5.5. Select the Impact font in the Font list and click on the OK button.

5

Figure 5.5.

Select a font for your text in the Font dialog box.

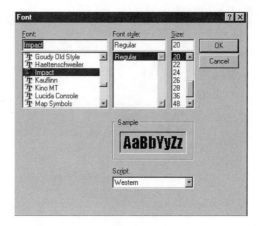

The color of Projects depends on the color to which your Current Color Swatch is set. By default, the Current Color Swatch is at the bottom left side of the Image Composer window (just beneath the Toolbox toolbar). Right-click on the Current Color Swatch and a color palette appears, as shown in Figure 5.6. Click on deep blue. The color that you clicked on appears in Current Color Swatch.

Figure 5.6.

Simply choose the color you want to use for your sprites.

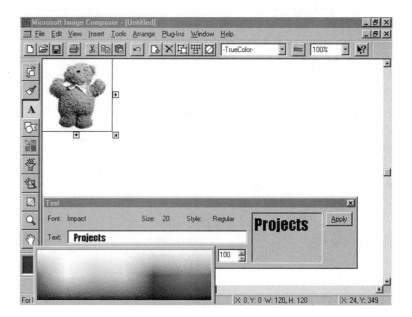

Click on the **A**pply button in the Text dialog box to add the Projects sprite to your composition. You probably need to move the sprite from on top of the teddy bear. Just grab it and move it anywhere in the composition through drag-and-drop techniques. Your composition contains two sprites like those in Figure 5.7.

Figure 5.7.

The Projects text is one sprite and the teddy bear image is another.

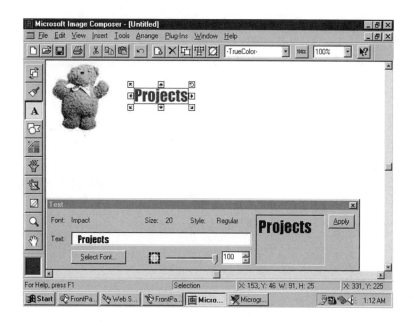

Save your composition by clicking on the Save toolbar button. The Save As dialog box appears. Enter a name such as `Personal Web Image` into the File **n**ame textbox and click on the **S**ave button.

Add another textual sprite, this time for the Hot List item. Type `What's Hot?` into the Text textbox. Right-click on the Current Color Swatch. Click on red in the color palette. Click on the **A**pply button on the Text dialog box. The What's Hot sprite is added to your composition.

Create a hot graphic for the Hot List item. The sun is hot. Create a sun sprite for your composition. Click on the Shapes button in the Toolbox. The Shapes dialog box appears, as shown in Figure 5.8.

Because you're creating a sun and the sun is round, click on the Oval button on the Shapes dialog box. Right-click on the Current Color Swatch and a color palette appears. Click on yellow. Drag your cursor across the image composition area to create a bounding box the size that you want your sun to be. Click on the **R**ender button on the Shapes dialog box. A yellow

5

circle is added to your composition, as shown in Figure 5.9. You can also use the Shapes dialog box to create other geometric shapes. You can create any four-sided figure by clicking on the Rectangle button. Shapes that are made up entirely of curves can be made with the Spline button. Multisided figures can easily be created with the Polygon button.

Figure 5.8.

Create shapes using the Shapes dialog box.

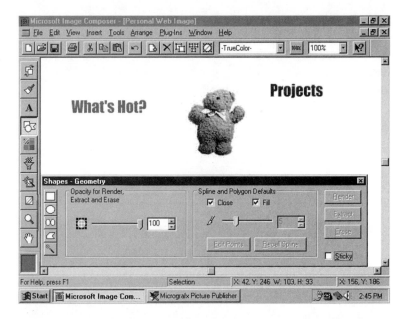

Figure 5.9.

Four sprites populate the Personal Web Image.

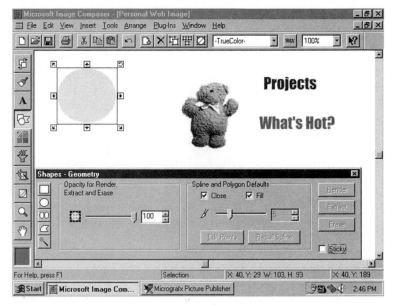

You now have a good start on a personal Web image. Rearrange the sprites, using drag-and-drop techniques. Move the sun sprite over to the top left, then move the What's Hot? sprite so that most of the first word overlaps the upper half of the sun.

Hey! What's Hot? disappears behind the sun! Image Composer images have depth in addition to area. The first sprite you added is the farthest back in depth. Each subsequent sprite that you add is on top of the previously added sprites.

You added the sun sprite after the What's Hot? sprite; therefore, the sun is in front of What's Hot?. Change their order in depth. Select the What's Hot? sprite by clicking on it; then select the Bring to Front command from the Arrange menu. The What's Hot? sprite now appears in front of the sun sprite, as shown in Figure 5.10.

Figure 5.10.

The What's Hot? sprite is moved to the front.

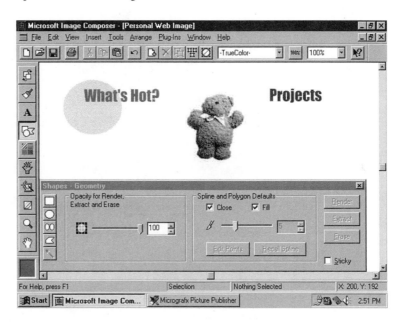

Move the teddy bear to the right of the sun and below the What's Hot? sprite. Place the Projects sprite over the arm on the right side of the teddy bear (the teddy bear's left arm) so that the first couple of letters overlap the arm, as shown in Figure 5.11.

Your composition is starting to come together, although it looks a bit stiff. Rotate the Projects sprite to loosen up the composition a bit. Click on the Projects sprite and notice the icon with the arrow that circles in the counterclockwise direction that appears at the upper right corner of the sprite. You rotate the sprite using your mouse at this icon. An arrow that circles in the counterclockwise direction attaches to your mouse cursor when it is over this icon. You hold down your left mouse button and move the mouse to rotate the icon. Click down on the

Project sprite's rotation icon and move your mouse to the left to rotate the text to roughly the angle that the teddy bear's arm projects. Your composition should look something like Figure 5.12.

Figure 5.11.

The sprites are placed in the desired arrangement.

Figure 5.12.

The Projects sprite is rotated.

The idea of the image is to let the user click on graphics that intuitively convey the content of the Web page with which they link. Text shouldn't play a prominent role in the image. Use text as a hint. Make the graphics stand out by washing out the text sprites.

Click on the Projects sprite, then click on the Warps and Filters button in the Toolbox. Select Color Enhancement in the drop-down list at the top left of the Warps and Filters dialog box. Select Wash in the list below the drop-down list you just used. You see a Wash Options area in the Warps and Filters dialog box, as shown in Figure 5.13.

Figure 5.13.

Wash out sprites to varying degrees through the Warps and Filters dialog box.

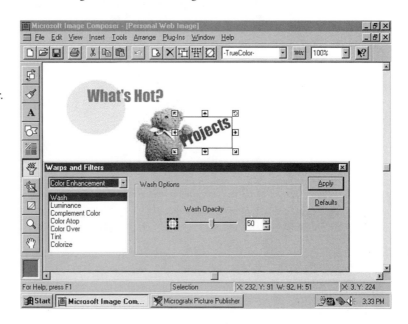

In the Wash Options area, there is a Wash Opacity value. You change the value by typing a new value, by using the slider, or by using the spin buttons. A wash opacity of 100 means that the color is completely opaque, whereas an opacity of 0 means that the color is completely absent—that is, the sprite is invisible. Set the Wash Opacity to 60, then apply it to the Projects sprite by clicking on the **A**pply button. Carry out the same procedure on the What's Hot? sprite. The Personal Web Image looks like the one in Figure 5.14.

Save your Personal Web Image to a file with the appropriate format. Set the image size so that it fits at the top of your personal Web page and so that it doesn't take too long to download over slow modem connections. First, save your work by clicking on the Save toolbar button. Now change the image's size. Select the Composition Properties command from the **F**ile menu. The Composition Properties dialog box appears, as shown in Figure 5.15.

Figure 5.14.

The Personal Web Image with two items ready for hyperlinks.

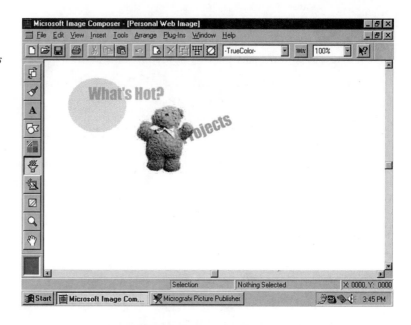

Figure 5.15.

Change the width and height of your composition in the Composition Properties dialog box.

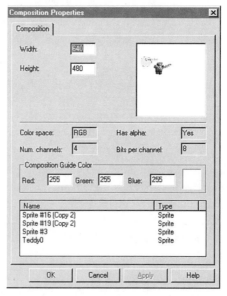

Type the new width, 600 pixels, in the Width textbox and type 200 pixels in the Height textbox. Click on the OK button. Your composition is now 600 pixels wide by 200 pixels high.

Save the Personal Web Image in GIF format. All Web browsers read the GIF format. You also can select a transparent color for GIF files. Select the Save **As** command from the **F**ile menu. The Save As dialog box appears, as shown in Figure 5.16. Select Compuserve GIF (*.gif) from the Save as **t**ype drop-down list.

Figure 5.16.

Image Composer's Save As dialog box presents some special options, including the Transparent color checkbox.

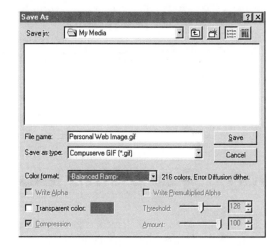

You can select from several options in Image Composer's Save As dialog box. This time, however, you keep the defaults. You will manipulate some of these parameters, such as background color transparency, while you're working with the image in the FrontPage Editor. Click on the **S**ave button. The File Format Limitation dialog box appears, as shown in Figure 5.17.

Figure 5.17.

The File Format Limitation dialog box warns you about Image Composer features not retained under certain file formats.

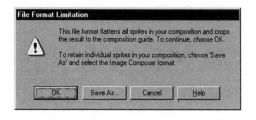

Image Composer supports features that aren't taken into account in many file formats. That's why you should always save your work in Microsoft Image Composer format (MIC) before you save it in any other format. You can go back to the MIC file and edit your compositions by using sprites and other Image Composer features. You already saved a version of the Personal Web Image as a MIC file. Click on the OK button. Your image is saved to a GIF file.

When you want to save JPG files, the Compression option is available to you. This option, when enabled, allows you to specify how much compression to use on the image. This is done with the Amount slider and spinner. The higher the compression value, the more degraded the image will appear, but the file size will be very small. The lower the compression value, the better the image, but the file size will be bigger.

You added two graphics to your Personal Web Image that represent two of the seven hyperlink items on your personal Web. Add the rest of the images any way you like—import graphics or create them in Image Composer. You learn how to create an image map using the image in the next section.

Creating a Client-Side Image Map

Make your personal Web look good and make it more intuitive to navigate by adding an image map. An image map is a graphic that, when you click on various locations, links to various URLs. Image maps are typically used to make navigation around a Web site easier to understand. Until now, image mapping was exotic and difficult to implement. You had to use special server programs. Now you can implement client-side image mapping that lets the user's Web browser do all the work. Better still, FrontPage provides tools that make creating image maps an intuitive and easy process.

Create an image map by using the Personal Web Image that you composed in the last section. Open your personal Web page in the FrontPage Editor. Highlight the horizontal bar, then the Image command from the Insert menu. The Image dialog box appears. Click on the Other Location tab if the Other Location sheet isn't displayed already, as shown in Figure 5.18.

Select the From File radio button, if it isn't already selected. If the image is on the Web or an Intranet, click the From Location button and type in its absolute URL. Add your Personal Web Image to the associated textbox by clicking on the Browse button. The Image dialog box appears. Select the My Media folder inside the Multimedia Files folder from the Look in drop-down list. Select GIF and JPEG (*.gif, *.jpg) from the Files of type drop-down list. Finally, select Personal Web Image from the Image dialog box file area, then click on the Open button. Press Enter twice to put blank space between the inserted image and the Contents list. Your personal Web page should look something like the one in Figure 5.19.

Figure 5.18.

Include image files that are not already part of the Web through the Other Location sheet.

Figure 5.19.

The Personal Web Image is inserted at the top of the personal Web page.

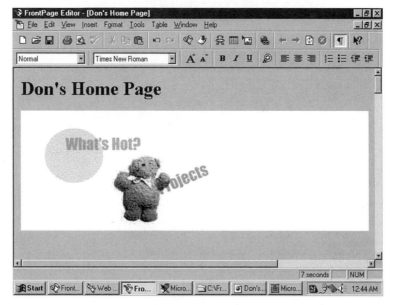

Save your work by clicking on the Save toolbar button. The Save Image to FrontPage Web dialog box appears. Click on the **Y**es button to save the Personal_Web_Image.gif to your personal Web.

The Image Toolbar

Create an image map that assigns a hyperlink from the sun to the Hot List heading and a hyperlink from the teddy bear to the Current Projects heading. The tools for creating image maps are available on the Image toolbar. Click on the Personal Web Image and the Image toolbar appears, as shown in Figure 5.20.

Figure 5.20.

Create image maps by using the tools available on the Image toolbar.

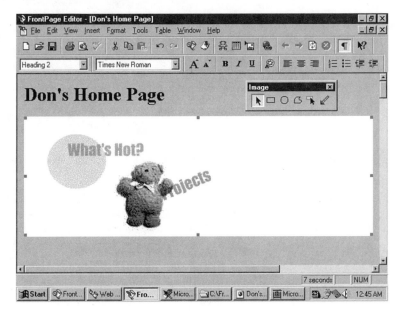

Start by creating a hyperlink from the sun to the Hot List heading. You create what is called a *hotspot* over the area of the image that, when a user clicks on it, will take the user to a bookmark or Web page. The Image toolbar provides three hotspot creation tools: the Rectangle, Circle, and Polygon tools. You create a hotspot with one of these tools, depending on the geometry of the part of the graphic that you want to hyperlink with something. For instance, you use the Circle tool to create a hotspot over the sun.

Click on the Circle button on the Image toolbar. Your mouse cursor changes into a pencil when it moves over the selected image. Wherever you first click will be the center of the circle hotspot, and the distance that you drag is the circle's radius. Click on the approximate center of the sun and drag to its edge. Don't worry if it's not exactly how you want it. You can move hotspots around the image, using drag-and-drop techniques. When you release your mouse button, the Create Hyperlink dialog box appears. Click on the Open Pages tab if the Open Pages sheet, as shown in Figure 5.21, isn't displayed already.

Select Don's Home Page (or the equivalent using your name) from the **O**pen Pages list and select Hot List from the **B**ookmark drop-down list. Click on the OK button. Adjust the placement of the hotspot, using drag-and-drop techniques. You added a hyperlink from the sun to the Hot List bookmark.

Figure 5.21.

Enter the hyperlink associated with the hotspot into the Create Hyperlink dialog box.

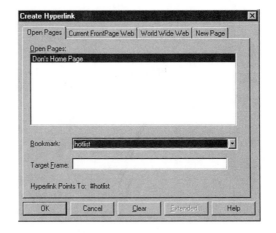

Add a hotspot to the teddy bear and create a hyperlink to the Hot List bookmark. Click on the Polygon button on the Image toolbar. Create a roughly rectangular-shaped hotspot over the teddy bear. Click once on the left ear (your left), then click on the right ear to create the first line segment. Click on the bottom-right edge of the right leg to create the second line segment; then click on the bottom-left edge of the left leg to create the third line segment. Finally, click on the same place on the left ear that you started. The Create Hyperlink dialog box appears. Click on the Open Pages tab if the Open Pages sheet isn't displayed already.

Select Don's Home Page (or the equivalent using your name) from the **O**pen Pages list and select projects from the **B**ookmark drop-down list. Click on the OK button. You added a hyperlink from the teddy bear to the Projects bookmark.

The Image toolbar's Rectangle tool works the same way that the Circle tool works except it creates a rectangular-shaped hotspot. Two other tools on the Image toolbar are new, however. When you click on the Highlight Hotspots button, the contents of the image you're working on disappear, and only the hotspot outlines are displayed, as in Figure 5.22.

When you click on the Make Transparent button, you can click on a color in your image and that color will be transparent. The background color in the Personal Web Image is white. Your cursor should change to the end of a pencil, with an eraser and an arrow pointing from the eraser when it's moved over the image. Click on the white background. The white should turn into whatever you set for your Web page's background color.

Save your work by clicking on the Save toolbar button. The Save Image to FrontPage Web dialog box appears asking if you want to save the Personal_Web_Image.gif file to your Web. Click on the **R**eplace button to replace the file with the newest version.

5

Figure 5.22.

The hotspots created over the Personal Web Image are highlighted when the Highlight Hotspots button is selected.

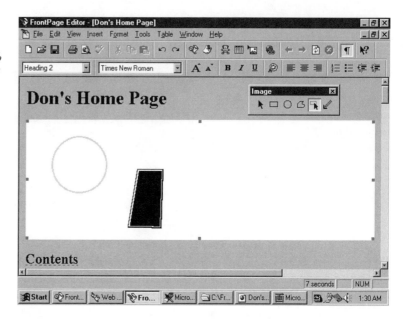

The new version of your personal Web page should look something like the one in Figure 5.23 when it's loaded into a Web browser. When you click on the sun, you go to the page's Hot List heading; when you click on the teddy bear, you go to the page's Current Projects heading.

Figure 5.23.

After you've created the image map, your home page will look something similar to this.

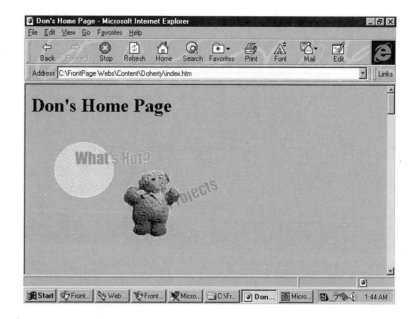

Summary

You just finished learning how to add interesting graphics to your Web pages and how to use those graphics as navigation tools. Image maps are a popular method for creating attractive and useful Webs at large sites. Traditionally, image maps were difficult to create and maintain. With client-side image mapping, that has changed. Also, the tools provided on the FrontPage Editor's Image toolbar make creating image maps as simple as drawing a circle or a square. The tools that you mastered in this chapter keep you at the forefront of using Web graphics.

Q&A

Q Am I forced to use Image Composer to make images for my FrontPage Webs?

A No, you can use any graphics program that you want that can create GIF or JPEG graphics.

Q Can I use Microsoft Image Composer files in the MIC format in my Web pages?

A No. Browsers don't recognize the MIC format. You always need to save the image file to a browser-recognized format—usually GIF or JPEG.

Q Can I create server-side image maps in FrontPage?

A Yes and no. You can do it, but there are no tools to make it especially easy.

Workshop

Image Composer is a full-featured program in its own right. Complete your Personal Web Image by including at least seven graphics objects. Experiment with Image Composer's large number of options while you finish the composition. Add hyperlinks to the graphic objects through hotspots.

Quiz

1. What graphics file format enables you to pick a color to be set as transparent?
2. Image Composer manipulates all graphic entities as objects. What are they called?
3. Areas that are hyperlinks on images are named what?

Chapter **6**

Adding Tables to Your Web Page

Tables are useful in their own right. You can present tables of data in your Web. This enables you to present data in an organized, and easy-to-understand, manner. Tables are probably even more important for the role they play in Web page layout, however. HTML is notoriously deficient in tags that help you in page layout. How can you place elements of your composition at particular locations on a page? You create a grid across your Web page with table tags. Then you place components of the page you're creating into the grid element at the appropriate location. Tables give you a lot of control over the layout of your Web page, and FrontPage makes it easy for you to add tables.

In this chapter, you

- ☐ Add tables to your Web page
- ☐ Use tables for page layout
- ☐ Create templates

Using Tables as Tables

You can add tables to your Web pages to display information. In fact, this is the most obvious use of tables. In this section, you add a weather tracking project to your personal Web. The project you set out for yourself is to keep track of your local weather on a daily basis with your own thermometer. You tabulate and display the data in a table on the Local Weather page in your personal Web.

Open your personal Web in FrontPage Explorer and then open your personal Web page in the FrontPage Editor. Go to the Current Projects heading in your personal Web page. Replace one of the project placeholders—Project 1, for instance—with `Local Weather Tracking`. Type a brief explanation of the project below, replacing the default text entered by the Personal Web template, as shown in Figure 6.1.

Figure 6.1.

Type the title and an explanation of your local weather tracking project.

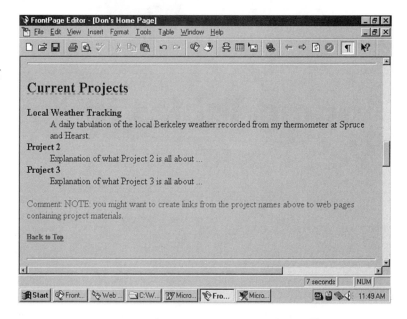

Add a new page to your personal Web by clicking on the FrontPage Editor's New toolbar button. Click on the Save toolbar button to save the new page. The Save As dialog box appears. Type `Local Weather` into the Save As dialog box's Page **T**itle textbox, and keep the suggested filename in the File **p**ath textbox. Click on the OK button.

Keep the new Local Weather page open in the FrontPage Editor, but activate your personal Web's Home Page. Create a hyperlink between the new project, Local Weather Tracking, that you added to your Current Projects list and the new Local Weather page.

Highlight Local Weather Tracking, then click on the Create or Edit Hyperlink toolbar button. The Create Hyperlink dialog box appears. Click on the Open Pages tab if the Open Pages sheet isn't displayed already. Select Local Weather from the **O**pen Pages list, then click on the OK button. The Local Weather Tracking project is linked to the Local Weather page.

You now create a table of local weather data on your Local Weather page. View the Local Weather page again in the FrontPage Editor. At the top of the page, add a level 1 heading with the words Local Weather. Select the **I**nsert Table command from the **T**able menu. The Insert Table dialog box appears, as shown in Figure 6.2.

Figure 6.2.

Add tables to your Web pages through the Insert Table dialog box.

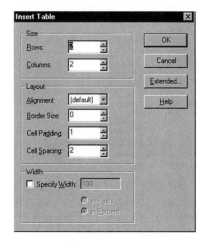

The main thing that you need to decide is the number of rows and columns that you want in the table. Start with three days of weather data. You need a row for the column headings plus three rows for the weather data—a total of four rows. Type 4 in the **R**ows textbox in the Insert Table dialog box's Size area. Each day of weather data includes the date, the high temperature, the low temperature, and then a call on how the sky looks—that is, sunny, hazy, cloudy, rain, and so forth. Each of these takes a column, so the table has four columns labeled Date, High, Low, and Sky. Type 4 into the **C**olumns textbox. Give the table a border size by adding 1 to the Border Size textbox in the Layout area. If this setting is 0, you can't see the table itself, just its contents. By default, the table will be put on the Web page, wherever it's created. You can change this behavior by clicking on the **A**lignment drop-down list. You can choose to have the table on the Left, the Right, or in the Center. Additionally, if you want to space out the table entries further, you should adjust the Cell Pa**d**ding and Cell **S**pacing values. The Cell Pa**d**ding entry controls how many pixels are between the cell border and the cell data. The Cell **S**pacing specifies the number of pixels between table cells. Finally, make the table fill the width of the Web page. Check the Specify **W**idth checkbox in the Width area. Select the in **P**ercent radio button if it isn't already selected and type 100 in the textbox next to the Specify **W**idth checkbox. Click on the OK button. Your Local Weather Web page should look something like Figure 6.3.

Figure 6.3.

A 4×4 table is added to the Local Weather Web page.

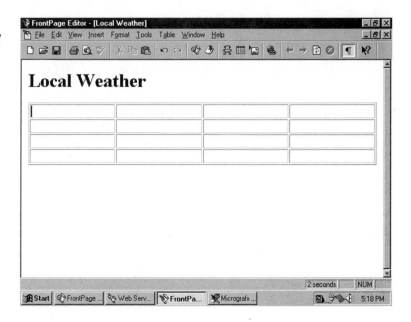

Type the table's column labels. Type Date into the table's top left cell. Then type High in the next cell to the right, Low in the next cell, and Sky in the top right cell. Make the labels stand out. Move your cursor so that it's over the table border to the left of Date. The cursor should change to a right pointing arrow. Click once and the entire first row should be highlighted. Select the **F**ont command from the F**o**rmat menu. Select Bold from the F**o**nt Style list and 4 (14 pt) from the **S**ize list. Click the OK button. Your Local Weather page with its labels should look something like Figure 6.4.

Now type the data. Three days of data are provided in Table 6.1. Recall that you can insert symbols into your Web pages, including the degree symbol, from the Symbol dialog box. Select the **S**ymbol command from the **I**nsert menu to open the Symbol dialog box. The easiest method is to insert the degree symbol (°) once, followed by F for Fahrenheit. Copy °F once and then paste it as many times as you need.

NOTE

While you're typing the weather information, in weather-related Web pages, such data is automated. Typically, such Web pages automatically retrieve, process, and integrate the information.

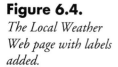

Figure 6.4.

The Local Weather Web page with labels added.

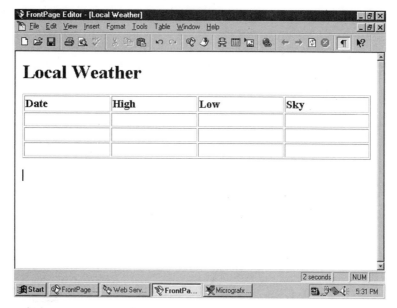

Table 6.1. Three days of weather data.

Date	High	Low	Sky
10-26-96	66°F	46°F	Sunny
10-27-96	69°F	48°F	Sunny
10-28-96	67°F	48°F	Sunny

The table on your Local Weather page should look something like the one in Figure 6.5.

There is a lot of empty space in the table. Too much empty space makes a table look shabby. No problem—once you insert a table, you can change its format through the Table Properties dialog box. Click anywhere in the table, then select the Table **P**roperties command from the T**a**ble menu. Alternatively, right-click on the table and select the Table Properties command from the shortcut menu. The Table Properties dialog box appears, as shown in Figure 6.6.

6

Figure 6.5.

The Local Weather Web page with the data added.

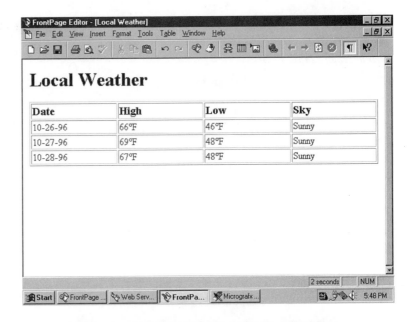

Figure 6.6.

Edit existing tables through the Table Properties dialog box.

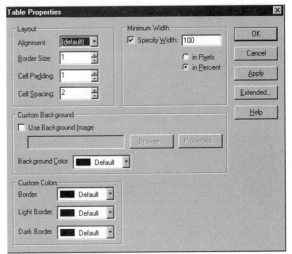

Change the value in the textbox next to the Specify **W**idth checkbox from 100 to 55. Click on the OK button. The table now spans 55 percent of the Web page's width as show in Figure 6.7.

Figure 6.7.

The resized table fits its data much better.

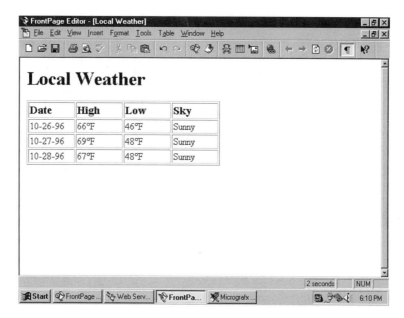

The Local Weather Tracking project is an ongoing project, so you'll obviously need more rows in the Local Weather table—in fact, a new row every day. In the FrontPage Editor, it's a simple matter to add new rows to an existing table.

Add one new row to your Local Weather table so that you can add the new day of data listed in Table 6.2. Click anywhere in the last row of the Local Weather table, then select the Insert Rows or Columns command from the Table menu. The Insert Rows or Columns dialog box appears, as shown in Figure 6.8.

Figure 6.8.

Add rows or columns to your table through the Insert Rows or Columns dialog box.

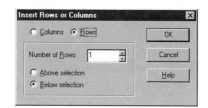

Table 6.2. A new day of weather data.

Date	High	Low	Sky
10-29-96	69°F	50°F	Sunny

Select the **R**ows radio button if it isn't already selected. You add one row, so leave the value in the Number of **R**ows textbox at 1. Finally, you want the new row added to the end of the table, so select the **B**elow selection radio button if it isn't selected already. Click on the OK button. You add a new row to the Local Weather table.

Type the data shown in Table 6.2 in the Local Weather table's new row. Your Local Weather page should look something like Figure 6.9.

Figure 6.9.

A new row of data is added to the Local Weather table.

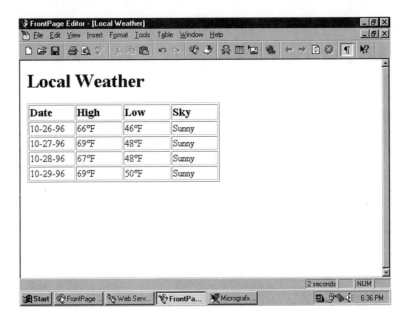

In this section, you learned how to create a new table of data. You also learned how to format and change an existing table. In the following sections, you use tables to control page layout.

Using Tables for Page Layout

Tables have become more important for helping in the creation of Web page layouts than for creating tables themselves. The lack of tags for placing text and other objects, such as images and form elements, at precise locations on the page has made using tables essential for this kind of task. For instance, what if you want to make a list that spans the width of the page, with each list element taking up the same amount of space? There are no tags that let you do this. However, you can create a table and place each list item in a single cell to get the same effect. You simply need to make the table's borders invisible. This is exactly what you do next.

Your personal Web's Home Page still contains a bulleted list under the image you added in Chapter 5, "Adding Graphics to Your Web Page." This kind of bulleted list isn't used at the major Web sites anymore. A list that spans the page is one preferred way to list hyperlinks to other locations in the same Web site. This method of listing hyperlinks takes much fewer lines, and the hyperlink list fits well beneath an image map. Notice that the Contents list takes up a good part of a page and isn't handy to a person using the image map above. It's ideal to keep all information related to a single goal or purpose on an area of a Web page small enough to see at once, without scrolling. The image map and the Contents list have the single purpose of telling the user what's in your Web and to give them hyperlinks to get there. They should both be visible at the same time. Achieve this effect by changing the Contents list on your personal Web's Home Page so that the list elements are listed across the width of the Web page under the image map.

Open your personal Web Home Page in the FrontPage Editor. First, delete the Contents heading over the Contents bulleted list. The heading was set to the top bookmark. Create a bookmark on the page heading—Don's Home Page in my case—and name the bookmark top. Highlight Don's Home Page and select the **B**ookmark command from the **E**dit menu. The Bookmark dialog box appears. Type top in the Bookmark Name textbox and click on the OK button. Now when you click on the hyperlinks that say Back to Top, you go up to the actual top of the page where the image map and, soon, all the hyperlinks are listed.

Create a layout for the Contents list by clicking on the line right under the image map and inserting a table. Click on the Insert Table toolbar button. A palette drops down, as shown in Figure 6.10.

Figure 6.10.

Select the number of rows and columns in your table by high-lighting boxes in the Insert Table toolbar button's palette.

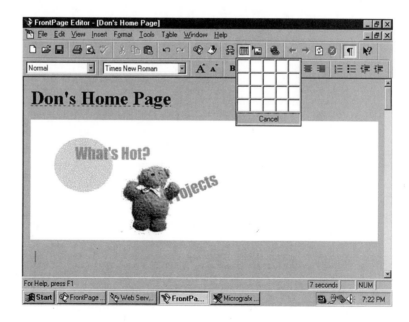

There are six list items, so highlight two rows by three columns. Click on the upper left box and, while holding down the mouse button, drag across one more box down and two more boxes to the right. The size of the table selected is shown at the bottom of the palette while you make the selection. When you've selected a 2-by-3 table, release your mouse button. A 2-by-3 table that spans the entire width of your Web page is entered below the image map, as shown in Figure 6.11.

Figure 6.11.

Your selected table will appear under the image.

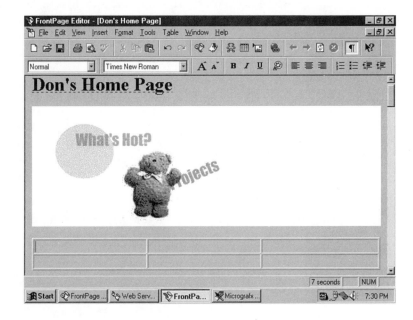

Move each item of the Contents list to a cell in the table. Use drag-and-drop or cut-and-paste methods. The links remain intact. Once you move all the list items, delete the remnants of the bulleted list. Make the table itself invisible by clicking anywhere in the table, then selecting the Table **P**roperties command from the T**a**ble menu. Type 0 into the **B**order Size textbox in the Layout area. Click on the OK button. The table's borders are represented by dotted lines in the FrontPage Editor, but they're invisible when a Web browser displays the page, as shown in Figure 6.12.

You can format table cells in addition to the table as a whole. Each hyperlinked item is left-aligned in the table's cell. What if you want them centered in their cells? Highlight all the cells in the table, then select the **C**ell Properties command from the T**a**ble menu. Alternatively, right-click on the highlighted table, then select the Cell Properties command from the shortcut menu. The Cell Properties dialog box appears, as shown in Figure 6.13.

Figure 6.12.

Both the personal Web's image map and the list of hyperlinks fit on a single visible portion of a Web page.

Figure 6.13.

Format a cell in a table through the Cell Properties dialog box.

Select Center in the Horizontal Alignment drop-down list in the Cell Properties dialog box's Layout area. Click on the OK button. The items are all centered in their cells, as shown in Figure 6.14. If you would rather have all the items take up all the space in their cells, that's not hard either. Simply put your cursor in a table cell and bring up the Cell Properties dialog box. Enable the Specify **W**idth checkbox, and type 100 in the text field. Next, click on the in **P**ercent radio button to use 100 percent of the cell width. Another useful feature of table cells that some Web authors use is the capability of controlling the cell's background color. This can also be easily done by selecting the cell you want to modify and bringing up the Cell Properties dialog box. Next click on the Background **C**olor drop-down list and select the color you want to use.

Figure 6.14.

All the items in the table are centered in their cells.

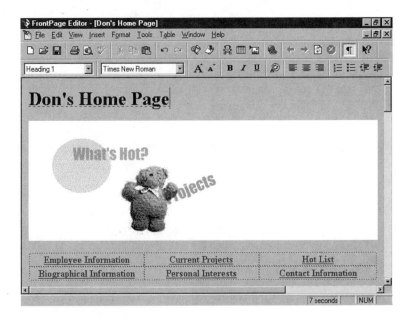

Creating Templates

You created your personal Web page using the Personal Web template in Chapter 1, "Building Your First Web." You've made several modifications to the original. The image map and your changes to the Contents list significantly change how a person sees and uses the page. What if you want to create every personal Web page you make like your modified page rather than the template that comes with FrontPage? It's probably no big deal if you make only your own personal Web, but what if you're in the business of building personal Web pages for other people? You can save your own Web design as a template and reuse it anytime you want.

6

Save your personal Web page as a template. Open your personal Web page in the FrontPage Editor. Select the Save **As** command from the **F**ile menu. The Save As dialog box appears. Click on the As Te**m**plate button to open the Save As Template dialog box, as shown in Figure 6.15.

Figure 6.15.

Create templates through the Save As Template dialog box.

Type Personal Page in the **T**itle textbox and type a description into the **D**escription scrolling textbox. Click on the OK button. When the Save Image to File dialog box appears, click on Yes if you want it included in your template; otherwise, click on No.

You can open the Personal Page template by selecting **N**ew from the **F**ile menu. The New Page dialog box appears. Select Personal Page from the Template or Wizard list, then click on the OK button. Your version of a personal Web page is loaded in the FrontPage Editor.

Summary

In this chapter, you learned how to insert tables into your Web pages and how to use tables to create page layouts. The FrontPage Editor provides tools to make adding and modifying tables a simple matter of point and click. Tables give you control over where text and other objects, such as graphics, are placed on a page. Frames are another useful and sophisticated way to control page layouts. You learn about frames tomorrow in Chapter 7, "Including Frames in Your Web."

Q&A

Q Can I insert images into table cells?

A Yes. Just click inside the cell where you want the image. Then use the same techniques that you use for inserting images anywhere.

Q Can each cell be formatted differently in a table?

A Yes. Click on a cell that you want to format, then open the Cell Properties dialog box. Set the properties the way you want them for that cell, then click on the OK button. The new property settings are applied to only the cell you selected.

Q Is it possible to create a Web template in FrontPage Explorer?

A No. You are able to create Web page templates in the FrontPage Editor, but there are no facilities to create a Web template in FrontPage Explorer.

Workshop

Think of any kind of data that you might like to hold in a table and build a table for it. You might build a table of your friends and their e-mail addresses, a table of birds that you've sighted, or maybe a table of mountains that you've climbed. Create a template of the table if you come up with a particularly good one that can be used over and over in various Webs.

Quiz

1. What are the two ways in which tables can be used?
2. Why do people use tables to help with page layouts?
3. When should you create a template?

6

DAY

4

Chapter 7

Including Frames in Your Web

Creating frames is a way to divide a Web browser's window into tiled areas. Each frame in a window contains a Web page or image. In contrast, the tables you worked with in Chapter 6, "Adding Tables to Your Web Page," divide a single Web page into areas. Some of the best Webs on the Internet today use frames. There are a couple of drawbacks, however. First, frames can be difficult to create by hand and, second, only a couple of the most powerful Web browsers available can read frames. In particular, the latest versions of Explorer and Netscape Navigator provide support for frames. FrontPage renders both of these drawbacks moot by providing you with tools that make creating frames a snap and make adding alternate pages for browsers without frame support as easy as point-and-click.

In this chapter, you

☐ Build frames using the Frames Wizard

☐ Use frames templates

☐ Create custom frames

☐ Add alternate pages

Using Frames

Frames provide the best combined methods for information display and ease of navigation. When you build Webs, you try to display information attractively and effectively on some pages, and you try to build attractive and intuitive lists or image maps on other pages that tell the user what information is available and how to get to it. Frames enable the display of both the information and the navigation tools at once. Usually, at least one frame displays data and at least one frame displays lists of hyperlinks that show the Web's contents and give you easy access to those contents.

The Cool Company Web is a prime example of a Web that can benefit from frames. It consists of a Home Page with a list of hyperlinks to three other pages in the Web. The Home Page is used only as a navigation tool; it tells users what information is available in the Web and gives them an easy way to get to the information. Frames let you show the list and the content at the same time. In the following section, you build frames for the Cool Company Web.

Using Frames Wizard

FrontPage provides a Frames Wizard that lets you build frames in minutes rather than in hours. Add frames to your Cool Company Web (the Basics Web) by using the Frames Wizard available in the FrontPage Editor.

Open your Basics Web (which is, by now, a misnomer) in FrontPage Explorer. Click on the Show FrontPage Editor toolbar button to open the FrontPage Editor. Create frames by selecting the **N**ew command from the FrontPage Editor's **F**ile menu. The New Page dialog box appears. Select Frames Wizard from the Template or Wizard dialog box, then click on the OK button. The Frames Wizard displays its Choose Technique sheet, as shown in Figure 7.1.

Figure 7.1.

The first sheet displayed by the Frames Wizard is the Choose Technique sheet.

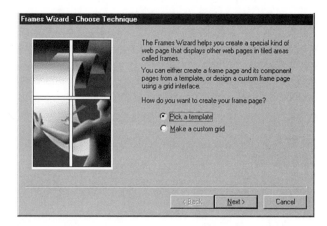

Frames Templates

You choose between using a previously designed frame layout or using a layout that you design in Frames Wizard's Choose Technique sheet. Select the **P**ick a template radio button to choose a previously designed frame layout and then click on the **N**ext button. The Frames Wizard displays the Pick Template Layout sheet, as shown in Figure 7.2.

Figure 7.2.

Choose a template from the Pick Template Layout sheet.

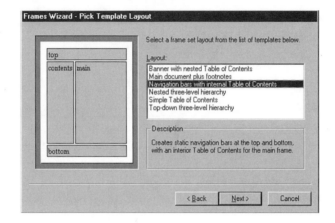

You choose from six templates from the **L**ayout list on the Pick Template Layout sheet. The templates include the following:

- ☐ Banner with nested Table of Contents
- ☐ Main document plus footnotes
- ☐ Navigation bars with internal Table of Contents
- ☐ Nested three-level hierarchy
- ☐ Simple Table of Contents
- ☐ Top-down three-level hierarchy

The layout of the template you select in the **L**ayout list is displayed in the area to the left of the list. You can change the relative size of each of the frames by moving the frame borders around in the layout display. Move your cursor over a border and the cursor turns into a double-headed arrow pointing in the directions that you can move the border. Click down on your left mouse button and drag the border until it's in a position you like. A brief description of the template is displayed in the Description area below the list.

Select the Navigation bars with internal Table of Contents template from the **L**ayout list. This is one of the most universally useful layouts. In the header and footer frames, include information that you want users to see wherever they might be in the Web. At left, in the

7

contents frame, display a kind of table of contents to your Web with hyperlinks. Display information requested by your viewers in the main frame. Click on the **N**ext button. The Choose Alternate Content sheet appears, as shown in Figure 7.3.

Figure 7.3.

Select an alternate page to be displayed if the Web browser doesn't recognize frames.

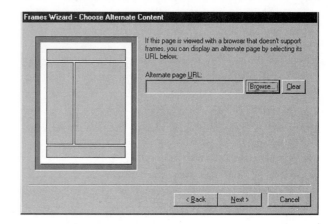

Select the Basics Web's current Home Page as the alternate page. Click on the **Br**owse button. The Choose Source URL dialog box appears, as shown in Figure 7.4.

Figure 7.4.

Select an alternate page from the pages in your current Web from the Choose Source URL dialog box.

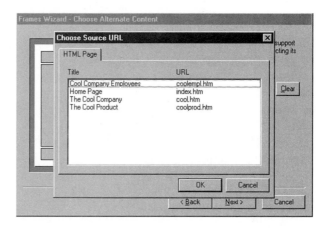

Click on Home Page to select Basics Web's Home Page, then click on the OK button. Click on the **N**ext button on the Choose Alternate Content sheet. Frames Wizard's Save Page sheet appears, as shown in Figure 7.5.

Figure 7.5.

Provide the frames window with a title and a filename in Frames Wizard's Save Page sheet.

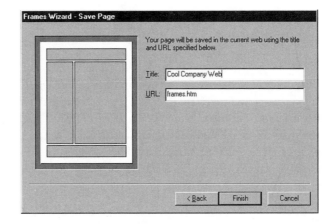

Give your frames window the same title that you gave to your Basics Web. Type Cool Company Web in the Save Page sheet's **T**itle textbox. Leave the default filename in the **URL** textbox. Click on the Finish button. Frames Wizard constructs your Cool Company Web frames. Nothing will appear in the FrontPage Editor window, but if you look at FrontPage Explorer you see the new frames, as shown in Figure 7.6.

Figure 7.6.

The Cool Company Web frames consist of five new files displayed in FrontPage Explorer.

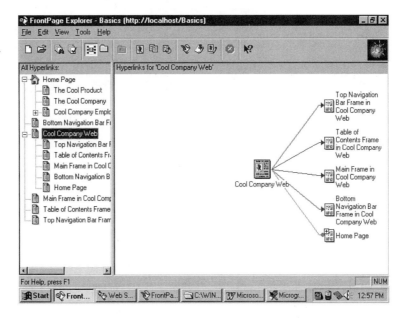

Five new files are added to your Basics Web. The FRAMES.HTM file (or the equivalent, if you named yours something else) is the frames file itself, and it appears in FrontPage Explorer as Cool Company Web. This file is unlike other HTML files because it doesn't describe an HTML page layout; it defines the frames layout in your browser window. Tags in the FRAMES.HTM file tell a Web browser the number of frames in a window, the frames' sizes and locations, and the Web pages that are loaded into the frames. Load Basics Web's frames window into your browser to get a better idea of what this means. Unfortunately, you can't launch frames into a Web browser from inside the FrontPage Web authoring and publishing environment. You need to go to the Front Page Webs\Content\Basics folder and double-click on the FRAMES.HTM file to launch Basics Web's frame window, as shown in Figure 7.7.

Figure 7.7.

The Cool Company Web frames display the default Web pages.

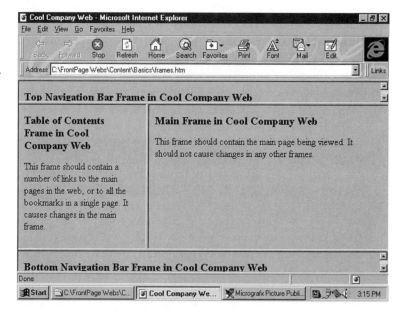

Frames Wizard provides default Web pages for each frame. It's up to you to fill in the Web pages with the appropriate information and hyperlinks. Most of what you need you already have in your Basics Web.

Adding Content to the Header Frame

Load the Top Navigation Bar Frame in Cool Company Web into the FrontPage Editor and add content to the page. This Web page displays in the frames window's header frame. It displays its contents at all times. Copy the heading from Basics Web's Home Page and paste it in the Top Navigation Bar Frame in Cool Company Web, in place of the placeholder text. The text is too large for the frame, so highlight the text and open the Font dialog box. Select Normal from the **S**ize list, then click on the OK button. Now the text is too small. Apply the Heading 1 style to Cool Company Web. Your completed Top Navigation Bar Frame in Cool Company Web page should look like the one in Figure 7.8.

Figure 7.8.

The completed Top Navigation Bar Frame in Cool Company Web page displayed in the FrontPage Editor.

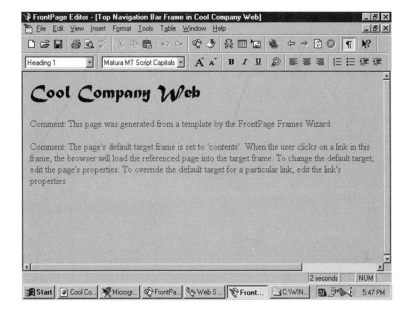

Adding Content to the Footer Frame

Load the Bottom Navigation Bar Frame in Cool Company Web into the FrontPage Editor and add content to the page. This Web page displays in the frames window's footer frame. You add author and copyright information along with a Timestamp WebBot on the left side of this page, and you add the Site Created with Microsoft FrontPage logo on the right side. A WebBot is a program, or script, provided by FrontPage to simplify the use of advanced Web page components. Using WebBots is covered in detail in Chapter 14, "Using WebBots with an Extended Server."

Delete all the placeholder text and add a table that spans across the entire page and has one row and two columns. Right-click on the new table and select the Table Properties command from the shortcut menu. Type 0 in the **B**order Size textbox in the Table Properties dialog box's Layout area. Click on the OK button. The tables borders are now invisible when displayed by Web browsers. You use the table for page layout.

7

Type Copyright, a space, and then insert the copyright symbol in the left cell of the table. To insert the copyright symbol, select the **S**ymbol command from the **I**nsert menu. The Symbol dialog box appears. Select the copyright symbol from the Symbol dialog box, then click on the **I**nsert button. Close the Symbol dialog box by clicking on the **C**lose button. Type a space, then type Cool Company. followed by a line break.

NOTE

> Recall that you enter line breaks by holding down the Shift key while you press the Enter key.

Add the Timestamp WebBot

On the new line, type Revised: followed by a space, then insert the Timestamp WebBot. Enter the WebBot by selecting the **W**ebBot Component command on the **I**nsert menu. The Insert WebBot Component dialog box appears, as shown in Figure 7.9.

Figure 7.9.

Insert WebBots from the Insert WebBot Component dialog box.

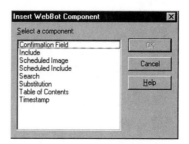

Select Timestamp from the **S**elect a component list, then click on the OK button. The WebBot Timestamp Component Properties dialog box appears, as shown in Figure 7.10.

Figure 7.10.

Set when the date is updated and set format properties in the WebBot Timestamp Component Properties dialog box.

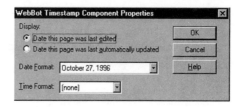

When the Date this page was last **e**dited radio button is selected in the WebBot Timestamp Component Properties dialog box's Display area, the WebBot updates the timestamp each time the page is edited in the FrontPage Editor. Alternatively, the timestamp is updated each time the page is automatically updated on the server when you select the Date this page was last **a**utomatically updated radio button. Select the Date this page was last **e**dited radio button. Select your favorite date format in the Date **F**ormat drop-down list. Leave (none) in the **T**ime Format drop-down list. Click on the OK button. Your Bottom Navigation Bar Frame in Cool Company Web page should look like the one in Figure 7.11.

Figure 7.11.

The Bottom Navigation Bar Frame in Cool Company Web page in the FrontPage Editor after adding text and a WebBot.

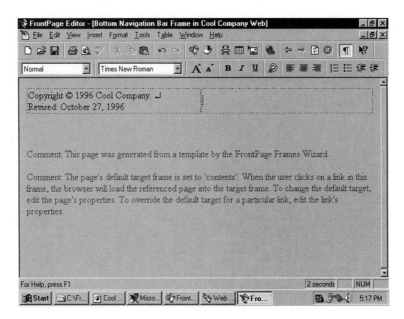

Inserting a Logo

Insert the Site Created with Microsoft FrontPage logo in the right table cell. Click in the right cell, then select the **I**mage command from the **I**nsert menu. The Image dialog box appears. Click on the Clip Art tag if the Clip Art sheet isn't displayed already. Select Logos from the **C**ategory drop-down list. Select the Microsoft FrontPage.gif from the Co**n**tents area, then click on the OK button. The logo is inserted in the right table cell, but it's aligned left. Right-click in the right table cell and select the Cell Properties command from the shortcut menu. The Cell Properties dialog box appears. Select Right from the Hori**z**ontal Alignment drop-down list in the Layout area. Click on the OK button. Your completed Bottom Navigation Bar Frame in Cool Company Web page should look like the one in Figure 7.12.

7

Figure 7.12.

The completed Bottom Navigation Bar Frame in Cool Company Web page displayed in the FrontPage Editor.

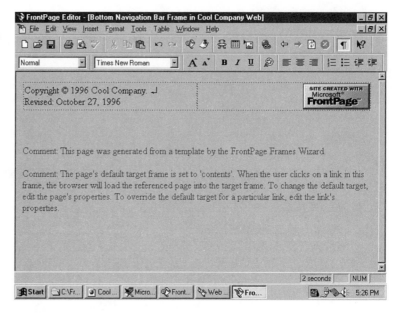

Adding Content to the Contents Frame

Load the Table of Contents Frame in Cool Company Web into the FrontPage Editor and add content to the page. A sort of table of contents to the Web, with each entry a hyperlink, goes on this page. Simply copy the list of hyperlinks from Basics Web's Home Page and paste it on this page. You probably want to get rid of the blank line between The Cool Product hyperlink and The Cool Company hyperlink. Finally, delete all the placeholder text.

Add one new item at the top of the list. You need a hyperlink to the opening page in the main frame. Type Welcome at the top of the page. Then add a hyperlink by highlighting Welcome and clicking on the Create or Edit Hyperlink toolbar button. Click on the Current FrontPage Web tab if the Current FrontPage Web sheet isn't displayed already. Click on the B**r**owse button and the Current Web dialog box appears, as shown in Figure 7.13.

Find Main Frame in Cool Company Web under the Title label. This title is associated with the FRMAIN.HTM file, the default main frame Web page. Click on FRMAIN.HTM in the Name column, then click on the OK button. FRMAIN.HTM is entered into the Current FrontPage Web sheet's **P**age textbox.

There is one more thing that you need to do before you finish creating the hyperlink. You need to specify the frame that FRMAIN.HTM is loaded into when the hyperlink is activated.

You specify the target frame by typing the frame's name, such as main, into the Current FrontPage Web sheet's Target **F**rame textbox. Type main into the Target **F**rame textbox (see Figure 7.14). Click on the OK button.

Figure 7.13.

Select a page from the current Web through the Current FrontPage Web sheet in the Edit Hyperlink dialog box.

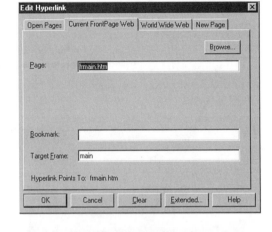

Figure 7.14.

Type the name of the frame that the Web page will load into in the Target Frame textbox.

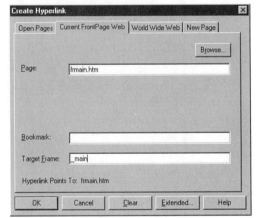

You need to go through the other four hyperlinks on the Table of Contents Frame in Cool Company Web page and set them so that they load into the main frame also. For example, click on The Cool Product hyperlink, then click on the Create or Edit Hyperlink toolbar button. The Edit Hyperlink dialog box appears. Click on the Current FrontPage Web tab if the Current FrontPage Web sheet isn't displayed. Type main into the Target Frame textbox, then click on the OK button. Repeat these steps for the remaining three hyperlinks.

Shorten a couple of the hyperlink names so that they fit into the contents frame. Change Cool Company Employees to Cool Employees, and change The Cool Company President to The Cool President. Your completed Table of Contents Frame in Cool Company Web page should look like the one in Figure 7.15.

Figure 7.15.

The completed Table of Contents Frame in Cool Company Web page displayed in the FrontPage Editor.

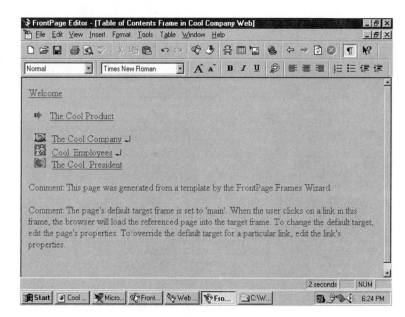

Adding Content to the Main Frame

Load the Main Frame in Cool Company Web into the FrontPage Editor and add content to the page. Highlight the placeholder text in the heading and type Welcome to the Cool Company. Delete the rest of the placeholder text, then copy the marquee from Basics Web's Home Page to below the heading in the Main Frame in Cool Company Web page. Your completed Main Frame in Cool Company Web page should look like the one in Figure 7.16.

Figure 7.16.

The completed Main Frame in Cool Company Web page displayed in the FrontPage Editor.

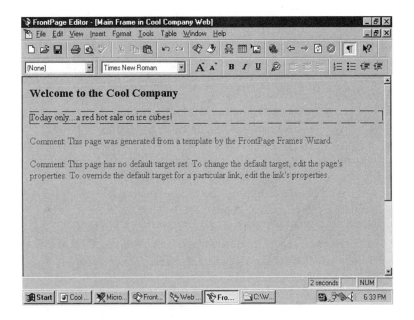

Editing Frames

Load the Cool Company Web frames into your Web browser again, now that you've added content to the frames' pages. You see something like Figure 7.17.

Figure 7.17.

These frames need some adjusting.

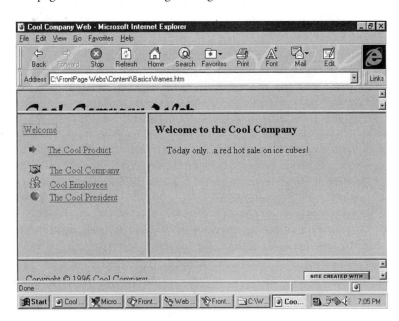

The size of your screen, in pixels, helps determine how a frames layout looks, because the size of each frame is set by a percentage of the browser window's width and height. It's clear that with the 640×400 screen resolution in Figure 7.17 the frames need some adjustment. In particular, the contents of the header and footer frames aren't visible. You can edit several aspects of existing frames, including frame size.

View the Basics Web in FrontPage Explorer. Click on Cool Company Web, the frame page, in the All Hyperlinks pane. Double-click on the Cool Company Web icon in the Hyperlinks for pane, or right-click on the icon and select Open from the shortcut menu. The Frames Wizard opens to the Edit Frameset Grid sheet, as shown in Figure 7.18.

Figure 7.18.

Change the frames layout through the Edit Frameset Grid sheet.

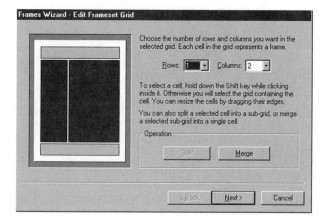

Adjust the horizontal frames borders in the Edit Frameset Grid sheet's visual editing area so that the header and footer are larger. Move your cursor over the top horizontal border until it turns into a double-headed arrow pointing up and down. Click down and hold your left mouse button as you drag the border down. Release your mouse button when you're satisfied with the size of the header. Go through the same steps for the bottom horizontal border to change the size of the footer.

You don't change anything else, but you can completely change your frames layout through the Edit Frameset Grid sheet. You can decrease the number of frames by using the **M**erge button or increase the number of frames by using the **S**plit button. You can also change the number of frames and how they're arranged by increasing or decreasing the number of rows and columns through the **R**ows and **C**olumns drop-down lists. Follow instructions on the sheet to select specific frames or sets of frames. Click on the **N**ext button. The Edit Frame Attributes sheet appears, as shown in Figure 7.19.

Figure 7.19.

Manipulate several frame attributes through the Edit Frame Attributes sheet.

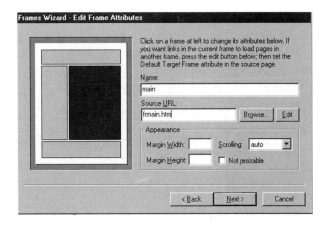

You aren't editing anything else this time. Nevertheless, you get an overview of what you can do in each sheet so that you know where to go when you do want to edit some aspect of frames that you don't edit at this time.

In the Edit Frame Attributes sheet, you click on a particular frame in the visual editing area, then change its attributes in the various textboxes, checkboxes, and so forth found on the sheet. The Name textbox contains the name of the frame. The Source URL textbox contains the filename of the default Web page loaded into the frame. In the Appearance area, there are two textboxes that enable you to set a margin around a frame. A *margin* is an area that is left unoccupied by frame content. Set the margin width in the Margin Width textbox, and set the margin height in the Margin Height textbox. You can set the Scrolling drop-down list to auto, no, or yes. If Scrolling is set to auto, the default, scrollbars will appear around a frame when they are needed. If Scrolling is set to no, scrollbars never appear; if Scrolling is set to yes, they're always present. Finally, if the Not resizable checkbox is checked, users cannot change the size of the frame when it's loaded into their browsers. Click on the Next button. The Choose Alternate Content sheet appears, as shown in Figure 7.20.

You can do one thing in the Choose Alternate Content sheet. That is, you can add or change the Web page used as an alternative to the frames. That way, people using browsers that don't recognize frames can still view your Web. Click on the Next button. The Save Page sheet appears, as shown in Figure 7.21.

7

Figure 7.20.

*Add or change the
Web page used as an
alternate for browsers
that don't recognize
frames in the Choose
Alternate Content
sheet.*

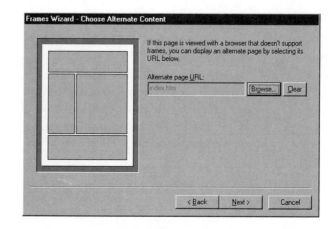

Figure 7.21.

*Change the frame's
title or filename in
the Save Page sheet.*

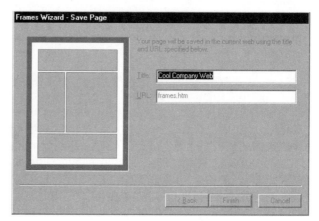

In the Save Page sheet, you can change the frame's title in the **T**itle textbox or change its
filename in the **U**RL textbox. Click on the Finish button. The Frames Wizard dialog box
appears, as shown in Figure 7.22.

Figure 7.22.

*A Frames Wizard
dialog box asks
whether you want
to overwrite the
old frames file.*

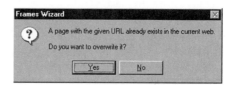

You do want to overwrite the old frames file, so click on the **Y**es button.

Load the Cool Company Web frames into your Web browser again, now that you've edited the size of the header and footer frames. You see something like Figure 7.23.

Figure 7.23.

The Cool Company Web frames now look good.

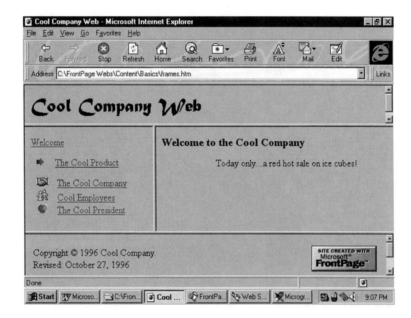

Custom Frames Pages

Build custom frames by selecting the **M**ake a custom grid radio button in the Frames Wizard's Choose Technique sheet. The rest of the sheets are identical to and follow the order of the Frames Wizard sheets that appear during editing, described in the previous section, Editing Frames.

Summary

You added frames to your Web in this chapter. In fact, the frames window uses mostly the same content pages. Hyperlinks load old Web pages unchanged into the main frame. Frames change how people look at your Web. They see a list of the contents of your Web at the same time that they look at the contents. You've just completed building one of the most sophisticated Web constructs available. Next, you add new sights and sounds to your Web through multimedia.

7

Q&A

Q **The frames that I created looked perfect on my computer, but when a friend loaded my Web it didn't look right. Help!**

A Frames layouts depend on screen size. Your screen size, in pixels, is probably different from your friend's. Usually, people target their frames to look the best displayed in what they think will be the most common screen resolution used.

Q **When I click on a hyperlink in my contents frame, the new page fills the whole browser window and the frames disappear. What's going wrong?**

A You forgot to type in the name of the frame that you want the page to load into when someone clicks on the hyperlink. Type the name of the target frame in the Target **F**rame textbox on the Edit Hyperlink dialog box's Current FrontPage Web sheet.

Q **Why can't I load the frames Web page?**

A The frames file defines how a frames browser window is arranged and isn't a Web page itself. If you try to open a frames file by double-clicking on its icon in FrontPage Explorer, the Frames Wizard opens instead, giving you the opportunity to edit the way the frames are arranged.

Workshop

Experiment with a variety of frames templates or try your own custom arrangements. See what kind of unique combinations of Web pages you can arrange in your frames.

Quiz

1. A table divides a Web page into separate areas. What do frames do?

2. What can you do for people who use Web browsers that don't recognize frames?

3. How do you set the frame that a page is loaded into when a hyperlink is activated?

7

Chapter 8

Adding Multimedia to Your Web Page

One of the great things about publishing on the Web is that you can include more than static text and pictures; you can include sound, animations, and video. You should, however, be careful about using such objects in your Web pages. All the features mentioned in this chapter are supported with Internet Explorer and Netscape. In some cases, you need to install special programs, such as plug-ins, to get this support so that if you do use sound, animations, and video, not everybody will be able to see, or hear, everything. FrontPage provides you with tools to incorporate multimedia in your Webs easily.

In this chapter, you

- ☐ Add background sound to your Web
- ☐ Add PowerPoint animations to your Web
- ☐ Add video to your Web

Adding Sound

You can create hyperlinks to sound files in the same way that you can create a hyperlink to another Web page. When users click on the hyperlink, the sound file downloads to their computers and the sound is played. This method of adding sounds to your Web can be useful in some situations, but often it's not what you had in mind. You might want sound to be more integrated with your Web page so that when someone opens your page, sound is immediately part of the experience. The background sound tag was designed to provide sound as an integral part of a Web page. Best of all, the most recent versions of Microsoft Internet Explorer and Netscape Navigator support background sounds.

Background Sound

Add background sound to your personal Web's home page. When a person opens your page, you greet them with "Welcome to my home page."

NOTE

> If your computer can play sounds, it can record them. If your computer can't play sounds, you need to buy a soundcard. Plug a microphone into your soundcard's microphone jack and run the Sound Recorder program provided with Microsoft Windows. You can record anything you want! It's recommended that you keep sound files for background sounds short so that they load quickly.

Open your personal home page in the FrontPage Editor. Select the Background Sound command from the **I**nsert menu. The Background Sound dialog box appears. The sound file that you're using is not part of the Web yet, so click on the Other Location tab to display the Background Sound dialog box's Other Location sheet, as shown in Figure 8.1.

You have the choice of adding a sound file from your file system or from the World Wide Web. Select the From **L**ocation radio button and type a URL in the associated textbox if you want to use a sound file on the World Wide Web. Select the From **F**ile radio button to add a sound file from your file system. Type the path and filename of your sound file in the associated textbox or click on the **B**rowse button to open the Background Sound dialog box, shown in Figure 8.2.

Figure 8.1.

Include a sound file from any folder through the Other Location sheet.

Figure 8.2.

Select a sound file through this Background Sound dialog box.

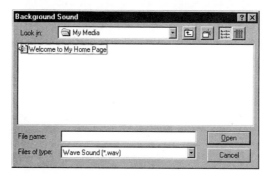

Select a sound file and click on the **O**pen button. The file is added to your Web page as a background sound. Save your work by clicking on the Save toolbar button. The Save File to Web dialog box appears, as shown in Figure 8.3, and asks if you want to save the sound file to your Web.

Figure 8.3.

Add the sound file to your Web through the Save File to Web dialog box.

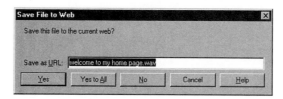

Click on the **Y**es button to save the sound file to your Web. Now your sound file plays when your personal home page is loaded into a Web browser.

NOTE
You can add a background sound through the Page Properties dialog box rather than the Background Sound dialog box. Using the Page Properties dialog box is an advantage if you want to set specific background sound properties. However, you can edit background sound properties through the Page Properties dialog box at any time after inserting a background sound. See the next section, Editing Background Sound Properties.

Editing Background Sound Properties

You can set the number of times a background sound plays, through the Page Properties dialog box. You want the Welcome to My Home Page sound file to play only once after loading the page in a browser.

Right-click anywhere on your personal Web's home page displayed in the FrontPage Editor and select the Page Properties command from the shortcut menu. Alternatively, select the Page Properties command from the **F**ile menu. The Page Properties dialog box appears. Click on the General tab if the General sheet isn't displayed already, as shown in Figure 8.4.

Figure 8.4.

Your Web page's background sound file displays in the Page Properties dialog box's Location textbox in the Background Sound area.

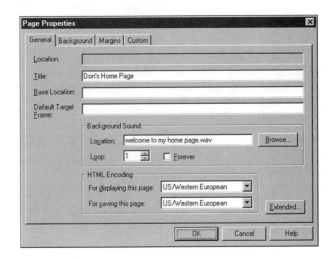

The background sound file you inserted in your Web page earlier in this chapter displays in the Page Properties dialog box's Location textbox in the Background Sound area. If you hadn't already added a background sound file, you could add one by typing a sound file's path and name into the Location textbox or by clicking on the **B**rowse button and browsing for the sound file.

Set the number of times a browser plays the background sound file on loading your Web page in the L**o**op box in the Background Sound area. You want the Welcome to My Home Page sound file to play once when the page is loaded. Type 1 in the L**o**op box if it isn't set to 1 already. There also is a **F**orever checkbox available. Check the **F**orever checkbox if you want the background sound file played over and over for as long as the Web page is open in a browser. Leave the **F**orever checkbox unchecked. Click on the OK button.

Adding Animation

You can create your own animation and add it to your Web pages. In Chapter 4, "Decorating and Expanding Your Web," you added animation to Web pages, but they were clip-art animation that was small and not of your own creation. There are several ways to create and package animation that you display on Web pages, and FrontPage supports many, including PowerPoint animation, Java applets, and ActiveX controls. You learn more about the last two on Day 6 in Chapter 11, "Adding Java Applets and ActiveX Controls." Here, you add PowerPoint animation to your Web page.

PowerPoint Animation

Show off data or create a quick and splashy logo with PowerPoint animation. People viewing your Web page must have the PowerPoint Animation ActiveX control or plug-in. However, the good news is that they are available for both Microsoft's Internet Explorer and Netscape's Navigator.

NOTE

> Create PowerPoint animation using Microsoft PowerPoint. For more information, see http://www.microsoft.com/powerpoint/.

Create a new Web page for The Dancing Teddy Bear project. Click on the New toolbar button in the FrontPage Editor, then save the new page by clicking on the Save toolbar button. The Save As dialog box appears. Type The Dancing Teddy Bear in the Page **T**itle textbox and keep the default filename in the File **p**ath textbox. Click on the OK button.

You add a Java applet to The Dancing Teddy Bear page in Chapter 11. In this section, you add the Dancing Teddy Bear logo. The logo is a PowerPoint animation. The title slides into place from the right side of the logo accompanied by a whoosh sound; then a GIF image of the teddy bear fades into existence accompanied by clapping.

NOTE   The Dancing Teddy Bear logo is available on this book's CD-ROM as the Dancing Teddy Bear.ppz file.

Select the **O**ther Components submenu from the **I**nsert menu. Then select the **P**owerPoint Animation command from the **O**ther Components submenu. The PowerPoint Animation dialog box appears, as shown in Figure 8.5.

Figure 8.5.

Add PowerPoint animation to your Web page through the PowerPoint animation dialog box.

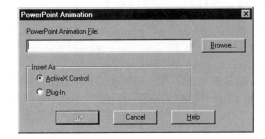

Type the path and filename of the PowerPoint animation file you're inserting in the PowerPoint Animation **F**ile textbox, or click on the **B**rowse button and browse for the file. You're inserting the Dancing Teddy Bear.ppz file.

You have two choices in the Insert As area. You can either insert the PowerPoint animation as an ActiveX control by selecting the **A**ctiveX Control radio button or you can insert it as a Netscape plug-in by selecting the **P**lug-in radio button. If you insert it as an ActiveX control, the person viewing it must have the PowerPoint Animation ActiveX control; if you insert it as a plug-in, the person viewing must have the PowerPoint Animation Netscape plug-in. The plug-in works with either Internet Explorer 3.0 or Netscape Navigator 2.0 or later. You can download the plug-in by pointing your Web browser to `http://www.microsoft.com/kb/softlib/mslfiles/pptvw32.exe`.

Inserting as an ActiveX Control

Insert the Dancing Teddy Bear PowerPoint animation as an ActiveX control by selecting the **A**ctiveX Control radio button. Click on the OK button. An ActiveX control field is inserted

8

into the Web page, but it's far too large for the logo. Right-click on the ActiveX control field and select the ActiveX Control Properties command from the shortcut menu or select the ActiveX Control Properties command from the **E**dit menu. The ActiveX Control Properties dialog box appears, as shown in Figure 8.6.

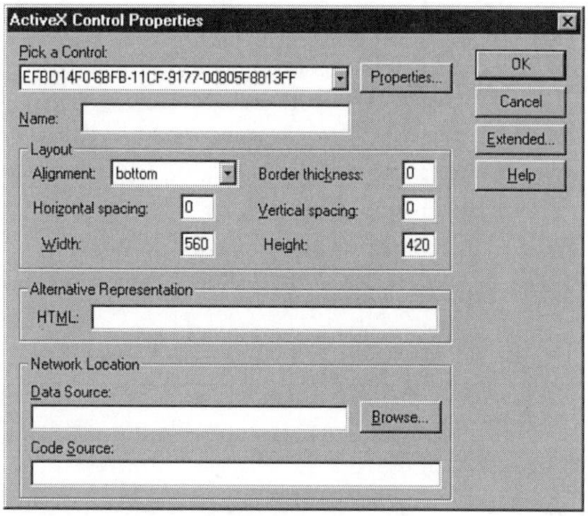

Figure 8.6.

Change the PowerPoint animation's display dimensions through the ActiveX Control Properties dialog box.

You can manipulate several ActiveX control properties. You learn more about them in Chapter 11. For now, stick to changing the dimensions of the Dancing Teddy Bear logo by typing **200** into the **W**idth textbox and **200** into the Hei**g**ht textbox in the ActiveX Control Properties dialog box Layout area. The logo is set at 200 pixels by 200 pixels. Select right in the A**l**ignment drop-down list so that the logo appears in the upper right corner of the Web page. Click on the OK button. In the FrontPage Editor, The Dancing Teddy Bear Web page should look like Figure 8.7.

Open The Dancing Teddy Bear page into an ActiveX control-enabled Web browser and be sure that the PowerPoint Animation ActiveX control is installed on your computer. You should see and hear the Dancing Teddy Bear logo right after the page loads. When the animation is finished, the page should look like Figure 8.8.

The Dancing Teddy Bear page appears in FrontPage Explorer with links to the Dancing Teddy Bear.ppz file and the PowerPoint Animation ActiveX control, as shown in Figure 8.9. The PowerPoint ActiveX control is represented by its class identification number (CLSID). You learn about class CLSIDs in Chapter 11.

Figure 8.7.

The Dancing Teddy Bear Web page in the FrontPage Editor.

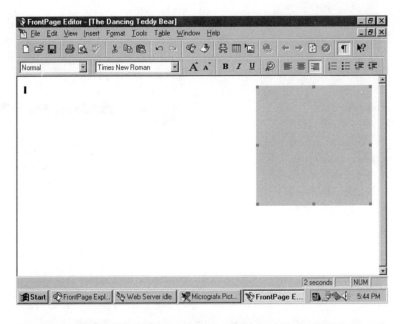

Figure 8.8.

The Dancing Teddy Bear logo introduces the dancing teddy bear.

Figure 8.9.

ActiveX controls added to your Web display in FrontPage Explorer.

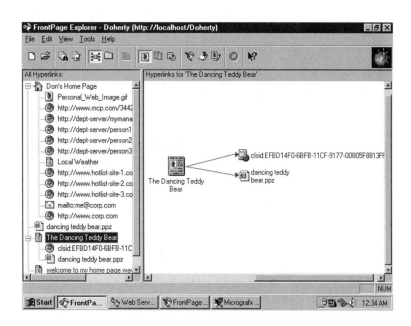

Inserting as a Netscape Plug-In

Insert the Dancing Teddy Bear PowerPoint animation as a Netscape plug-in by selecting the **P**lug-in radio button. Click on the OK button. A Netscape plug-in field is inserted into the Web page. It's far too large for the logo. Right-click on the Netscape plug-in field and select the Plugin Properties command from the shortcut menu, or select the Plugin Properties command from the **E**dit menu. The Plug-In Properties dialog box appears, as shown in Figure 8.10.

Figure 8.10.

Change the PowerPoint animation's display dimensions through the Plug-In Properties dialog box.

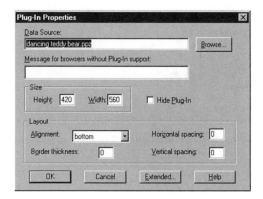

You can manipulate several Netscape plug-in properties. Change the dimensions of the Dancing Teddy Bear logo by typing 200 into the **W**idth textbox and 200 into the Heigh**t** textbox in the Plug-In Properties dialog box Size area. The logo is set at 200 pixels by 200 pixels. Select right in the **A**lignment drop-down list in the Layout area so that the logo appears in the upper right corner of the Web page. Click on the OK button. In the FrontPage Editor, The Dancing Teddy Bear Web page should look like Figure 8.11.

Figure 8.11.

The Dancing Teddy Bear Web page using the PowerPoint Animation Netscape plug-in.

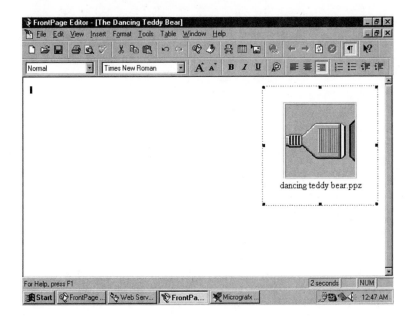

Open The Dancing Teddy Bear page in the Netscape plug-in–enabled Web browser and be sure that the PowerPoint Animation Netscape plug-in is installed on your computer. You should see and hear the Dancing Teddy Bear logo right after the page loads.

Adding Video

You can insert a video into your Web page so that it plays automatically when the page is loaded into a Web browser. FrontPage's video support is similar to the background sound you inserted into your personal home page earlier in this chapter. In fact, the videos can include sound.

NOTE

There are a variety of ways to create your own videos. One relatively inexpensive way is to use QuickCam. The video used in this section was created using black-and-white Quickcam, which is available for less than $100. A color version is available for less than $200. Learn more about Quickcam by Connectix at `http://www.connectix.com`.

Greet people that view your personal home page with a video of yourself saying "Welcome to My Home Page" rather than just a background sound that says the same thing. First, remove the background sound that you inserted into your personal home page. Right-click on your personal Web page and select the Page Properties command from the shortcut menu or select the Page Properties command from the **F**ile menu. The Page Properties dialog box appears. Click on the General tab if the General sheet isn't displayed already. Delete the path and filename displayed in the Lo**c**ation textbox of the Background Sound area. Click on the OK button to close the Page Properties dialog box.

You also should remove the sound file used for the background sound from your Web. You can see the Welcome to My Home Page sound file (welcome to my home page.wav) in FrontPage Explorer, as shown in Figure 8.12.

Figure 8.12.

The background sound file is part of your personal Web.

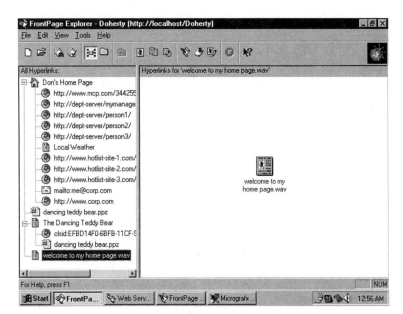

Select the welcome to my home page.wav file in FrontPage Explorer's All Hyperlinks window, then press the Delete key. The Confirm Delete dialog box opens, as shown in Figure 8.13.

Figure 8.13.

Confirm your decision to delete a file in the Confirm Delete dialog box.

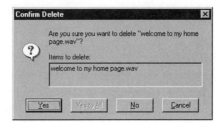

Click on the **Ye**s button. The sound file is removed from your Web.

Add a video to your home page. Open your personal home page in the FrontPage Editor. Insert your mouse cursor at the end of the page's heading, then select the **V**ideo command from the **I**nsert menu. The Video dialog box appears. Click on the Other Location tab if the Other Location sheet, as shown in Figure 8.14, isn't displayed already.

Figure 8.14.

Add a video file to your Web page through the Video dialog box.

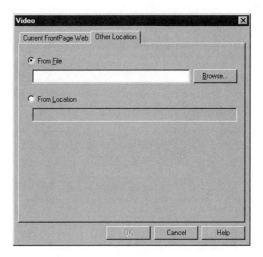

You have the choice of adding a video file from your file system or from the World Wide Web. Select the From **L**ocation radio button and type a URL in the associated textbox if you want to use a video file on the World Wide Web. Select the From **F**ile radio button to add a video file from your file system. Type the path and filename of your video file in the associated textbox or click on the **B**rowse button to open the Video dialog box shown in Figure 8.15.

Select a video file and click on the **O**pen button. The file is added to your Web page. Save your work by clicking on the Save toolbar button. The Save File to Web dialog box appears and asks if you want to save the video file to your Web. Click on the **Ye**s button to save the video file to your Web.

Figure 8.15.

Select a video file through the Video dialog box.

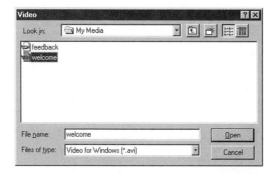

You inserted a video into a Web page; however, the video isn't placed at an aesthetically pleasing location. Move the Welcome video so that it plays at the top right corner of your personal Web page. Right-click on the video area and select the Image Properties command from the shortcut menu or select the Image Properties command from the **E**dit menu. The Image Properties dialog box appears. Click on the Appearance tab if the Appearance sheet isn't displayed already. Select right from the **A**lignment drop-down list in the Layout area. Click on the OK button. Your welcoming video is better positioned on your personal home page, as shown in Figure 8.16.

Your video file plays when your personal home page is loaded into a Web browser.

Figure 8.16.

The Welcome video runs when the page is loaded into a Web browser.

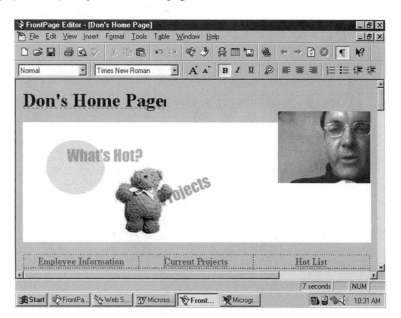

Editing Video Properties

You can set a number of video properties through the Image Properties dialog box, including the number of times it plays and when it plays.

You want the Welcome video file to play only once after loading the page in a browser. Right-click on the video area. Select the Image Properties command from the shortcut menu or select the Image Properties command from the **E**dit menu. The Image Properties dialog box appears. Click on the Video tab if the Video sheet isn't displayed already, as shown in Figure 8.17.

Figure 8.17.

Set video properties through the Image Properties dialog box's Video sheet.

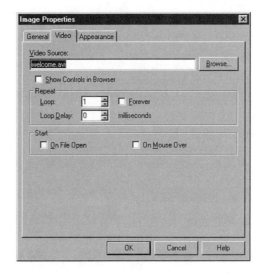

The video file you inserted in your Web page earlier displays in the **V**ideo Source textbox on the Image Properties dialog box's Video sheet. The **S**how Controls in Browser checkbox is below the **V**ideo Source textbox. Check the **S**how Controls in Browser checkbox if you want the video player controls to display on your Web page.

Set the number of times a browser plays the video file in the L**o**op box in the Repeat area. You want the Welcome video file to play once when the Web page is loaded. Type 1 in the L**o**op box if it isn't set to 1 already. You can set a delay between each playing of your video. Type the number of milliseconds of delay in the Loop **D**elay box. Type 0 in the Loop **D**elay box, because your video doesn't repeat. There is also a **F**orever checkbox available. Check the **F**orever checkbox if you want the video file played over and over for as long as the Web page is open in a browser. Leave the **F**orever checkbox unchecked.

You can set when the video is played. Check the **O**n File Open checkbox in the Start area if you want the video to play automatically when it's loaded into a Web browser. Check the On

Mouse Over checkbox if you want the video to play whenever the user's mouse passes over the video. You can check both checkboxes if you want the video to play on loading the Web page and when a user moves a mouse over the video. Checking both is a good idea when you automatically play the video once on loading. If users want to hear the video again, they can easily play it. Check the On Mouse Over checkbox, then click on the OK button.

Summary

You added sound, animation, and video to your Web. You also got an introduction to content that uses ActiveX controls and Netscape plug-ins. These advanced objects, along with Java applets, give you the opportunity to build far richer multimedia Webs. You learn more about them in Chapter 11.

Q&A

Q Are background sounds the only kind of sound that I can add to my Web pages?

A You can add sound in all sorts of ways to your Web page. The background sound feature is a simple way to add sound that is integrated into your Web page, but even in this chapter you added sound played through a PowerPoint animation and through video. In Chapter 11, you learn how to add sound played in real time through an ActiveX control.

Q Is PowerPoint animation the only kind of animation that I can add to my Web pages?

A You can add several types and packages of animation to your Web pages, using FrontPage. You added clip-art animation to your Web in Chapter 4. In this chapter, you added PowerPoint animation. Later, especially in Chapter 11, you add other types of animation.

Q Isn't creating digital video prohibitively expensive?

A The cost of digital camera and video equipment has become relatively reasonable recently. Several options are available. Look around—you may be surprised.

Workshop

Experiment with inserting different combinations of media covered in this chapter into your Web pages. Play with the various properties and see what kind of effects you can obtain.

Quiz

1. It's a good idea to keep background sounds short. Why?
2. PowerPoint animation must be played by special applications. What are the generic names for the applications?
3. What are three ways that a video can be activated?

8

DAY 5

Chapter 9

Adding Forms and Other Interactive Elements

Forms were the first addition to HTML that allowed Web pages to be truly interactive beyond hyperlinks, and the FrontPage Editor makes it easy to enter forms. Forms are defined by the `<FORM>` tag and `</FORM>` end-tag. A form is just an area where form fields can be added and, on its own, isn't displayed on a Web page. Forms are made useful by the special interactive graphics user interface elements known as form fields. These graphics can appear as buttons, textboxes, drop-down lists, and other interactive elements. FrontPage supports building any kind of form by adding form fields. Forms can quickly and easily be created by using wizards and templates.

In this chapter, you

- ☐ Add forms to your Web
- ☐ Add form fields to your forms
- ☐ Use the FrontPage Editor's Forms toolbar
- ☐ Use the Form Page Wizard
- ☐ Use the Feedback Form template

Adding Forms

You add forms to your Web pages in the FrontPage Editor. You actually add forms by adding form fields. The FrontPage Editor adds a form to your Web page the first time you add a form field to it. You can then either add more form fields to the same form or you can add new forms by adding new form fields outside the first form.

NOTE
> The form itself becomes useful when you set it up to interact with a server, as discussed in the Setting Up Forms to Interact with Servers section later in this chapter.

Form Fields

Inserting form fields, sometimes called form elements, into your Web page is as easy as selecting the name of the form field from the Form Field submenu of the Insert menu. For instance, insert a pushbutton in a Web page by selecting the **P**ush Button command from the Form Field submenu of the **I**nsert menu. The result is a pushbutton added to your Web page, as shown in Figure 9.1.

Figure 9.1.

New pushbuttons are submit buttons by default.

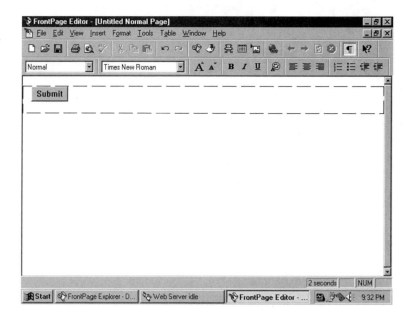

A form that contains the pushbutton is automatically added to the page. A dashed line represents the perimeter of the form. If you look at the source code, as shown in Figure 9.2, you can see that a `<FORM>` tag marks the start of the form containing the pushbutton element and a `</FORM>` end-tag marks the end.

Figure 9.2.

The source code for a single pushbutton in a form is displayed in the View or Edit HTML dialog box.

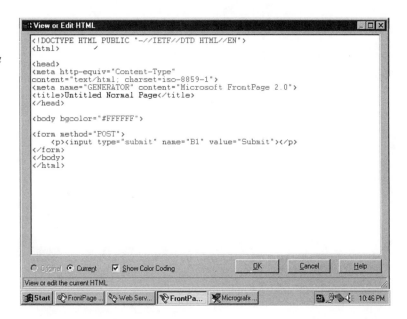

The `<INPUT>` tag between the `<FORM>` tag and the `</FORM>` end-tag defines the pushbutton form field. In fact, most form fields or elements are defined using the `<INPUT>` tag with the type of element set by the TYPE attribute.

You can add new fields to the same form or you can create a new form when you add a new field. Add a one-line textbox field on the same form under the pushbutton. With your cursor inserted after the Submit pushbutton, press the Enter key. Then select the One-Line Text Box command from the Form Field submenu on the Insert menu. A textbox is added on the same form as the pushbutton, as shown in Figure 9.3.

In the source code shown in Figure 9.4, you can see that a new `<INPUT>` tag with the TYPE attribute set to `"text"` is added between the same `<FORM>` tag and `</FORM>` end-tag as the old `<INPUT>` tag with the TYPE attribute set to `"submit"`.

Figure 9.3.

One form is displayed with a Submit pushbutton and a textbox.

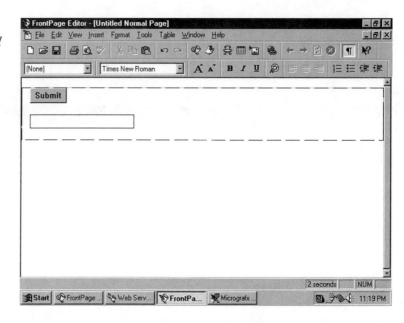

Figure 9.4.

The source code of a Web page with one form containing a Submit pushbutton and a textbox.

Insert another pushbutton, but this time add the new form field outside the existing form. Place your cursor on the line below the bottom dashed line that represents the bottom of the form. Select the **P**ush Button command from the Form Fiel**d** submenu of the **I**nsert menu.

A new form with a pushbutton is added below the old form with the pushbutton and textbox, as shown in Figure 9.5.

Figure 9.5.

The Web page now has two forms on it.

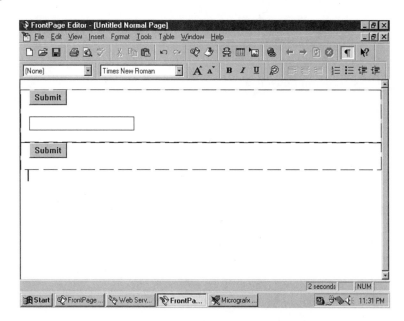

When you look at the source code, as shown in Figure 9.6, you see two sets of `<FORM>` tags and `</FORM>` end-tags, each set defining a separate form.

Figure 9.6.

The source code for the Web page with two forms on it.

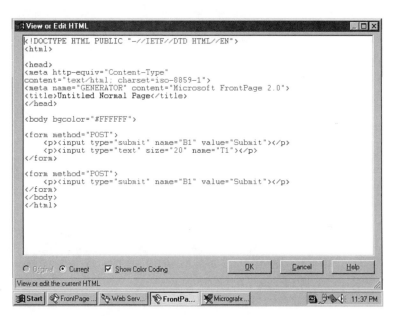

Seven form fields are available to add to your forms:

- ☐ One-line textbox
- ☐ Scrolling textbox
- ☐ Checkbox
- ☐ Radio button
- ☐ Drop-down menu
- ☐ Pushbutton
- ☐ Image

Each form field or element differs in the kinds of properties you can set and the kinds of tasks they can do. You learn more about events and procedures involving form elements in Chapter 10, "Tying It Together with Scripts." The following sections briefly describe the seven form elements, their properties, and their data validation methods.

One-Line Textboxes

The one-line textbox is used as a single-lined text entry field. The <INPUT> tag's TYPE attribute has its value set to "TEXT". Insert a one-line textbox by selecting the One-Line **T**ext Box command from the Form Fiel**d** submenu on the **I**nsert menu. A one-line textbox is inserted into your Web page, as shown in Figure 9.7.

Figure 9.7.

This Web page contains a one-line textbox.

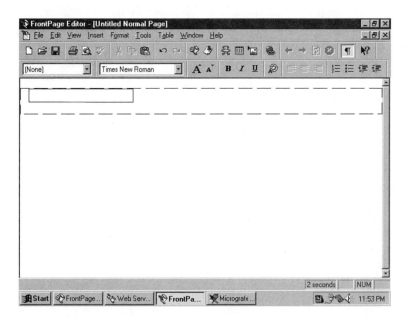

Properties

Edit the one-line textbox's properties by right-clicking on the textbox and selecting the Form Field Properties command from the shortcut menu or by clicking on the textbox and selecting the Form Field Properties command from the Edit menu. The Text Box Properties dialog box appears, as shown in Figure 9.8.

Figure 9.8.

Change a one-line textbox's properties through the Text Box Properties dialog box.

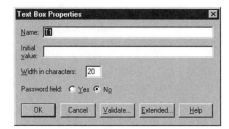

Type a name for the textbox into the **N**ame textbox. Use a name that describes the data that the textbox will hold, such as First Name, Last Name, or Address. Scripts use the name entered into the **N**ame textbox as the element's name.

Type an initial value into the Initial **v**alue textbox if you want the textbox to open containing a number or some text.

The number in the **W**idth in characters textbox defines the width of the textbox by the number of characters it can hold.

Finally, you can set the textbox as a password field by selecting the **Y**es radio button in the Password field area. If you do, only asterisks will display when a person types into the textbox; otherwise, select the N**o** radio button and text will display normally.

Data Validation

You can validate data entered into the one-line textbox. If the Text Box Properties dialog box remains open, click on the **V**alidate button; otherwise, right-click on the one-line textbox and select the Form Field Validation command. The Text Box Validation dialog box appears, as shown in Figure 9.9.

Enter a name that refers to the textbox into the Display **N**ame textbox. The name is used to refer to the one-line textbox in validation warning messages presented to users.

Select a data type in the Data **T**ype drop-down list if you want to limit the type of data a person can enter into the one-line textbox. Four options are available: No Constraints, Text, Integer, and Number. Select No Constraints if you don't want to limit the type of data entered into the textbox; otherwise, the data type you select is the type of data that the user is allowed to enter.

Figure 9.9.

Set the textbox field validation rules in the Text Box Validation dialog box.

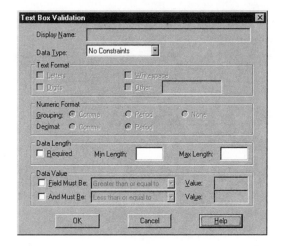

If you constrained the data to Text, you can set options in the Text Format area. Only the features you specify by checking their checkboxes can be entered into the textbox.

Options in the Numeric Format area can be set if the textbox is constrained to receive only Numeric or Integer data.

The Data Length area contains options for restricting the length of any data type. Data must be entered into the textbox if the **R**equired checkbox is checked.

You can set restrictions on any data type in the Data Value area.

Scrolling Textboxes

The scrolling textbox is used as a text entry field. Unlike other form elements, the `<INPUT>` tag isn't used. The `<TEXTAREA>` tag and the `</TEXTAREA>` end-tag define the scrolling textbox. Insert a scrolling textbox by selecting the **S**crolling Text Box command from the Form Field submenu on the **I**nsert menu. A scrolling textbox is inserted into your Web page, as shown in Figure 9.10.

Figure 9.10.

This Web page contains a scrolling textbox.

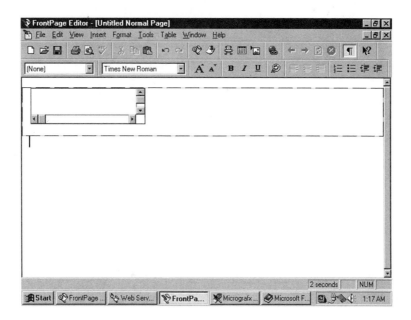

Properties

Edit the scrolling textbox's properties by right-clicking on the textbox and selecting the Form Field Properties command from the shortcut menu or by clicking on the textbox and selecting the Form Field Properties command from the Edit menu. The Scrolling Text Box Properties dialog box appears, as shown in Figure 9.11.

Figure 9.11.

Change scrolling textbox properties through the Scrolling Text Box Properties dialog box.

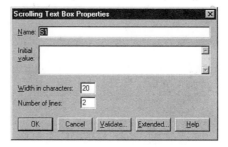

Type a name for the textbox into the Name textbox. Use a name that describes the data that the textbox will hold, such as Address. Scripts use the name entered into the Name textbox as the element's name. Type an initial value into the Initial value textbox. The number in the

Width in characters textbox defines the width of the textbox by the number of characters it can hold. Set the number of lines that the scrolling textbox displays in the Number of lines textbox.

Data Validation

You can validate data entered into the scrolling textbox. If the Scrolling Text Box Properties dialog box remains open, click on the Validate button; otherwise, right-click on the scrolling textbox and select the Form Field Validation command. The Text Box Validation dialog box appears. All the validation properties are the same as in the one-line textbox. Refer to the previous Data Validation section for the one-line textbox.

Checkboxes

The checkbox is used as a way to give yes or no answers, usually to select an item or not. Checkboxes can also be used to enable the user to select multiple selections. The <INPUT> tag's TYPE attribute is set to "CHECKBOX". Insert a checkbox by selecting the Check Box command from the Form Field submenu on the Insert menu. A checkbox is inserted into your Web page, as shown in Figure 9.12.

Figure 9.12.
This Web page contains a checkbox.

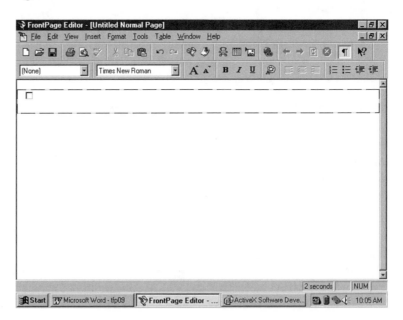

Properties

Edit checkbox properties by right-clicking on the checkbox and selecting the Form Field Properties command from the shortcut menu or by clicking on the textbox and selecting the Form Field Properties command from the Edit menu. The Check Box Properties dialog box appears, as shown in Figure 9.13.

Figure 9.13.

Change checkbox properties through the Check Box Properties dialog box.

Type a name for the checkbox into the **N**ame textbox. Use a name that describes what the checkbox selects for, such as `Send a Brochure`, `Married`, or `Available Weekends`. Scripts use the name entered into the **N**ame textbox as the element's name.

The **V**alue textbox holds the value that the checkbox passes when it's checked. The value of a checked checkbox is `ON` by default.

Finally, you can set the initial state of the checkbox in the Initial State area. The checkbox is checked by default if you select the **C**hecked radio button; otherwise, if you select the **N**ot Checked radio button, the checkbox is not checked by default.

Radio Buttons

The radio button is used to select a single value from a set of alternatives. The `<INPUT>` tag's `TYPE` attribute is set to `"RADIO"`. Insert a radio button by selecting the **R**adio Button command from the Form Field submenu on the **I**nsert menu. A checkbox is inserted into your Web page, as shown in Figure 9.14.

There must be at least two radio buttons in a group so that there are alternatives to select from. A group of radio buttons is placed in the same form and given the same name in the Radio Button Properties dialog box.

Figure 9.14.

This Web page contains two radio buttons in a single group.

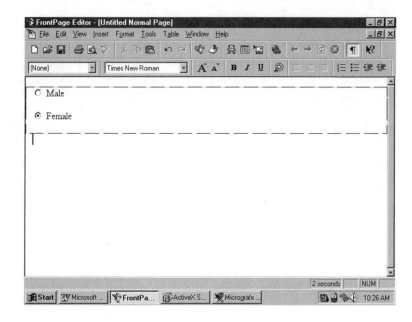

Properties

Edit radio button properties by right-clicking on the radio button and selecting the Form Field Properties command from the shortcut menu or by clicking on the textbox and selecting the Form Field Properties command from the **E**dit menu. The Radio Button Properties dialog box appears, as shown in Figure 9.15.

Figure 9.15.

Change radio button properties through the Radio Button Properties dialog box.

Type a group name for a set of radio buttons into the Group **N**ame textbox. Use a name that describes the type of data you select from the group of radio buttons, such as `Sex`, `Marriage Status`, or `Day of Week`. Scripts use the name entered into the Group **N**ame textbox as the element's name. Be sure to add the same group name to each radio button in the same group.

The **V**alue textbox holds the value that the radio button group passes when that radio button is selected. Each radio button should contain a value.

Finally, you can set the initial state of the radio button in the Initial State area. The radio button is selected by default if you select the **S**elected radio button; otherwise, if you select the N**o**t Selected radio button, the radio button is not selected by default. Only one radio button in a group can be selected at any one time.

Data Validation

You can use data validation on radio button groups. If the Radio Button Properties dialog box remains open, click on the **V**alidate button; otherwise, right-click on the radio button and select the Form Field Validation command. The Radio Button Validation dialog box appears, as shown in Figure 9.16.

Figure 9.16.

Set the radio button validation rules in the Radio Button Validation dialog box.

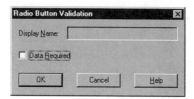

There is only one type of validation procedure that you can have performed on radio button groups. You can check the Data **R**equired checkbox to require that a radio button is selected. If you check the Data **R**equired checkbox, you can enter a name into the Display **N**ame textbox that is used for the data validation warning messages presented to users.

Drop-Down Menus

The drop-down menu, also known as a drop-down list, is used to present several alternatives from which the user can select. The `<SELECT>` tag and `</SELECT>` end-tag are used to define a drop-down menu. Insert a drop-down menu by selecting the **D**rop-Down Menu command from the Form Fiel**d** submenu on the **I**nsert menu. A drop-down menu is inserted into your Web page, as shown in Figure 9.17.

Figure 9.17.

This Web page contains a drop-down menu.

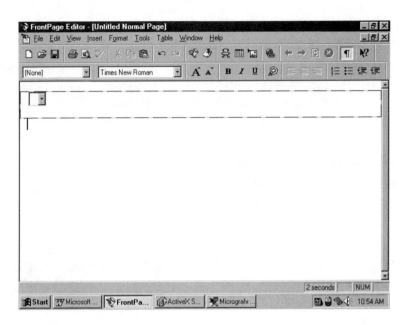

Properties

Edit drop-down menu properties by right-clicking on the drop-down menu and selecting the Form Field Properties command from the shortcut menu or by clicking on the drop-down menu and selecting the Form Field Properties command from the **E**dit menu. The Drop-Down Menu Properties dialog box appears, as shown in Figure 9.18.

Figure 9.18.

Change drop-down menu properties through the Drop-Down Menu Properties dialog box.

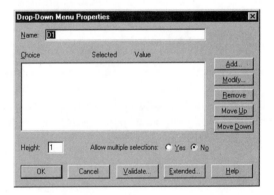

Type a name for the drop-down menu into the **N**ame textbox. Use a name that describes the type of data you select from the drop-down menu, such as Country, Month, or Day of Week. Scripts use the name entered into the **N**ame textbox as the element's name.

Use the large list area of the Drop-Down Menu Properties dialog box to add choices that are listed in the drop-down menu. Add the choices by clicking on the **A**dd button. The Add Choice dialog box appears, as shown in Figure 9.19.

Figure 9.19.

Add items to be listed in the drop-down menu through the Add Choice dialog box.

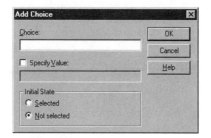

Type the name of the choice in the **C**hoice textbox—for example, Monday. The choice is listed on the drop-down menu. By default, the value passed by the drop-down menu is the same as the name of the selected menu choice as it was typed into **C**hoice. You can specify a different value by checking the Specify **V**alue checkbox and typing the value into the textbox under the Specify **V**alue checkbox. You can also set whether the menu choice is selected by default. Select the **S**elected radio button in the Initial State area if you want the menu choice selected by default; otherwise, select the **N**ot Selected radio button. You can select only one menu choice by default if the N**o** radio button is selected in the Allow multiple selections area of the Drop-Down Menu Properties dialog box. If you select the **Y**es radio button, you can select as many menu choice items by default as you want.

Add any number of menu choices as you want to a drop-down menu. You can modify a menu choice's properties by selecting the menu choice in the Drop-Down Menu Properties dialog box's list, then clicking on the **M**odify button. The menu choices are listed in the drop-down menu in the same order that they're listed in the Drop-Down Menu Properties dialog box's list. You can modify the menu choice order. Move a menu choice up in the list by clicking on the menu choice, then clicking on the Move **U**p button. Move a menu choice down in the list by clicking on the menu choice then clicking on the Move **D**own button. Finally, you can delete a menu choice by clicking on the menu choice, then clicking on the **R**emove button.

The drop-down menu can show a different number of items without opening. Type the number of menu choices that you want to show at once in the He**i**ght textbox on the Drop-Down Menu Properties dialog box.

Data Validation

You can use data validation on drop-down menus. If the Drop-Down Menu Properties dialog box remains open, click on the **V**alidate button. Otherwise, right-click on the drop-down menu and select the Form Field Validation command. The Drop-Down Menu Validation dialog box appears, as shown in Figure 9.20.

Figure 9.20.

Set the drop-down menu validation rules in the Drop-Down Menu Validation dialog box.

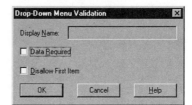

You can check the Data **R**equired checkbox to require that at least one menu choice is selected. You can also check the **D**isallow First Item checkbox to make it impossible for a person to select the first item on the menu. Check this box if you want to use the first item to label the menu, for instance. If you check the Data **R**equired checkbox or the **D**isallow First Item checkbox, you can enter a name in the Display **N**ame textbox that is used for the data validation warning messages presented to users.

Pushbuttons

The pushbutton is a graphically represented button that, when clicked on, usually results in the running of a procedure. The <INPUT> tag's TYPE attribute is set to "SUBMIT" by default. The "SUBMIT" type creates the Submit pushbutton. A Submit pushbutton is used for submitting the contents of the form in which it resides. You learn about the two other types of buttons and how to set them in the Properties section.

Insert a pushbutton by selecting the **P**ush Button command from the Form Fiel**d** submenu on the **I**nsert menu. A Submit pushbutton is inserted into your Web page, as shown in Figure 9.21.

Figure 9.21.

This Web page contains a Submit pushbutton.

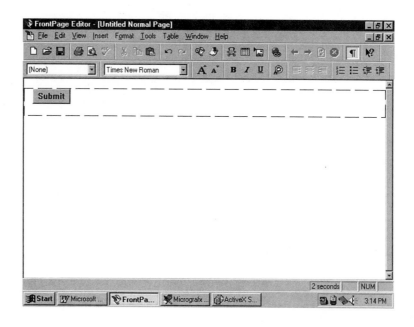

Properties

Edit pushbutton properties by right-clicking on the pushbutton and selecting the Form Field Properties command from the shortcut menu or by clicking on the pushbutton and selecting the Form Field Properties command from the **E**dit menu. The Push Button Properties dialog box appears, as shown in Figure 9.22.

Three kinds of pushbuttons are available: Normal, Submit, and Reset. The default is the Submit pushbutton. Make a Submit pushbutton by selecting the **S**ubmit radio button in the Button type area. Submit pushbuttons display the Submit label by default, entered in the Push Button dialog box's **V**alue/Label textbox. The Submit pushbutton is used for submitting the contents of the form in which it resides.

Make a Normal pushbutton by selecting the **N**ormal radio button in the Button type area. Normal buttons are defined when the <INPUT> tag's TYPE attribute is set to "Button". Submit pushbuttons display the Button label by default, entered in the Push Button dialog box's **V**alue/Label textbox. The Normal pushbutton is used for custom actions defined by you. You use the Normal pushbutton when you learn scripting in Chapter 10.

Figure 9.22.

*Change pushbutton
properties through the
Push Button Proper-
ties dialog box.*

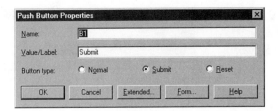

Make a Reset pushbutton by selecting the **R**eset radio button in the Button type area. Reset buttons are defined when the <INPUT> tag's TYPE attribute is set to "Reset". Reset pushbuttons display the Reset label by default, entered in the Push Button dialog box's **V**alue/Label textbox. The Reset pushbutton resets the fields in the form that it resides to specified default values.

Type a name for the pushbutton into the **N**ame textbox. Use a name that describes what clicking on the pushbutton does. Scripts use the name entered into the **N**ame textbox as the element's name.

Type a label into the **V**alue/Label textbox if you want the pushbutton to display a label different from the default.

Images

The image form field is used to display an image that you can click on to cause an event to occur. The <INPUT> tag's TYPE attribute is set to "IMAGE". Insert an image by selecting the **I**mage command from the Form Fiel**d** submenu on the **I**nsert menu. The Image dialog box appears. Select an image through the Image dialog box. An image is inserted into a form on your Web page, as shown in Figure 9.23.

WARNING

The ability to set the <INPUT> tag's TYPE attribute to "IMAGE" is a convention introduced in HTML 3.2. That means that if you use it, it may not be supported on many browsers yet.

9

Figure 9.23.

This Web page contains an image form field.

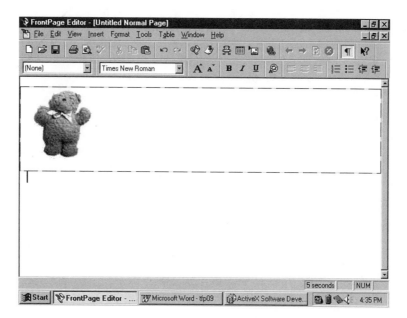

Properties

Edit image form field properties by right-clicking on the image and selecting the Form Field Properties command from the shortcut menu or by clicking on the image and selecting the Form Field Properties command from the **E**dit menu. The Image Form Field Properties dialog box appears, as shown in Figure 9.24.

Figure 9.24.

Change image form field properties through the Image Form Field Properties dialog box.

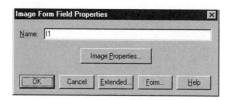

Type a name for the image form field into the **N**ame textbox. Use a name that describes the event initiated by clicking on the image. Scripts use the name entered into the **N**ame textbox as the element's name. You can edit image properties by clicking on the Image **P**roperties dialog box to open the Image Properties dialog box.

Using the Forms Toolbar

All the form fields, except the image form field, are available from the Form Fields toolbar, as shown in Figure 9.25.

Figure 9.25.

Add form fields to
your Web page from
the Form Fields
toolbar.

Display the Form Fields toolbar by selecting the F**o**rms Toolbar command from the **V**iew menu.

Setting Up Forms to Interact with Servers

Each form can hold a collection of data. The data gathered through the various form fields can be communicated to a server for storage and later retrieval. For instance, the forms may collect personal information, such as name, address, and telephone number. All the personal information entered by various people can be stored on the server so that the Web's owner can add the data to their databases. Form fields can also receive data from a server to be displayed as default values. Either way, there must be a mechanism for a form to interact with a server. You select a mechanism or form handler in the Form Properties dialog box, as shown in Figure 9.26.

You select a form handler from the drop-down list in the Form Handler area. You can use custom form handlers, the Internet Database Connector, or WebBots. Custom form handlers are beyond the scope of this book; however, FrontPage supports them, so you can use them if you want to. The other form handlers, the Internet Database Connector and WebBots, require the server to provide the FrontPage Server Extensions and are described in detail on Day 7.

Figure 9.26.

Select the ways that a form interacts with a server in the Form Properties dialog box.

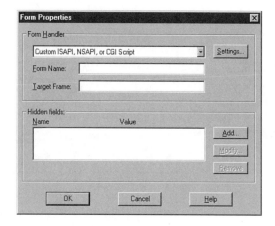

Using the Form Page Wizard

Create any kind of form by using the FrontPage Editor's Form Page Wizard. Tell it the types of information that you need to collect and the Form Page Wizard builds you a custom form page.

Begin creating a new form page by selecting the **N**ew command from the **F**ile menu. The New Page dialog box appears. Select Form Page Wizard from the Template or Wizard list. Click on the OK button. The Form Page Wizard dialog box appears, as shown in Figure 9.27.

Figure 9.27.

The first Form Page Wizard sheet tells you about the Form Page Wizard.

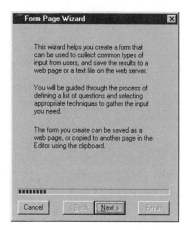

The first sheet presents a blurb on the Form Page Wizard. Click on the **N**ext button. The second Form Page Wizard sheet appears, as shown in Figure 9.28.

Figure 9.28.

Enter the form page's title and filename into the second Form Page Wizard sheet.

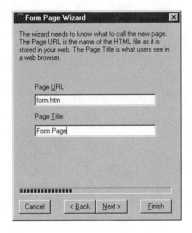

Page Names and URLs

Enter the filename you want to give to your form page in the Page **U**RL textbox; otherwise, keep the default filename. Enter the title you want to give your form page in the Page **T**itle textbox. Click on the **N**ext button. The third Form Page Wizard sheet appears, as shown in Figure 9.29.

Figure 9.29.

Add the questions that you want the form to ask in the third Form Page Wizard sheet.

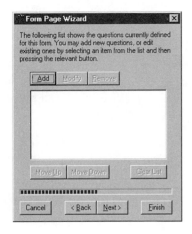

Asking Questions

The third Form Page Wizard sheet contains a list of questions that define the information gathered by the form you're building. Start adding questions to the list by clicking on the **A**dd button. A question sheet appears, as shown in Figure 9.30.

Figure 9.30.

Select a question type on the first question sheet.

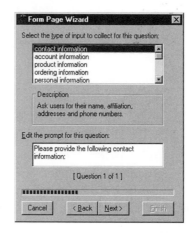

Fourteen question types are listed in the Select the **t**ype of input to collect for this question list. Select a question type in this list, then edit the way the question is asked on the form page in the **E**dit the prompt for this question textbox. The next step depends on which question type you select.

Contact Information

Select the Contact Information question type if you want to collect information from visitors to your Web page that gives you a means of contacting them, such as name, address, and telephone number. When you click on the Next button, the Contact Information Properties sheet appears, as shown in Figure 9.31.

Choose the contact information that your form page collects through the checkboxes and radio buttons on the Contact Information Properties sheet. The name you enter in the Enter the base name for this group of **v**ariables textbox at the bottom of the sheet is the name of the form where all the fields will reside. Click on the **N**ext button to return to the first information sheet, with the contact information question added to its list.

Figure 9.31.

Choose the contact information your form page collects on the Contact Information Properties sheet.

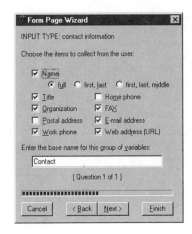

Account Information

Select the Account Information question type if you want to use the form page as a way to log into a password-protected area. It creates form fields that ask for username and password. When you click on the **N**ext button, the Account Information Properties sheet appears, as shown in Figure 9.32.

Figure 9.32.

Choose the account information your form page collects on the Account Information Properties sheet.

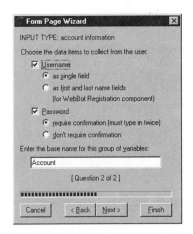

Choose the account information that your form page collects through the checkboxes and radio buttons on the Account Information Properties sheet. The name you enter in the Enter the base name for this group of **v**ariables textbox at the bottom of the sheet is the name of the form where all the fields will reside. Click on the **N**ext button to return to the first information sheet, with the account information question added to its list.

Product Information

Select the Product Information question type if you want to use the form page as a way to ask users which product they want to know more about. When you click on the **N**ext button, the Product Information Properties sheet appears, as shown in Figure 9.33.

Figure 9.33.

Choose the product information your form page collects on the Product Information Properties sheet.

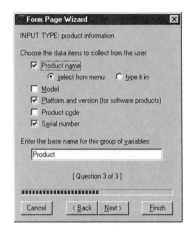

Choose the product information that your form page collects through the checkboxes and radio buttons on the Product Information Properties sheet. The name you enter in the Enter the base name for this group of **v**ariables textbox at the bottom of the sheet is the name of the form where all the fields will reside. Click on the **N**ext button to return to the first information sheet, with the product information question added to its list.

Ordering Information

Select the Ordering Information question type if you want to use the form page as a way of asking users what product they want to order and other order information. When you click on the **N**ext button, the Ordering Information Properties sheet appears, as shown in Figure 9.34.

Choose the ordering information that your form page collects through the checkboxes and radio buttons on the Ordering Information Properties sheet. The name you enter in the Enter the base name for this group of **v**ariables textbox at the bottom of the sheet is the name of the form where all the fields will reside. Click on the **N**ext button to return to the first information sheet, with the ordering information question added to its list.

Figure 9.34.

Choose the ordering information your form page collects on the Ordering Information Properties sheet.

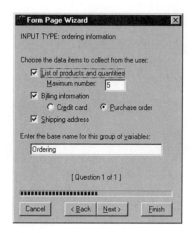

Personal Information

Select the Personal Information question type if you want to use the form page to ask users about their name, age, and other personal information. When you click on the **N**ext button, the Personal Information Properties sheet appears, as shown in Figure 9.35.

Figure 9.35.

Choose the personal information your form page collects on the Personal Information Properties sheet.

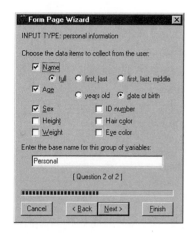

Choose the personal information that your form page collects through the checkboxes and radio buttons on the Personal Information Properties sheet. The name you enter in the Enter the base name for this group of **v**ariables textbox at the bottom of the sheet is the name of the form where all the fields will reside. Click on the **N**ext button to return to the first information sheet, with the personal information question added to its list.

One of Several Options

Select the One of Several Options question type if you want a user to select only one option of several. When you click on the **N**ext button, the One of Several Options Properties sheet appears, as shown in Figure 9.36.

Figure 9.36.

Add a list of options to the One of Several Options Properties sheet.

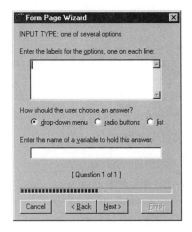

Add all the options you want users to choose from in the Enter the labels for the **o**ptions, one on each line listbox. Choose to present the options in a drop-down menu, radio buttons, or list. Finally, type a name of a variable that holds the option selected in the Enter the name of a **v**ariable to hold this answer textbox at the bottom of the sheet. Click on the **N**ext button to return to the first information sheet, with the one of several options question added to its list.

Any of Several Options

Select the Any of Several Options question type if you want a user to select from a list of several options. Users can select as many options as they want at the same time. When you click on the **N**ext button, the Any of Several Options Properties sheet appears, as shown in Figure 9.37.

Add all of the options you want users to choose from in the Enter the labels for the **o**ptions, one on each line listbox. Choose whether you want the options listed in multiple columns. The name you enter into the Enter the base name for this group of **v**ariables textbox at the bottom of the sheet is the name of the form where all the fields will reside. Click on the **N**ext button to return to the first information sheet, with the any of several options question added to its list.

Figure 9.37.

Add a list of options to the Any of Several Options Properties sheet.

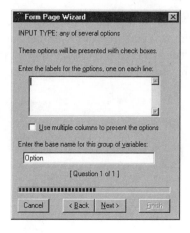

Boolean

Select the Boolean question type if you want a user to respond to a yes/no or true/false question. When you click on the **N**ext button, the Boolean Properties sheet appears, as shown in Figure 9.38.

Figure 9.38.

Select the kind of Boolean question asked in the Boolean Properties sheet.

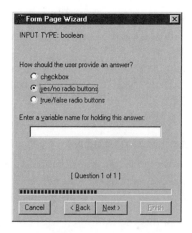

Choose whether you want the question asked to use checkboxes, yes/no radio buttons, or true/false radio buttons. Type a name of a variable that holds the option selected in the Enter a **v**ariable name for holding this answer textbox at the bottom of the sheet. Click on the **N**ext button to return to the first information sheet, with the Boolean question added to its list.

Date

Select the Date question type if you want a user to enter a date into your form page. W
you click on the Next button, the Date Properties sheet appears, as shown in Figure 9

Figure 9.39.

*Select a date format in
the Date Properties
sheet.*

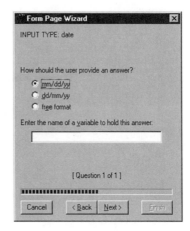

Select a date format. Then type the name of a variable that holds the date entered by a
in the Enter the name of a **variable** to hold this answer textbox at the bottom of the s
Click on the **N**ext button to return to the first information sheet, with the date que
added to its list.

Time

Select the Time question type if you want a user to enter a time into your form page. \
you click on the **N**ext button, the Time Properties sheet appears, as shown in Figure

Figure 9.40.

*Select a time format
in the Time Properties
sheet.*

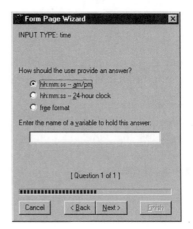

Select a time format. Then type the name of a variable that holds the time entered by a user in the Enter the name of a variable to hold this answer textbox at the bottom of the sheet. Click on the **N**ext button to return to the first information sheet, with the time question added to its list.

Range

Select the Range question type if you want a user to select a value from a range of values. When you click on the **N**ext button, the Range Properties sheet appears, as shown in Figure 9.41.

Figure 9.41.

Select a range format in the Range Properties sheet.

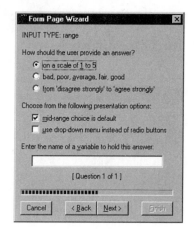

Select the range that a user can select from and how it's presented. Then type the name of a variable that holds the time entered by a user in the Enter the name of a variable to hold this answer textbox at the bottom of the sheet. Click on the **N**ext button to return to the first information sheet, with the range question added to its list.

Number

Select the Number question type if you want a user to enter a number in your form page. When you click on the **N**ext button, the Number Properties sheet appears, as shown in Figure 9.42.

Set the maximum size of the number and the kind of currency prefix it has, if any. Then type the name of a variable that holds the number entered by a user in the Enter the name of a variable to hold this answer textbox at the bottom of the sheet. Click on the **N**ext button to return to the first information sheet, with the number question added to its list.

Figure 9.42.

Select number question properties in the Number Properties sheet.

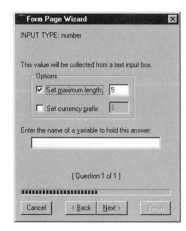

String

Select the String question type if you want a user to enter a string into a single-line textbox on your form page. When you click on the **N**ext button, the String Properties sheet appears, as shown in Figure 9.43.

Figure 9.43.

Set the maximum length of an entered string in the String Properties sheet.

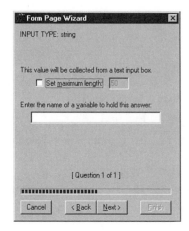

You can set the maximum length of an entered string by checking the Set **m**aximum length checkbox and typing the maximum length in the textbox to the right. Type the name of a variable that holds the text entered by a user in the Enter the name of a **v**ariable to hold this answer textbox at the bottom of the sheet. Click on the **N**ext button to return to the first information sheet, with the string question added to its list.

Paragraph

Select the Paragraph question type if you want a user to enter one or more paragraphs into a scrolling textbox on your form page. When you click on the **N**ext button, the Paragraph Properties sheet appears, as shown in Figure 9.44.

Figure 9.44.

Enter the name of a variable in the Paragraph Properties sheet.

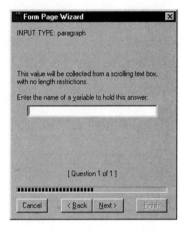

Type the name of a variable that holds the text entered by a user in the Enter the name of a **v**ariable to hold this answer textbox at the bottom of the sheet. Click on the **N**ext button to return to the first information sheet, with the paragraph question added to its list.

Presentation Options

When you finish adding all the question types you want to the Form Wizard's list, click on the **N**ext button on the question sheet. The Presentation Options sheet appears, as shown in Figure 9.45.

Figure 9.45.

Choose how you want the list of questions to be presented.

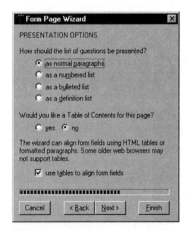

Select options so that your form page is presented the way you want it to look. Click on the Next button.

Output Options

The Output Options sheet, as shown in Figure 9.46, enables you to select the way your form page interacts with the server. Be sure that you have the custom server setup necessary or that you have the FrontPage Server Extensions available on your server.

Figure 9.46.

You get to specify where, and how, the user-returned information will be stored.

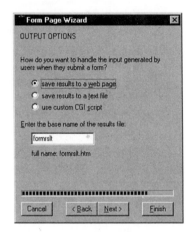

Enter the name of the file, without an extension, that holds the forms output in the **E**nter the base name of the results file textbox. Click on the **N**ext button. You've answered all of Form Wizard's questions. Click on the **F**inish button and your new form page is created.

Using the Feedback Form Template

The Feedback Form template makes it easy for you to set up a Web page containing a form that gathers feedback from visitors to your Web site. The feedback could be comments on your Web site, for instance, or questions about a product.

Create a Web page with a feedback form by selecting the **N**ew command from the **F**ile menu in the FrontPage Editor. The New Page dialog box appears. Select Feedback Form from the Templates or Wizard list. Click on the OK button. A generic feedback form is created, as shown in Figure 9.47. Edit the placeholder text in the new form to reflect the kind of feedback you want users to enter in the form.

Figure 9.47.

Edit the generic feedback form to fit your needs.

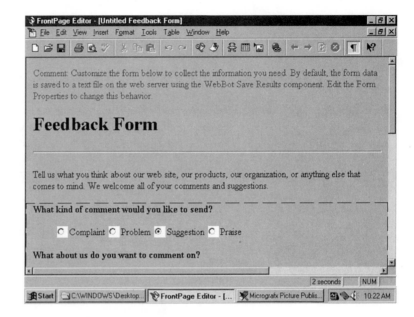

Summary

In this chapter, you learned about all the form fields available and how to create and work with forms. You now know how to set a wide range of properties and you understand the flexibility that the FrontPage Web authoring and publishing environment gives you in choosing the way that your forms interact with your server. You learn how to pull together forms into a powerful interactive interface using scripts in Chapter 10. You learn about interactive user interfaces in Chapter 11, "Adding Java Applets and ActiveX Controls," that go beyond HTML and are available for your Web page.

Q&A

Q Forms, form fields, and form elements? What are all of these things?

A It's a bit confusing because different names are often used for the same thing. There are two main parts to a form: the form itself, and the objects in the form, such as buttons, lists, and so forth. The objects are sometimes referred to as form fields and sometimes referred to as form elements.

9

Q I've created Web pages with forms and published them on my server, but no data is sent from the forms to the server. What's wrong?

A Your server must support custom interactions with your form through the Common Gateway Interface (CGI) and other mechanisms or the FrontPage Server Extensions. Custom services are beyond the scope of this book. Learn to use features provided by the FrontPage Server Extensions on Day 7.

Q My server doesn't provide any kind of support for interactions with forms. Are forms useful at all for me?

A Yes, forms can still be useful to you. Form fields can provide graphic user interface elements for scripts. You learn about scripts in Chapter 10.

Workshop

If your server supports interactions with form pages, think about what information you would like to get back from people visiting your Web. Design a form that gathers the information.

Quiz

1. What's the difference between a form and a form field?
2. What are the seven form fields available in FrontPage?
3. Why would you name a form field?

Chapter 10

Tying It Together with Scripts

You've built Webs with hyperlinks, forms, and other objects that enable users to interact with your Web pages. However, all the disparate elements that you've learned about must work together if you want them to do something useful. Scripts tie these elements together. A script forms the intermediary that talks with both HTML and the compiled applets and controls used on the Web. Scripting languages provide the thread that connects page layout with complex procedural objects. They're also useful for creating simpler procedures within an HTML document.

In this chapter, you

☐ Learn the Internet Explorer Object Model

☐ Learn about object-based scripting

☐ Build event-driven scripts

☐ Use both VBScript and JavaScript

☐ Use the Script Wizard

Language Overview

Scripts are interpreted languages that are typed directly into your HTML document. When users open your Web page, their Web browsers download your HTML document, then interpret your script. The script runs on the client machine after it's downloaded and leaves the server that provided the document free to do other things.

There is one hitch: A Web browser must have the interpreter for the scripting language to be able to run it. Therefore, to run VBScript, your Web browser must have access to a VBScript interpreter. To run JavaScript, your Web browser also must have access to a JavaScript interpreter. The current version of Microsoft Internet Explorer has both a VBScript and a JavaScript interpreter. Current versions of Netscape Navigator have access to only a JavaScript interpreter. Consider who your audience is. Additionally, Internet Explorer's support for VBScript is limited to only Windows 95/NT. That means that Mac and Windows 3.1 users who are using Internet Explorer won't be able to see your VBScript code. If you want the broadest possible audience today, use JavaScript. If you want to reach an audience that uses the Microsoft Internet Explorer, use either VBScript or JavaScript. FrontPage supports both scripting languages.

Object-Based

Your key to effective scripting is to understand objects and how they are used. A large part of your programming task is to know what objects to use and how to use them.

Both VBScript and JavaScript are object-based. This means that they use and manipulate objects but, in contrast to object-oriented languages, they don't support class libraries or inheritance. You can build objects, but you can't build classes. You rarely, if ever, need to build objects, because the scripting languages have the Internet Explorer Object Model available to them.

NOTE

> The Internet Explorer Object Model is based on the Navigator Object Model introduced by Netscape along with JavaScript. Compatibility across browsers and across scripting languages is maintained this way.

Event-Driven

VBScript and JavaScript are object-based languages with objects that include methods for doing things—but how does a user access a method? How do you get an object to do something? The short answer is that VBScript and JavaScript are also event-driven languages.

Something happens—usually a user action—that triggers an object to activity. That is the essence of event-driven languages and, for that matter, event-driven environments.

Today's operating systems, including Microsoft Windows, Mac OS, and UNIX X-Windows, are event-driven environments. They sit and wait for you to click on an icon or select a menu option. When you do, you cause a user-initiated event to occur, and the operating system or program can respond to the event.

The event-driven model is reflected in the programming methods used for event-driven environments. You could write a program that just cranks through a procedure and doesn't respond to user-initiated events. Users of your program will be very upset, however, when their operating systems effectively lock up and they are unable to interact with the program until it's finished with the procedure. In VBScript and JavaScript, events are handled through the Internet Explorer Object Model event handlers.

The Internet Explorer Object Model

Objects and events are central to creating scripts that interact between your Web page and the user. The Internet Explorer Object model provides scripts with browser objects and event handlers.

Objects

Scripts use objects that are very similar to objects in the world around you. Because you'll be programming in the virtual world of your computer and the Web, contemplate what you might consider to be an object in that world. Your browser is an object. It's the thing that you use to surf the Web. In fact, the browser is an object in the Internet Explorer Object Model. The browser object is named `navigator`.

 NOTE | The `navigator` object is named after the original object model's browser.

Browsers have *properties*. A browser has a name and a version, for instance. The objects that form the Internet Explorer Object Model also have properties. Properties are a part of an object. You can observe software object properties by calling the object's property by name. To call an object's property, you write the object's name (`objectName`), then a period, followed by the property's name (`propertyName`):

```
objectName.propertyName
```

You can program your Web page to look up the name of the browser under which it's running by adding the following line:

```
navigator.appName
```

The browser object, `navigator`, has an `appName` property that holds the name of the browser. You might also find another `navigator` object property useful. The `appVersion` property returns the version of the browser.

NOTE   The code listed in this section is the same for both VBScript and JavaScript except for one thing: for JavaScript, add a semicolon (;) to the end of each line.

Objects can be made up of other objects. A computer is an object that is built from other objects, such as a monitor and a hard disk. A Web browser is also an object made up of other objects. A Web browser is composed of a window, for instance. The Internet Explorer Object Model includes a window object named `window`.

Like the browser object, the window object has properties. It also does things. You can get a software object to do something by calling on the object's *method* of doing it. A method is actually a function that is a part of the object. To call an object's method, you write the object's name (*objectName*), then a period, followed by the name of the object's method (*methodName*):

```
objectName.methodName( parameters)
```

For example, a window can open and close. The Internet Explorer Object Model's `window` object has a method to open a new browser window named `open`. To open a new browser window, you add the following code:

```
window.open("URL", "windowName", ["windowFeatures"])
```

NOTE   The parameter list between parentheses is method-specific. These issues are addressed when you actually write scripts later in the chapter.

A `window` object is, of course, made up of other objects. A `window` object can contain a document (usually an HTML document); the document can be made up of forms, anchors, links, and so on. The list of objects makes up an *object hierarchy*. A chart of The Internet Explorer Object Model's object hierarchy is provided in Figure 10.1. Refer to this chart often while you're learning the objects and their properties and methods.

Figure 10.1.

The Microsoft Internet Explorer Object Model's object hierarchy allows easy manipulation of browser-related objects.

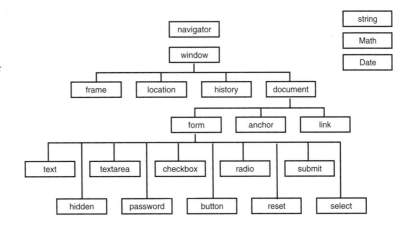

Event Handlers

Scripts respond to events through *event handlers*. The Internet Explorer Object Model includes event handlers that can tell your scripts when a specific event occurs. Your script can respond to events in specific ways. You might want to have Caution! appear in the browser's status bar when a user's mouse pointer is over a sensitive part of your Web page, for example; or you might want to run a sound file that says "Thank you!" when a user submits a form. Table 10.1 lists the Internet Explorer Object Model's event handlers.

Table 10.1. Internet Explorer Object Model event handlers.

Event Handler	Description
mouseMove	A mousemove event fires whenever the mouse pointer moves over a link.
onBlur	A blur event fires when an element loses focus.
onChange	A change event fires when an element has been modified.
onClick	A click event fires when an object on a form is clicked.
onFocus	A focus event fires when a field receives input focus by tabbing with the keyboard or clicking with the mouse.
onLoad	A load event fires when the browser finishes loading a window or all frames within a frameset.

continues

Table 10.1. continued

Event Handler	Description
onMouseOver	A mouseover event fires once each time the mouse pointer moves over an object from outside that object.
onSelect	A select event fires when a user selects some of the contents of an element.
onSubmit	A submit event fires when a user submits a form.
onUnload	An unload event fires when the contents of a window are unloaded.

A subset of objects in the Internet Explorer Object Model is associated with event handlers. Furthermore, each object that is associated with event handlers is generally associated only with a subset of them. For instance, only the window, form, link, and element objects are associated with event handlers. Of these, window is associated only with the onLoad and onUnload event handlers, and form is associated only with onSubmit. Objects and their associated event handlers are listed in Table 10.2.

Table 10.2. Objects and their event handlers.

Object	Event Handler
window	onLoad
	onUnload
form	onSubmit
link	mouseMove
	onClick
	onMouseOver
element	onBlur
	onChange
	onClick
	onFocus
	onSelect

The event methods supported by element depend on the kind of element employed. If element is a button, the onClick event is valid and all the others are invalid. If element is a textbox, all the element object's event handlers are valid except for onClick.

Now that you know that scripts are event-driven and object-based, your main conceptual tasks are accomplished. You can build effective scripts by using the Internet Explorer Object

Model methods, properties, and event handlers. You also can extend the power of scripts by using Java applets or ActiveX controls. Java applets and ActiveX controls provide new objects for you to manipulate through the scripting language.

Using VBScript and JavaScript

FrontPage supports scripting in both VBScript and JavaScript. Although each scripting language is unique in some ways, its similarity to the other is more striking. VBScript is familiar to Basic programmers, particularly Visual Basic programmers. JavaScript is similar to C and C++. Both manipulate objects in a similar manner, and both scripting languages use the Internet Explorer Object Model. In this section, you write scripts in both VBScript and JavaScript so that you can compare and contrast the scripting languages as you learn how to use them.

Object-Based Scripting

Follow tradition and write your first scripts to print Hello World!. The scripts print the message to the document window in your Web browser.

FrontPage makes it easy to add scripts to your Web pages. Create a new blank Web page in the FrontPage Editor by clicking on the New toolbar button. Add a script to the new page through the Script dialog box. Select the Script command from the Insert menu. The Script dialog box appears, as shown in Figure 10.2.

Figure 10.2.

Enter scripts into the Script dialog box.

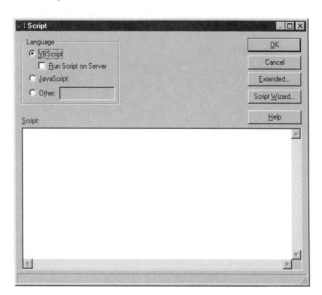

First, add the VBScript version of Hello World!. Select the **V**BScript radio button in the Language area of the Scripting dialog box. Leave the **R**un Script on Server checkbox unselected; the script will run in the user's Web browser. Type this line of VBScript code into the **S**cript scrolling textbox:

```
document.write "VBScript says ""Hello World!"""
```

Click on the **O**K button. You've added your first script to a Web page. A small icon indicates that VBScript code resides on your Web page, as shown in Figure 10.3. You can double-click on the icon to display the code in the Script dialog box.

NOTE

> By an arbitrary convention, scripts are presented first in VBScript followed by their JavaScript equivalent.

Figure 10.3.

The VBScript icon displays wherever VBScript is added to your Web page.

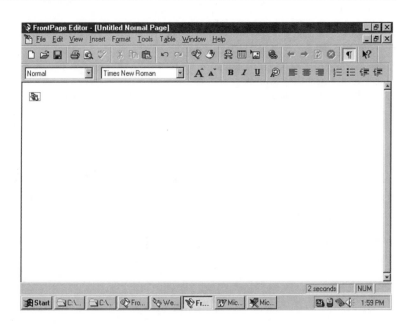

Save your Web page by clicking on the Save toolbar button. When prompted by the Save As dialog box, type `Hello World!` in the Page **T**itle textbox and keep the default HELLO.HTM in the File **P**ath textbox. Click on the OK button.

View your new Web page in your Web browser by clicking on the Preview in Browser toolbar button. You see `VBScript says "Hello World!"` displayed, as shown in Figure 10.4.

Figure 10.4.

*The output from your
VBScript code displays
in the browser
window.*

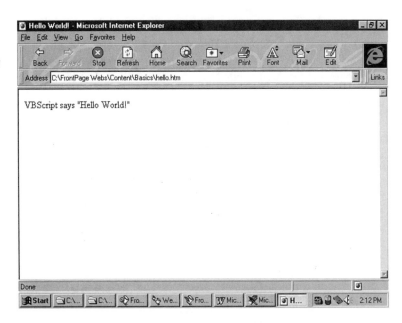

Place your cursor on the next line of the Web page, below the VBScript icon, in the FrontPage
Editor and type HTML says "Hello World!" and press the Enter key. Your Hello World! Web
page should look similar to Figure 10.5.

Figure 10.5.

*Type some text below
the VBScript code you
entered earlier.*

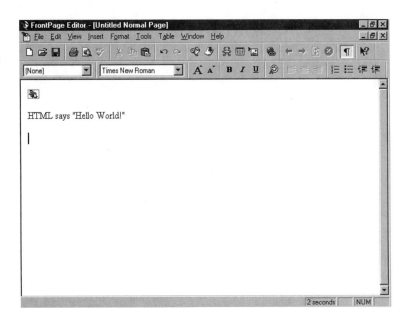

Enter your first JavaScript code. Place your cursor on the line following the text that you just entered. Select the Script command from the Insert menu. The Script dialog box appears. Select the JavaScript radio button in the Language area of the Scripting dialog box. Type the following JavaScript code in the Script scrolling textbox:

```
document.write("JavaScript says \"Hello World!\"");
```

Click on the OK button. A small icon with a J on it indicates that JavaScript code resides on your Web page. You can double-click on the icon to display the code in the Script dialog box. The completed page in the FrontPage Editor is shown in Figure 10.6.

Figure 10.6.

The complete Hello World! Web page displayed in the FrontPage Editor.

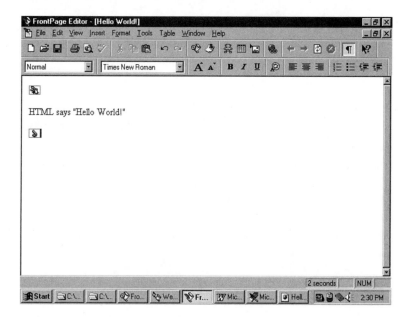

View your completed Hello World! Web page in your Web browser by clicking on the Preview in Browser toolbar button. You see output from three code types displayed, as shown in Figure 10.7.

Display the complete source code of the Hello World! Web page. Select the HTML command from the View menu in the FrontPage Editor. The View or Edit HTML dialog box appears, as shown in Figure 10.8.

Figure 10.7.

The complete Hello World! Web page displayed in a Web browser.

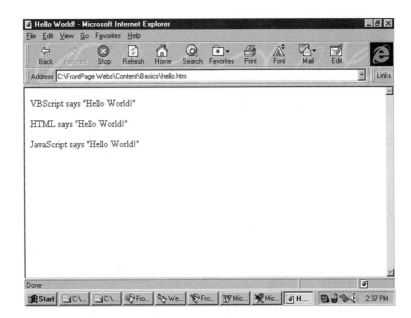

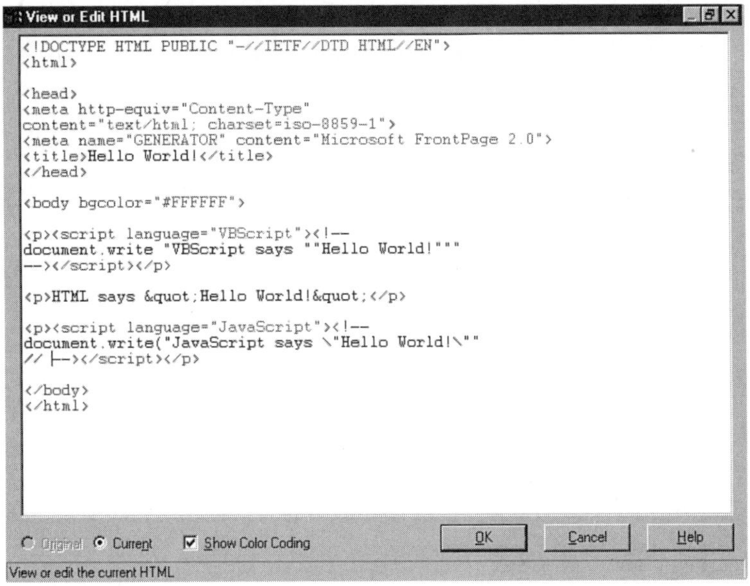

Figure 10.8.

Display the source code for your completed Hello World! Web page.

Nearly all the source code in the Hello World! Web page is familiar from Chapter 3, "Web Publishing Basics: Text, Lists, and Links." The code you entered is all in the document's body. After the <BODY> tag, you first come across the VBScript-specific code:

```
<P><SCRIPT LANGUAGE="VBScript"><!--
document.write "VBScript says ""Hello World!"""
--></SCRIPT></P>
```

The VBScript-specific code is followed by some HTML code corresponding to the text that you typed directly into the page in the FrontPage Editor:

```
<P>HTML says &quot;Hello World!&quot;</P>
```

This is followed by the JavaScript-specific code:

```
<P><SCRIPT LANGUAGE="JavaScript"><!--
document.write("JavaScript says \"Hello World!\"");
// --></SCRIPT></P>
```

These code fragments are mostly made up of HTML tags. The <SCRIPT> tag signals that the code that follows is a scripting language up to the </SCRIPT> end-tag. The <SCRIPT> tag's LANGUAGE argument specifies the scripting language used. The argument is set equal to "VBScript" to specify VBScript and "JavaScript" to specify JavaScript.

The <!-- after the <SCRIPT> tag and the --> (// --> for JavaScript) before the </SCRIPT> end-tag tell the browser to ignore the script between them if the browser does not recognize the scripting language. Including these tags is very important; otherwise, people who have browsers that don't run the script you use will see the scripting code presented in their browser windows when they load your Web page. Using the tags enables all users to view your Web page, even if they don't get the added functionality provided by your scripts.

The key line in the VBScript code is the following:

```
document.write "VBScript says ""Hello World!"""
```

and in the JavaScript code it's this:

```
document.write("JavaScript says \"Hello World!\"");
```

These lines invoke the document object's write method.

Look at the Internet Explorer Object Model's object hierarchy in Figure 10.1. Notice that the document object is under the window object. This means that a window object can be composed of a document object, along with frame, location, and history objects. In fact, the window object is implied in the line of code but is not required in this instance. You could just as well write the following:

10

```
window.document.write "VBScript says ""Hello World!"""
```

or

```
window.document.write("JavaScript says \"Hello World!\"");
```

The document object's write method includes a single parameter: the string "VBScript says ""Hello World!""" or "JavaScript says \"Hello World!\"". The write method displays the expression in a document window. This string includes two "" in VBScript—one set before Hello and one set after World!. Doubling up the double quotation marks enables you to include quotation marks inside the string. The string itself is delimited by quotation marks. The final result is that VBScript displays the string VBScript says "Hello World" in your browser's document window. In JavaScript, the string includes two \" . This is called an *escape sequence,* and it enables you to include quotations inside strings in JavaScript. The string itself is delimited by the regular quotation marks. The final result is that JavaScript displays the string JavaScript says "Hello World" in your browser's document window.

You see that the VBScript and JavaScript codes are nearly identical. You generally find only small syntactical differences between the two scripting languages—using two double quotation marks versus an escape sequence, for instance. Another example is JavaScript's convention of ending each line with a semicolon (;), as in C. There are other differences in syntax between VBScript and JavaScript, but they are minor and can easily be looked up.

Event-Driven Scripts

As pointed out previously, VBScript and JavaScript are event-driven scripting languages. Your first scripts don't do anything that plain old HTML can't do, except maybe hide some output in certain cases. They simply print messages to the browser's document window. No user interaction is required. No events trigger the scripts to do something. Usually, when you add a script to your Web page, you do so because you want the users to be able to do something. You want them to interact with your Web page.

You build an interactive Web page in this section. You add a button that the user clicks on to open a dialog box. The user enters a response in the dialog box, and your script reacts according to the input.

Open a new blank Web page in the FrontPage Editor. Add a pushbutton to the page by selecting the **P**ush Button command from the **I**nsert, Form Fiel**d** menu. Double-click on the pushbutton to open the Push Button Properties dialog box, as shown in Figure 10.9. Type ClickMe into the **N**ame textbox and type Click Me into the **V**alue/Label textbox. Select the N**o**rmal radio button from the Button type area. Click on the OK button.

Figure 10.9.

Enter all the button information into the Push Button Properties dialog box.

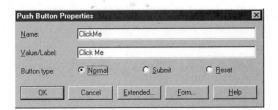

Your Web page in the FrontPage Editor should contain a form with a Click Me pushbutton, as shown in Figure 10.10.

Figure 10.10.

You can see the Click Me pushbutton in your Web page loaded in the FrontPage Editor.

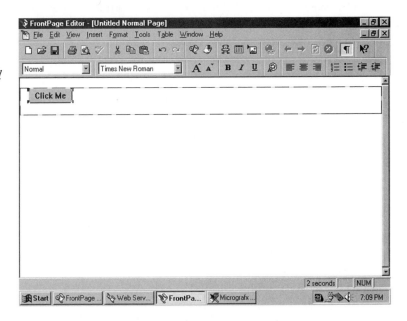

Save your Web page by clicking on the Save toolbar button. When prompted by the Save As dialog box, enter Test for Ten into the Page **T**itle textbox and modify the default file in the File **P**ath textbox to read TEN.HTM. Click on the OK button.

Click on the line just below the form. Then open the Script dialog box by selecting the Scrip**t** command from the **I**nsert menu. Select the **V**BScript radio button from the Language area and type the VBScript code in Listing 10.1 into the **S**cript scrolling textbox. Click on the O**K** button and save your work.

TYPE **Listing 10.1. Test for Ten (the VBScript part).**

```
Sub ClickMe_onClick
    ten = prompt("Enter 10", 0)
    If(ten <> "") Then
        If( ten = 10) Then
            strAlertMessage = "Thank you!"
        Else
            strAlertMessage = "That wasn't a 10!"
        End If
    Else
        strAlertMessage = "Input canceled!"
    End If
    alert strAlertMessage
End Sub
```

Add another pushbutton to your Test for Ten Web page. Click on the line just below the VBScript icon, then select the **P**ush Button command from the **I**nsert, Form Fiel**d** menu. Double-click on the pushbutton to open the Push Button Properties dialog box. Type ClickMeToo into the **N**ame textbox and type Click Me Too into the **V**alue/Label textbox. Select the N**o**rmal radio button from the Button type area. Click on the OK button. Your Test for Ten page should look like Figure 10.11.

Figure 10.11.

You can see the second pushbutton below the VBScript icon.

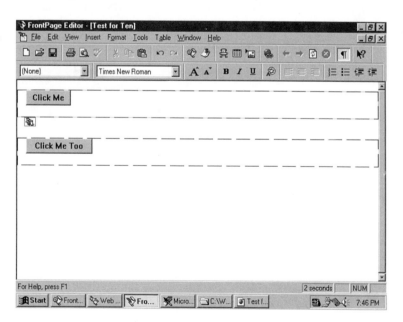

Click on the line just below the form with the Click Me Too pushbutton. Open the Script dialog box by selecting the Script command from the Insert menu. Select the JavaScript radio button from the Language area and then type the JavaScript code in Listing 10.2 in the Script scrolling textbox. Click on the OK button and save your work.

TYPE **Listing 10.2. Test for Ten (the JavaScript part).**

```
function ClickMeToo_onClick()
{
    ten = prompt("Enter 10", 0);
    if(ten)
    {
        if( ten == 10)
            strAlertMessage = "Thank you!";
        else
            strAlertMessage = "That wasn't a 10!";
    }
    else
        strAlertMessage = "Input canceled!";
    alert(strAlertMessage);
}
```

Load the Test for Ten Web page into your VBScript-enabled Web browser by clicking on the Preview in Browser toolbar button. The browser's document window contains two buttons, as shown in Figure 10.12.

Figure 10.12.

The Click Me and Click Me Too buttons display when you load the Test for Ten Web page into your browser.

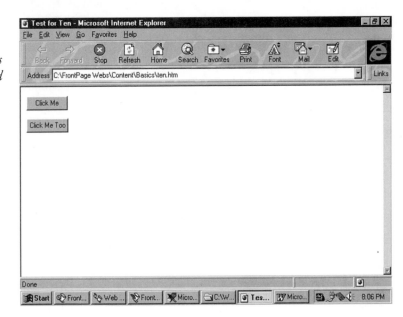

When you click on the Click Me button or the Click Me Too button, a dialog box appears with Enter 10 displayed above a textbox containing a 0, as shown in Figure 10.13.

NOTE

The VBScript associated with the Click Me button and JavaScript code associated with the Click Me Too button do the exact same things. The rest of this discussion cites the Click Me button, but you can use either the Click Me or the Click Me Too button.

Figure 10.13.

The Microsoft Internet Explorer dialog box asks the user to enter 10.

Type 10 into the textbox and click on the OK button. A dialog box appears with the words Thank you!, as shown in Figure 10.14.

Figure 10.14.

The Microsoft Internet Explorer dialog box says Thank you!

Click on the Click Me button again. This time, enter some number other than 10 and click on the OK button. A dialog box appears with the words That wasn't a 10!, as shown in Figure 10.15. The script checks your entry and sees that you didn't enter a 10.

Figure 10.15.

The dialog box announces that the user didn't enter a 10.

Click on the Click Me button one more time. This time, enter anything you want into the textbox and click on the Cancel button. A dialog box appears with the words `Input canceled!`, as shown in Figure 10.16. The script checks for canceled inputs.

Figure 10.16.

The dialog box confirms that the user canceled the input.

Scripts treat most items found on Web pages as objects. For instance, forms created by the `<FORM>` tag can contain all sorts of objects known as *elements*. The forms in Test for Ten contain buttons defined by the `<INPUT>` tag. The value of an `<INPUT>` tag's `TYPE` argument specifies its element type, which is set equal to `"button"`. The pushbutton form elements are connected to their respective scripts through the `onClick` event handler.

VBScript and JavaScript recognize the value of the `<INPUT>` tag's `NAME` argument as an object name. You added two buttons to the Test for Ten Web page, one named Click Me and the other named Click Me Too. Once you specify an element's `NAME` argument, scripts treat the element like another object in the Internet Explorer Object Model.

 A *button* is an `element` object named `button` in the Internet Explorer Object Model.

To connect the `button` object to an event, the event handler is appended to the object's name and defined as a function or procedure. Notice how the Click Me button name is appended with the `onClick` event handler in VBScript:

```
Sub ClickMe_onClick
    ...
End Sub
```

and in JavaScript:

```
function ClickMeToo_onClick()
{
    ...
}
```

An underscore connects the `button` object's name to the event handler, and the whole thing—`ClickMe_onClick` or `ClickMeToo_onClick`—is part of the procedure or function signature. Here, the differences in syntax between VBScript and JavaScript become obvious.

In VBScript, the `Sub` statement precedes `ClickMe_onClick`. The `Sub` statement is used to define a procedure. The `End Sub` statement marks the end of a procedure. Whenever you click on the ClickMe button, the `ClickMe_onClick` procedure runs.

In contrast, the JavaScript signature begins with the `function` statement and must be followed by the open and close parentheses, signifying that this is a function.

In VBScript, a procedure defined with `Sub` and `End Sub` is distinct from a function defined with `Function` and `End Function`. A function returns a value and a procedure doesn't. In JavaScript, there are only functions defined by the `function` statement. JavaScript also employs open and close brackets for defining blocks of script. Rather than signifying the end of a function with an `End Function` statement, as in VBScript, JavaScript signifies the end of a function with a close bracket that matches an open bracket set at the beginning of a function right after the function's signature.

The `button` object can use only the `onClick` event handler, but other types of objects can use one or more of an array of event handlers available in the Internet Explorer Object Model.

The `ClickMe_onClick` procedure and the `ClickMeToo_onClick` function demonstrate several points on scripting. Take a closer look at the VBScript `ClickMe_onClick` procedure:

```
Sub ClickMe_onClick
    ten = prompt("Enter 10", 0)
    If(ten <> "") Then
        If( ten = 10) Then
            strAlertMessage = "Thank you!"
        Else
            strAlertMessage = "That wasn't a 10!"
        End If
    Else
        strAlertMessage = "Input canceled!"
    End If
    alert strAlertMessage
End Sub
```

and the JavaScript `ClickMeToo_onClick` function:

```
function ClickMeToo_onClick()
{
    ten = prompt("Enter 10", 0);
    if(ten)
    {
        if( ten == 10)
            strAlertMessage = "Thank you!";
        else
            strAlertMessage = "That wasn't a 10!";
    }
    else
        strAlertMessage = "Input canceled!";
    alert(strAlertMessage);
}
```

The first expression in the body of both the VBScript and JavaScript code includes `prompt`, a `window` method. Again, `window` can be left off when you use `window` child objects or methods.

The current `window` object is assumed.

The `prompt` method takes up to two parameters and returns either the text—in this case a number—entered into a dialog box's textbox, or an empty string (`""`) in VBScript or `false` in JavaScript if the user clicks on the Cancel button. The first and required `prompt` parameter is the message shown on the dialog box. `"Enter 10"` is entered as the first `prompt` parameter. The second and optional parameter is a default value, in this case `0`, to be placed in the dialog box's textbox. Values returned by `prompt` are assigned to the `ten` variable.

Notice that variables are not defined before they are used. There is no strong type checking. You can simply write the variable where you need it.

NOTE

> VBScript has one variable type named `Variant`. The `Variant` type variable can contain one of several subtypes. Find details on the VBScript variable types and subtypes in the Variables section of Appendix C, "VBScript Reference." The section also shows how you can avoid errors that can arise due to automatic variable assignment.

The script acts on the result returned to the `ten` variable after a value is prompted for and entered (or not). Nested program control statements—the `If...Else...End If` statement in VBScript and the `if...else` statement in JavaScript—are used first to test whether the user clicked on the Cancel button and then to test whether the user entered `10`. Here are the relevant lines of VBScript code:

```
If(ten <> "") Then
    If( ten = 10) Then
        strAlertMessage = "Thank you!"
    Else
        strAlertMessage = "That wasn't a 10!"
    End If
Else
    strAlertMessage = "Input canceled!"
End If
```

and here are the relevant lines of JavaScript code:

```
if(ten)
{
    if( ten == 10)
        strAlertMessage = "Thank you!";
    else
        strAlertMessage = "That wasn't a 10!";
}
else
    strAlertMessage = "Input canceled!";
```

These code segments display differences in syntax between VBScript and JavaScript.

Nevertheless, they also look very similar.

NOTE Find details on VBScript statements and operators in Appendix C. Find details on JavaScript statements and operators in Appendix D, "JavaScript Reference."

In VBScript, if the user clicks on the Cancel button, the prompt method assigns an empty string ("") to the ten variable. The not equal comparison operator (<>) used in the If statement tests the ten variable to see that it's not equal to "". If the ten variable is not equal to "", the script interpreter skips the code block after If(ten <> "") Then and reads the expression after Else where the strAlertMessage variable is assigned the "Input Canceled!" string.

In contrast, when a user clicks on the Cancel button while the JavaScript code is running, the prompt method assigns false to the ten variable; otherwise, it assigns true. The if statement checks to see whether ten is true or false. If the user clicked on the Cancel button, ten is false; the script interpreter skips the code block after if(ten) and reads the expression after else where the strAlertMessage variable is assigned the "Input Canceled!" string.

If the OK button is clicked while either VBScript or JavaScript is running, the script's interpreter reads the code block following If(ten <> "") Then or the if(ten) expression. The If...Else...End If or if...else statement inside this block of code checks the value of the ten variable to see whether it is equal to 10. If it is, "Thank you!" is assigned to the strAlertMessage variable. On the other hand, if the value of the ten variable is anything other than 10, "That wasn't a 10!" is assigned to the strAlertMessage variable.

Finally, the last line in both the VBScript and the JavaScript code calls the window object's alert method with the strAlertMessage variable as its parameter:

```
alert strAlertMessage
```

Whatever was assigned to the strAlertMessage variable is sent as output to the alert dialog box.

This script does a lot of work for relatively little effort. It includes a button, a dialog box that prompts for input, and a dialog box that responds to the different possible outcomes. To build the script, you need to know (or look up) the right objects to use and the right event handler to use. In addition, you need to include some program control to test user input. Test for Ten uses comparison operators and program control statements. These are common elements in scripts. You can look them up in the script references in the appendixes (Appendix C for VBScript and Appendix D for Javascript). In the next section, you learn how to use FrontPage's special scripting tool, the Script Wizard.

Using the Script Wizard

The Script Wizard enables you intuitively to connect object events to actions. Start getting an intuitive feeling for the power of Script Wizard by creating a new Web page with a button and a VBScript procedure. Use Script Wizard to connect a click on the button with the procedure.

Create a new blank Web page in the FrontPage Editor. Add a pushbutton to the page by selecting the **P**ush Button command from the **I**nsert, Form Fiel**d** menu. Double-click on the pushbutton to open the Push Button Properties dialog box. Type ClickMe into the **N**ame textbox and type Click Me into the **V**alue/Label textbox, just as you did in the last section. Select the **N**ormal radio button from the Button type area. Click on the OK button.

Save your Web page by clicking on the Save toolbar button. When prompted by the Save As dialog box, enter Ten Again into the Page **T**itle textbox and accept the default file in the File **P**ath textbox. Click on the OK button.

Click on the line just below the form, then open the Script dialog box by selecting the Scrip**t** command from the **I**nsert menu. Select the **V**BScript radio button from the Language area. Then type the VBScript code in Listing 10.3 into the **S**cript scrolling textbox. The code is exactly the same as in Listing 10.1, except that the procedure's name is TestForTen rather than ClickMe. Click on the **O**K button and save your work.

TYPE   **Listing 10.3. Ten Again.**

```
Sub TestForTen_onClick
    ten = prompt("Enter 10", 0)
    If(ten <> "") Then
        If( ten = 10) Then
            strAlertMessage = "Thank you!"
        Else
            strAlertMessage = "That wasn't a 10!"
        End If
    Else
        strAlertMessage = "Input canceled!"
    End If
    alert strAlertMessage
End Sub
```

If you load the Ten Again Web page into a browser and click on the Click Me button, nothing happens. You've added a button and a procedure to the page, but you didn't concern yourself with making sure that they were connected. This is, in fact, very handy. You can add several generic procedures and functions to a Web page without concern for the exact elements that will use them. Likewise, you can add several elements to a page without worrying about the exact procedures or functions to which you'll connect them. In the end, you open Script Wizard and tie them all together. Try it!

Open Script Wizard by selecting the Script command from the Insert menu. The Script dialog box opens, as shown in Figure 10.17.

Figure 10.17.

Open Script Wizard by clicking on the Script Wizard button in the Script dialog box.

Click on the Script Wizard button. The Script Wizard dialog box opens, as shown in Figure 10.18.

Figure 10.18.

The Script Wizard dialog box includes a Select an Event list and an Insert Actions list.

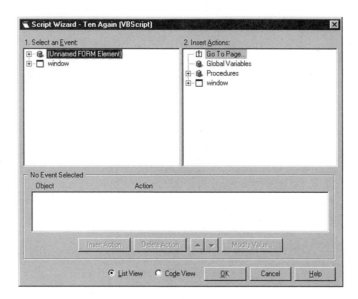

Look at the hierarchical lists in the Select an **E**vent and Insert **A**ctions lists in the Script Wizard dialog box. They work like the hierarchical list in FrontPage Explorer's All Hyperlinks pane and in Windows Explorer's All Folders pane. Click on the little plus sign to expand a tree of a list's hierarchy and click on the little minus sign to collapse a tree.

In the Select an **E**vent list you see two objects: an unnamed form and a window. Three-dimensional box icons represent objects, like the form field. Two-dimensional window icons represent browser windows. The unnamed form is the form that the pushbutton is part of. Expand the Unnamed FORM Element by clicking on the plus sign next to it.

Inside the unnamed form hierarchy, you should see two items listed: onSubmit and ClickMe. Next to onSubmit is an open diamond that represents events. onSubmit is a form event handler, the only one that the form object has. The ClickMe object is the pushbutton. Remember that ClickMe is the name that you gave the pushbutton when you added it to the page. Recall that scripts recognize your added objects by the name that you give them. Click on the plus sign next to ClickMe. Inside ClickMe is the onClick event handler, the only button event handler. Your Script Wizard dialog box should look something like Figure 10.19.

Figure 10.19.

*The expanded Unnamed FORM Element hierarchy is displayed in Script Wizard dialog box's Select an **E**vent list.*

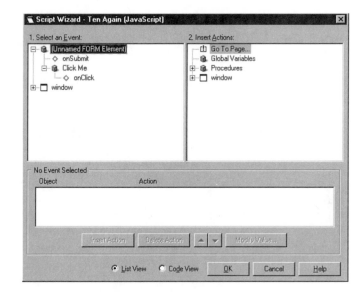

In the Insert Actions list you see four items: a Go To Page action, a Global Variables object, a Procedures object, and a window. The only new icon, an exclamation mark, represents an action. The Go To Page action is a top-level Web browser action. The Global Variables object contains any global variables that you might add. You haven't added any, so there are none. The Procedures object contains any procedures that you might add. You have added one: the TestForTen procedure. Expand the Procedures object hierarchy by clicking on the plus sign next to it. You should see something like Figure 10.20.

Figure 10.20.

The expanded Procedures hierarchy is displayed in the Script Wizard dialog box's Insert Actions list.

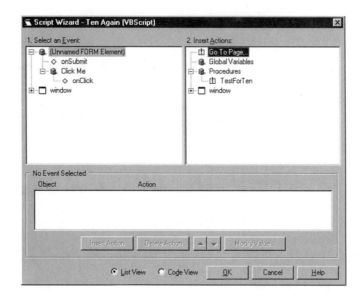

There's your TestForTen procedure. It's a type of action. That is, if something calls the procedure, the procedure carries out an action. When someone clicks on the button object ClickMe, you want it to call TestForTen. Here's where the beauty of Script Wizard enters the scene. Tie the ClickMe onClick event to the TestForTen action. First, click on onClick in the Select an Event list. onClick should be highlighted. Now click on TestForTen in the Insert Actions list. TestForTen should be highlighted. Now that the event and the action that you want to tie together are highlighted, click on the Insert Action button. Your Script Wizard dialog box should look something like Figure 10.21.

Figure 10.21.

The onClick event is tied together with the TestForTen action.

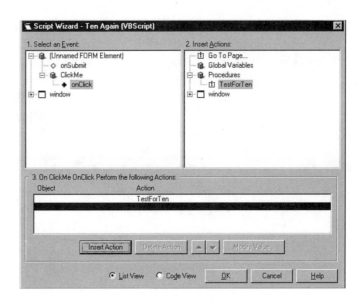

Click on the **OK** button. Be sure to save your work.

Load the Ten Again Web page into your browser by clicking on the Preview in Browser toolbar button in the FrontPage Editor. Clicking on the Click Me button results in the same behavior as clicking on the buttons in the Test for Ten Web page earlier in this chapter.

Summary

You covered a lot of ground in this chapter. You learned about the Internet Explorer Object Model, VBScript, and JavaScript. You learned how to enter scripts using the FrontPage Editor's scripting tools, including Script Wizard. You can apply these skills to tie together Web page components that you learned about earlier in the book, such as forms, form elements, frames, and ActiveX controls. In the next chapter, you use these skills while learning about Java applets and more about ActiveX controls.

Q&A

Q What scripting language should I use: VBScript or JavaScript?

A As you saw in this chapter, these two scripting languages do the same thing, so your choice can be boiled down to two considerations:

1. Which language is easiest for you to use?

2. Does your target audience use a browser that includes the language's interpreter?

10

The first question is personal. Usually, if you're a C or C++ fan, JavaScript is the most intuitive language; otherwise, usually VBScript is more intuitive. If your target audience uses the current version of the Internet Explorer, either language can be used. If your audience uses Netscape's Navigator, you might want to use JavaScript.

Q If I use the Internet Explorer Object Model, will browsers other than the Internet Explorer be able to run my scripts?

A The Internet Explorer Object Model uses the same object hierarchy as the object model used by Netscape's Navigator. Microsoft built the object model so that the Internet Explorer can run existing JavaScript code. Browsers built to run VBScript or JavaScript code can use the Internet Explorer Object Model.

Q Where do object actions come from?

A When programmers build controls or other objects, they write procedures or functions—often called methods—into them. An object's procedures or functions show up as actions in the Script Wizard dialog box.

Workshop

Experiment with the Script Wizard. Try manipulating windows and frames and other objects by connecting events and actions. The possibilities are nearly endless.

Quiz

1. There are two major characteristics of the VBScript and JavaScript scripting languages. What are they?

2. How do scripts recognize a form element as an object?

3. Script Wizard gives you the point-and-click capability of tying what two things together?

DAY

6

Chapter 11

Adding Java Applets and ActiveX Controls

Java applets and ActiveX controls take your Web pages far beyond the interactive and presentation capabilities that they could ever achieve with HTML. Forms combined with scripting languages bring users the ability to interact with Web pages in more meaningful ways than simply clicking on links. However, as the name implies, forms remain similar to printed pages. HTML multimedia capabilities are impressive, but many yearn for the ability to present sound, animation, and even their own worlds outside the constraints imposed by the printed page-like format of Web pages. Java applets and ActiveX controls provide the opportunity to break out of the traditional printed page format by enabling you to incorporate programs into your Web. It's simple to incorporate Java applets and ActiveX controls into your Webs using the FrontPage Web authoring and publishing environment.

In this chapter, you

☐ Add animation to your Web with a Java applet

☐ Use ActiveX controls instead of form fields

☐ Explore a virtual world using an ActiveX control and a Netscape plug-in

Adding Java Applets

Java applets are special programs designed specifically for running in your Web browser. They derive their name from the fact that they are programmed using the Java language. When you open a page containing a Java applet, the applet is downloaded from the Internet to your computer where it runs. The page with the Java applet doesn't actually hold the Java applet itself. The applet is referenced by an <APPLET> tag. The <APPLET> tag tells your browser where to get the applet itself, a file with the CLASS extension. FrontPage makes it a point-and-click procedure to add Java applets to your Web.

NOTE

> Don't confuse the Java programming language with the JavaScript scripting language. They are two different things. JavaScript is not a subset of the Java language. They were developed by two different companies and are very different. Sun developed Java as a programming language. Netscape developed LiveScript as a scripting language. When Netscape added Java to its browsers, it changed the name of LiveScript to JavaScript and made LiveScript more Java-like. Nevertheless, they remain distinct. (In contrast, VBScript is a subset of the Visual Basic programming language.)

Add an animation to your personal Web using The Dancing Teddy Bear Java applet. Open your personal Web in FrontPage Explorer. Add the files for The Dancing Teddy Bear to your personal Web. Open FrontPage Explorer and select the **I**mport command from the **F**ile menu. The Import File to FrontPage Web dialog box appears, as shown in Figure 11.1.

Figure 11.1.

Add files to your Web through the Import File to the FrontPage Web dialog box.

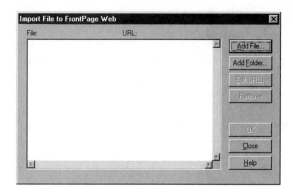

Tip

Get The Dancing Teddy Bear applet from the CD-ROM accompanying this book or from the Java pages of my Web at

`http://ourworld.compuserve.com/homepages/Brainstage/ddoherty.htm`.

The complete applet includes the `TEDDY.CLASS` and the three images `TEDDY0.JPG`, `TEDDY1.JPG`, and `TEDDY2.JPG`.

Click on the **A**dd File button and the Add File to Import List dialog box appears, as shown in Figure 11.2. The complete applet includes the TEDDY.CLASS and the three images TEDDY0.JPG, TEDDY1.JPG, and TEDDY2.JPG. Select all the files at once or one at a time (if they're in different folders, for instance) through the Add File to Import List dialog box. Click on the **O**pen button.

Figure 11.2.

Select all four files at once in the Add File to Import List dialog box.

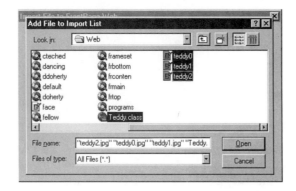

The files you select are listed in the Import File to the FrontPage Web dialog box's list. Add more files using the same method if you need to; when you're finished, click on the OK button.

All The Dancing Teddy Bear files go in the same folder. However, some applets are designed so that the image files, for instance, go into a different folder than the applet itself. Applets should be provided with information on file placement, whether they take parameters, and the optimal size of the applet's window.

Open The Dancing Teddy Bear page you created in Chapter 8, "Adding Multimedia to Your Web Page," in the FrontPage Editor. If you didn't create the page in Chapter 8, create it now. Select the Java Applet command from the **O**ther Components submenu on the **I**nsert menu. The Java Applet Properties dialog box appears, as shown in Figure 11.3.

Figure 11.3.

Insert Java applets through the Java Applet Properties dialog box.

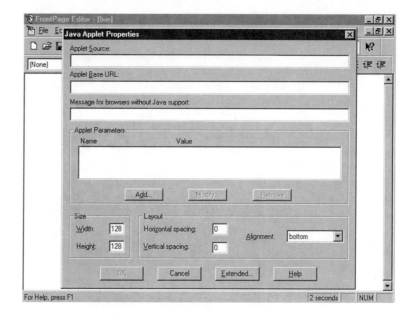

Type the name of the applet, TEDDY.CLASS, in the Applet **S**ource textbox. Add the URL for the applet in the Applet **B**ase URL textbox if it's different from your Web's base URL. Leave the Applet **B**ase URL textbox blank. Type a message such as Your browser doesn't support Java for people without a Java-enabled browser into the Messa**g**e for browsers without Java support textbox. Add applet parameters in the Applet Parameters area. The Dancing Teddy Bear applet doesn't take any parameters. Set the size of the applet's window in the Size area. The Dancing Teddy Bear Applet looks best when viewed through an applet window 750 pixels wide and 200 pixels high. Type 750 into the **W**idth textbox and 200 in the Heigh**t** textbox in the Size area. You can modify the layout properties in the Layout area. Leave these at their default settings and click on the OK button. The applet information is added to your Web page and represented by a J icon with the name of the class listed under it, as shown in Figure 11.4.

11

Figure 11.4.

The J icon shows that the area outlined by the dotted line is the window area of a Java applet.

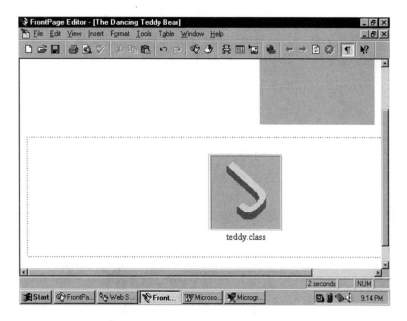

Load The Dancing Teddy Bear page into your Web page and watch a teddy bear dance.

Adding ActiveX Controls

Add a wide range of interactive and multimedia capabilities to your Web pages with ActiveX controls. ActiveX controls include code signing so that users can be sure that the control they use is safe; otherwise, they're the same thing as an OLE control. Keep in mind, however, that most browsers don't support ActiveX natively. Only Microsoft's Internet Explorer provides built-in support for ActiveX. Other browsers either don't support it at all or require a special plug-in for such support. FrontPage makes it simple to add ActiveX controls. In the following sections, you take a quick survey of the Microsoft Forms 2.0 ActiveX controls and you add a virtual world to your Web by using a Virtual Reality Modeling Language (VRML) ActiveX Control. Later in the chapter, you add a virtual world that uses a Netscape plug-in.

You use the same procedures to add any ActiveX control to your Web page using the FrontPage Editor. Work through the procedures using the Microsoft Forms 2.0 CheckBox ActiveX control.

NOTE

PowerPoint animation using the PowerPoint Animation ActiveX control is added to your page through a slightly different method than all other ActiveX controls. Adding PowerPoint animation to your Web is described in Chapter 8.

Insert the CheckBox ActiveX control in your Web page by selecting the **A**ctiveX Control command from the **O**ther Components submenu on the **I**nsert menu in the FrontPage Editor. The ActiveX Control Properties dialog box appears, as shown in Figure 11.5.

Figure 11.5.

Insert ActiveX controls into your Web page through the ActiveX Control Properties dialog box.

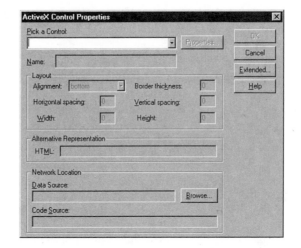

Select Microsoft Forms 2.0 CheckBox from the **P**ick a Control drop-down list. Type a unique name for the control in the **N**ame textbox. This is the name that you use when referring to the control in scripts. Specify the layout of the control in the Layout area. Not all browsers recognize ActiveX controls. Type an HTML filename in the HT**M**L textbox in the Alternative Representation area if you want to display, to those without ActiveX support, an alternate Web page in place of the one with an ActiveX control. Some ActiveX controls take runtime parameters. Enter the URL of the location of the file containing the runtime parameters into the **D**ata Source textbox in the Network Location area. If the file is part of your FrontPage Web, you simply type the filename. Some people browsing your Web will have an ActiveX-enabled browser, but they might not have the ActiveX controls that you use loaded onto their computer. In the Code **S**ource textbox in the Network Location area, type the URL that their Web browsers should use to download the ActiveX control if they don't already have it.

Click on the Properties button to open one of the most useful tools available on the ActiveX Control Properties dialog box. Two windows appear, as shown in Figure 11.6.

Figure 11.6.

Edit control properties through the Edit ActiveX Control and Properties windows.

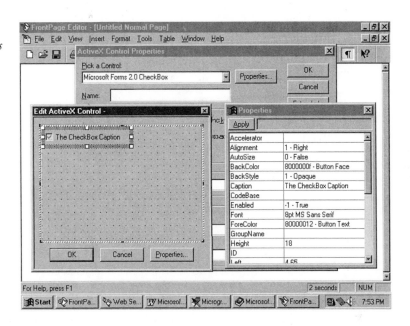

The ActiveX control is displayed the way it will be displayed on your Web page in the Edit ActiveX Control window. Visually manipulate the control in the Edit ActiveX Control window or change its various properties through the Properties window. The Properties window lists all the control's editable properties. Some of the properties are discussed when you examine individual controls. When you are finished editing the control, click on the OK button in the Edit ActiveX Control window.

Microsoft Form 2.0 ActiveX Controls

Yesterday, in Chapter 9, "Adding Forms and Other Interactive Elements," you learned about forms and all seven form fields you can add to Web pages. ActiveX enables you to go beyond the capabilities of HTML forms. The Microsoft Form ActiveX controls replace and extend the seven form fields available in HTML with the following fourteen controls:

- [ ] CheckBox
- [ ] ComboBox
- [ ] CommandButton
- [ ] Frame

☐ Image
☐ Label
☐ ListBox
☐ MultiPage
☐ OptionButton
☐ ScrollBar
☐ SpinButton
☐ TabStrip
☐ TextBox
☐ ToggleButton

Viewing Virtual Worlds

Add a virtual world to your personal Web. A virtual world is a space that you're able to move around in and explore. As with the real world, you can look at and manipulate objects. In this section, you add a virtual cow to your Web. In one instance you view the cow through an ActiveX control, and in the other instance you view it through a Netscape plug-in. Notice that you provide the content in your Web, and you link the content to an ActiveX control or Netscape plug-in through commands embedded in your Web page.

Using the VRML ActiveX Control

First, be sure that Microsoft's VRML 1.0 ActiveX control is installed on your computer. The Microsoft VRML 1.0 ActiveX control is available on the CD-ROM accompanying this book or at http://www.microsoft.com/ie/download/ieadd.htm. Double-click on the setup file and the Microsoft VRML 1.0 ActiveX control is installed on your computer.

Second, import the COW_WRL.WRL file to your Web. COW_WRL.WRL is a VRML 1.0 file that is available on the CD-ROM accompanying this book or at http://www.ocnus.com/models/Animals/. Open your personal Web in FrontPage Explorer, then select the **I**mport command from the **F**ile menu. The Import File to FrontPage Web dialog box appears. Click on the **A**dd File button. The Add File to Import List dialog box appears. Find COW_WRL.WRL and highlight it. Then click on the **O**pen button. The COW_WRL.WRL file should be listed in the Import File to FrontPage Web dialog box, as shown in Figure 11.7.

11

Figure 11.7.

COW_WRL.WRL is listed in the Import File to FrontPage Web dialog box.

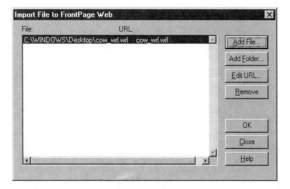

Click on the OK button. COW_WRL.WRL is added to your Web and is listed in the FrontPage Explorer window, as shown in Figure 11.8.

Figure 11.8.

COW_WRL.WRL displays in the FrontPage Explorer window as an icon.

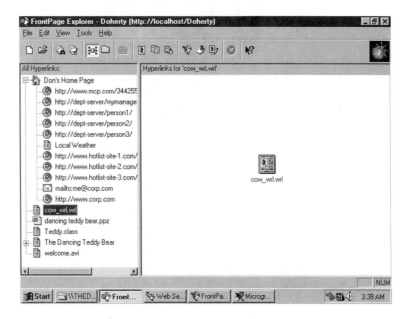

Open a new Web page in the FrontPage Editor. Select the **A**ctiveX Control command from the **O**ther Components submenu on the **I**nsert menu in the FrontPage Editor. The ActiveX Control Properties dialog box appears.

Select VrmlViewer Object\ from the **P**ick a Control drop-down list in the ActiveX Control Properties dialog box. Click on the **P**roperties button to open the Edit ActiveX Control and Properties windows, as shown in Figure 11.9.

Figure 11.9.

Edit control properties through the Edit ActiveX Control and Properties windows.

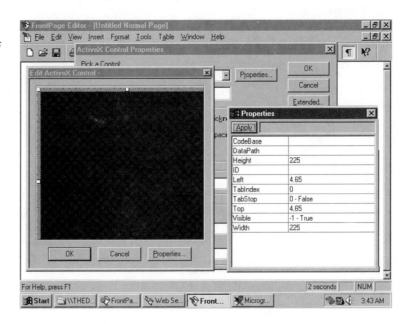

Add the full path and filename of the VRML 1.0 file in the DataPath property field in the Properties dialog box. Highlight the DataPath property, then type a URL into the textbox at the top of the Properties window next to the **A**pply button. The URL should be something like `http://localhost/Doherty/cow_wrl.wrl` where `localhost` is the name of the server and `Doherty` is the name of the FrontPage Web that the `cow_wrl.wrl` VRML 1.0 file resides in. Click on the **A**pply button. The data file should load into the ActiveX control and display in the Edit ActiveX Control window, as shown in Figure 11.10.

Click on the OK button in the Edit ActiveX Control to accept the current property settings. Click on the OK button in the ActiveX Control Properties dialog box. The COW_WRL.WRL file is added to your Web page. Save the Web page by clicking on the Save toolbar button. Give the Page **T**itle a value such as The Virtual Cow. The Virtual Cow Web page displays a hyperlink to the Microsoft VRML 1.0 ActiveX Control, represented by its class identification number (CLSID) in FrontPage Explorer, as shown in Figure 11.11. View the cow by clicking on the Preview in Browser toolbar button.

Figure 11.10.

The cow should appear in the Edit ActiveX Control window.

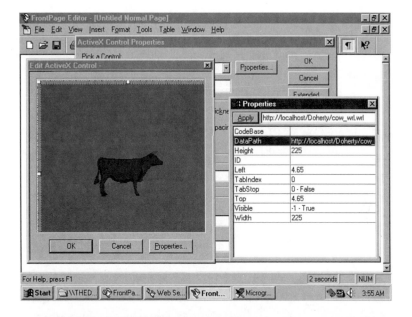

Figure 11.11.

A hyperlink appears between The Virtual Cow Web page and the Microsoft VRML 1.0 ActiveX control.

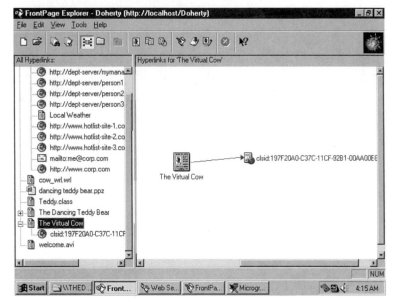

Using the VRML Netscape Plug-In

First, install the Silicon Graphics, Inc. Cosmo Player Netscape plug-in on your computer. The Cosmo Player Netscape plug-in is available on the CD-ROM accompanying this book or at http://webspace.sgi.com/cosmoplayer/download.html. Double-click on the setup file and the Cosmo Player Netscape plug-in is installed on your computer.

The COW_WRL.WRL file should already be a part of your Web. If not, refer to the beginning of the previous section on where to get the file and how to import it into your Web.

Open The Virtual Cow Web page from the previous section in the FrontPage Editor. Click on the ActiveX control area from the last section, then press the Delete key. Your page is blank again. Add the virtual cow to the page, but this time use the Netscape plug-in to view it. Select the **P**lug-In command from the **O**ther Components submenu on the **I**nsert menu in the FrontPage Editor. The Plug-In Properties dialog box appears, as shown in Figure 11.12.

Figure 11.12.

Enter Netscape plug-in properties in the Plug-In Properties dialog box.

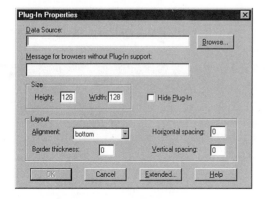

Add the name of the data file in the **D**ata Source textbox. Either type COW_WRL.WRL or browse for the file by clicking on the **B**rowse button. Click on the OK button in the Plug-In Properties dialog box. An electronic plug represents the Netscape plug-in area. Click on the icon and resize the plug-in's window by dragging the resize boxes until you have something similar to Figure 11.13.

Figure 11.13.

The icon represents the Netscape plug-in area with the data file listed below.

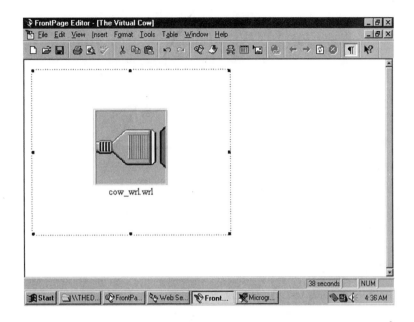

Save the Web page by clicking on the Save toolbar button. View the cow by clicking on the Preview in Browser toolbar button.

Summary

In this chapter, you added a Java applet, ActiveX controls, and a Netscape plug-in to your Web. These small programs open up nearly endless possibilities for your Webs. You provide content and then link the content to an applet, control, or plug-in. Because all these are powerful miniprograms, they are able to go far beyond HTML in the way they present your content—even as far as letting people walk around and explore it.

Q&A

Q I inserted the Dancing Teddy Bear applet into my Web but I don't see anything. What's wrong?

A You must include all the files in your Web. The applet itself, TEDDY.CLASS, must reside in the same folder as three image files, TEDDY0.JPG, TEDDY1.JPG, and TEDDY2.JPG.

Q How come I don't see ActiveX controls listed in my Start menu as I do other programs?

A ActiveX controls are a special kind of program with an ALX extension rather than an EXE extension. ActiveX controls are software components that act as standalone miniprograms. Any software can ask an ActiveX control to carry out a task. Think of ActiveX controls as specialists that are asked by nonexpert software to do specific tasks that take special skills.

Q Why don't I need to select the name of a Netscape plug-in when I add a plug-in to a Web page?

A Netscape plug-ins are recognized through their file associations and not the specific plug-in software. This is different from ActiveX controls that are recognized through their unique class identification numbers.

Workshop

There is a lot of experimenting you can do just by surveying what Java applets, ActiveX controls, and Netscape plug-ins are available to you. Try them out and see what is useful to you.

Quiz

1. What extension do Java applets have?
2. Why use Microsoft Form 2.0 ActiveX controls rather than HTML form fields?
3. Where do ActiveX controls run as miniprograms or components?

Chapter **12**

Managing Your Web

A glance at a Web displayed in FrontPage Explorer gives you a detailed overview of the Web, making Web management a breeze. Webs grow rapidly. After working on it for less than a week, your Web includes many pages and even more hyperlinks. It also includes images, a PowerPoint animation, a Java applet, and a video file. With FrontPage Explorer, you can add or delete components and import or export files from your Web. You can even find and replace words or perform a spell check across the whole Web. Today, you learn to carry out these Web-wide procedures from FrontPage Explorer.

In this chapter, you

☐ Delete a Web

☐ Import and export files

☐ Spell check your Web

☐ Perform a find-and-replace procedure on your Web

Deleting a Web

You can delete only Webs that are loaded into FrontPage Explorer. Open the Web that you want to delete into FrontPage Explorer, then select the **D**elete FrontPage Web command from the **F**ile menu. The Confirm Delete dialog box appears, as shown in Figure 12.1.

WARNING

Don't try to delete a FrontPage Web from outside FrontPage (from Windows Explorer, for example). You'll succeed in deleting the folders and files, but FrontPage Explorer will expect them to still exist, which may lead to problems.

Figure 12.1.

Be sure you mean it before you click on the Yes button.

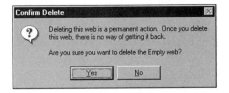

Click on the **Y**es button to delete the open Web. There is no turning back once you click on the **Y**es button, so make sure that you really want to before you do it. The files are not sent to the trashcan, so there is no way to recover them.

Importing Files to Your Web

Import Java applets, images, Web pages, or any other type of file to your Web. Open the Web that you want to import files into in FrontPage Explorer. Select the **I**mport command from the **F**ile menu. The Import File to FrontPage Web dialog box appears, as shown in Figure 12.2.

Figure 12.2.

Create a list of files to import into your Web in the Import File to FrontPage Web dialog box.

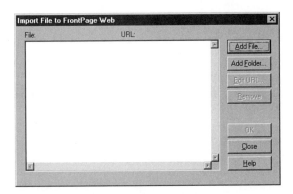

Click on the **A**dd File button to add files to your list of files to import in the Import File to FrontPage Web dialog box. The Add File to Import List dialog box appears, as shown in Figure 12.3.

Figure 12.3.

Select files to add to your list of files to import through the Add File to Import List dialog box.

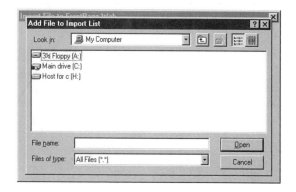

Select files in the usual way. You can select more than one at a time if you want. This can be done by holding down the Ctrl key while clicking on multiple selections. Once you finish selecting, click on the **O**pen button and the files are added to the files to import list. When you have all the files that you want to import in the files to import list, click on the OK button.

You can also add folders and their contents to your Web. To add folders and their contents to the Import File to FrontPage Web dialog box list, click on the Add **F**older button. The Browse for Folder dialog box appears, as shown in Figure 12.4.

Figure 12.4.

Select folders to add to your list of files to import through the Browse for Folder dialog box.

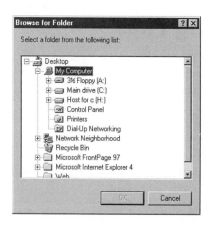

Select a folder and click on the OK button. All the files in the folder are listed in the Import File to FrontPage Web dialog box list. Click on the OK button, and the folder and all the files in the folder are copied to your Web.

12

Exporting Files from Your Web

Export any file from your Web. Highlight the file you want to export in FrontPage Explorer, then select the **E**xport command from the **F**ile menu. The Export Selected As dialog box appears, as shown in Figure 12.5.

Figure 12.5.

Give the file a name and choose a place for the file in the Export Selected As dialog box.

Select the folder where you want to export the file to, then type a name for the exported file in the File **n**ame textbox. Click on the **S**ave button. When FrontPage is finished exporting the file, a FrontPage Explorer dialog box appears, as shown in Figure 12.6.

Figure 12.6.

This FrontPage Explorer dialog box tells you the name of the file exported and the name and location of the new file.

Click on the OK button. The file is exported. The original file is still in your Web. The exported file is a copy of the original.

Spell Checking Your Web

Spell check your whole Web. Click on the Cross File Spelling toolbar button or select the **S**pelling command from the **T**ools menu. The Spelling dialog box appears, as shown in Figure 12.7.

12

Figure 12.7.

Select spell checking options from the Spelling dialog box.

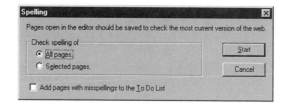

Select the **A**ll pages radio button in the Check spelling of area if you want the spell checker to check the spelling of all the pages in your Web. Select the S**e**lected pages radio button if you want to check the spelling of only selected files. Finally, check the Add pages with misspellings to the **T**o Do List checkbox and each page with a misspelling is added to the Web's To Do List.

Finding Words on Your Web

Find any word anywhere on your Web. Load your Web into FrontPage Explorer, then click on the Cross File Find toolbar button or select the **F**ind command from the **T**ools menu. The Find In FrontPage Web dialog box appears, as shown in Figure 12.8.

Figure 12.8.

Select options for finding words from the Find In FrontPage Web dialog box.

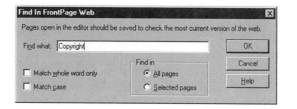

Type the word, or part of a word, that you want to look for in the Fi**n**d what text field. You can check the Match **w**hole word only or Match **c**ase checkboxes. In the Find in area, select the **A**ll pages radio button if you want to search across all the Web pages. Otherwise, select the **S**elected pages radio button to search across only the Web pages you selected in FrontPage Explorer. Once you're satisfied with your selections, click on the OK button. The Find Occurrences Of dialog box appears while your Web is being searched. The progress of your search is represented at the bottom of the dialog box by a graphic. The name of the Web page currently being searched is displayed along with the number of pages searched over the total number of pages in the Web. When the find operation is finished, the Find Occurrences Of dialog box looks something like Figure 12.9.

Figure 12.9.

*The Find Occurrences
Of dialog box after
searching for*
`copyright`.

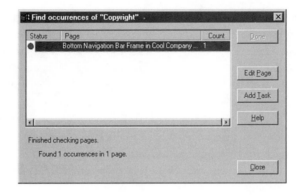

The name of the page or pages that contain the word you're searching for are listed in the Find
Occurrences Of dialog box, with the number of occurrences listed next to the page name in
the Count column. Highlight a page in the list and click on the Edit **P**age button to open
the page in the FrontPage Editor. Highlight a page and click on the Add **T**ask button to add
a linked task to the Web's To Do List.

Using Automatic Find and Replace on Your Web

Automatically find and replace any word anywhere on your Web. Load your Web into
FrontPage Explorer, then select the **R**eplace command from the **T**ools menu. The Replace
in FrontPage Web dialog box appears, as shown in Figure 12.10.

Figure 12.10.

*Set up an automatic
find-and-replace
procedure in the
Replace in FrontPage
Web dialog box.*

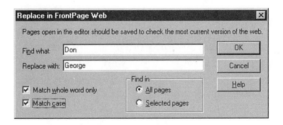

Type the word or phrase that you want to search for in the Fi**n**d what textbox, and type the
word or phrase that you want as a replacement in the Replace with textbox. You can check
the Match **w**hole word only or Match **c**ase checkboxes. In the Find in area, select the **A**ll pages
radio button if you want to search and replace across all the Web pages. Otherwise, select the
Selected pages radio button to search and replace across only the Web pages you selected in

12

FrontPage Explorer. Once you're satisfied with your selection, click on the OK button. The Find Occurrences Of dialog box appears while your Web is being searched. The progress of your search is represented at the bottom of the dialog box by a graphic. The name of the Web page currently being searched is displayed along with the number of pages searched over the total number of pages in the Web. Once the find operation is finished, highlight those pages on which you want to carry out the replace operation, then click on the Edit **P**age button. The page or pages open in the FrontPage Editor and the Replace dialog box appears, as shown in Figure 12.11.

Figure 12.11.

Carry out the replace operation through the Replace dialog box.

Click on the Replace **A**ll button if you want all the found words or phrases replaced automatically. Click on the **R**eplace button to replace the currently highlighted word or phrase. Click on **F**ind Next to skip replacing the currently highlighted word or phrase and go to the next one in the list.

Summary

In this chapter, you learned how to use FrontPage to carry out tasks across your entire Web. You checked your spelling across all your Web's pages, found words or phrases in your Web, and carried out a find-and-replace procedure.

Q&A

Q I've deleted a Web from FrontPage, but now I've decided that I still want the Web. What can I do?

A If you kept a backup, you're in luck; restore the backup files of your FrontPage Webs folder. Otherwise, you're out of luck. Once you delete a Web in FrontPage, it's gone forever. Be careful when you delete a Web! It's best to keep backups when you do.

Q   **Can I carry out a find operation on my Web to find specific objects—an ActiveX control, for instance?**

A   There is no find mechanism for anything but text; however, you should be able to find controls, images, and Web pages relatively easily through FrontPage Explorer's graphic interface.

Workshop

Use FrontPage Explorer's find capabilities to navigate through your Web and to find specific areas of your Web on which you want to work. Add each part of the Web that you want to work on as a linked task in your Web's To Do List.

Quiz

1. Can you recover a Web deleted from FrontPage Explorer?

2. You can import multiple files into a Web page, but can you export multiple files?

3. What basic text functions can you perform from FrontPage Explorer, across multiple Web pages?

DAY 7

Chapter 13

Connecting Your Web to a Database

Traditionally, the seventh day is one of rest and relaxation. Unfortunately, not for the readers of this book. Today is the day you learn how to bring your Web page alive with dynamic content. You'll do it by connecting your Web to a database. Once connected to a database, your Web pages can manipulate and display this data however you, or your users, want. Manually writing programs to access databases and output the data in a preformatted manner is difficult at best. FrontPage, however, makes it easy to connect your Web to a database.

In this chapter, you:

☐ Learn about Internet Database Connectors

☐ Connect your Web to a database using the Database Connector Wizard

☐ Add database data to your Web pages

☐ Create custom Web pages that enable database queries and return the results

☐ Create a guestbook Web page that users can sign when they visit your site

The Internet Database Connector

FrontPage is tightly integrated with a Web server extension that provides access to ODBC data sources. This is the *Internet Database Connector (IDC)*. This extension to Microsoft's Web servers provides a mechanism to access ODBC data sources.

What Is ODBC?

Open Database Connectivity (ODBC) is a system standard that provides a consistent method of retrieving and updating data using a wide array of databases. The benefit of using ODBC is that once your program is created, the underlying database can change without needing more program changes. This is true because of the standardized interface.

For example, suppose you wanted to create a program that retrieved data using ODBC from an Oracle database. You wrote your program and it's been running fine for months. Suddenly, your corporate standard changes, and you are forced to convert all your databases over to Microsoft Access. Well, fear not. Because you used ODBC, and as long as you do not change the layout of your database, your program will not have to change. You simply need to point it at the right data source.

For more information about ODBC and ODBC drivers, check out the ODBC home page at `http://www.microsoft.com/odbc`.

The IDC is the mechanism that the Microsoft Internet Information Server (MSIIS) and the Personal Web Server (PWS) use to retrieve data from an ODBC data source. It uses an external Windows program called HTTPODBC.DLL to interact with the database. When you make a database request through the Web server, it passes the request on to this program. This program then contacts the ODBC data source and performs the request. The resultant data is merged into the document and returned to the browser.

To facilitate database access, the IDC utilizes two special documents to retrieve and display data from databases. These two documents are the IDC definition file and the *HTML extension*, or *HTX*, file. You'll learn more about these in a moment. For now, let's focus on getting your system ready for creating these dynamic Web pages.

13

What You Need on Your Server

Before you can start adding database content to your Web pages, you need to

1. Configure ODBC to work with the database of your choice.
2. Create a directory from where your database queries can be executed.
3. Create the Internet Database Connector database query file.

Let's take a look at each one individually.

Configuring ODBC

The first thing you must do before you can connect your Web to a database is make sure you have access to a database. For this chapter, you are going to use ODBC to connect to a database. ODBC comes with Microsoft Office and is relatively easy to configure.

For this chapter, you're going to create a simple database table to implement your guestbook Web page. This database is called guestbook.mdb and is included on the CD-ROM. Before you can create your Web page, you need to provide Windows with information about this database.

 NOTE

> The mdb file extension indicates that the file is a Microsoft Access database file.

Your computer's hard drive is filled with folders and files. Each of these files represents one thing or another. However, Windows is not aware of what each file contains. ODBC data sources on your computer are different. You can configure a database to be available to all the programs on your computer by creating an ODBC *Data Source Name (DSN)*. This is done with the ODBC Data Source Administrator.

The ODBC Data Source Administrator

In order for your programs to know about sources of data on your computer, you need to add a System DSN for each of them. A *System DSN* creates a public label for your database. This label can be used by any ODBC program to retrieve and update data in your data source. Think of your database files (the mdb files) as little gold mines on your hard drive. They live all over the place, but none of your programs can find them. When you give them a System DSN, it's like creating a map of all your mines. Whenever you need one, each of your programs will be able to find it.

The ODBC Data Source Administrator is a program that is available through your Control Panel. Figure 13.1 shows the ODBC Data Source Administrator in the Control Panel.

Figure 13.1.

The ODBC Data Source Administrator, labeled 32bit ODBC, is usually the first item in the Control Panel.

When you double-click, or launch, the administrator, it shows the different data source information in a tab view. The first view, User DSN, shows the available ODBC drivers that are installed on your system. Figure 13.2 shows the User DSN tab display. Here you can add and remove new ODBC drivers.

Figure 13.2.

The User DSN enables you to add and remove ODBC drivers.

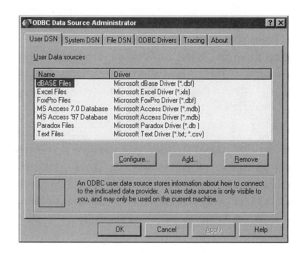

13

To create a new System DSN (which you need for FrontPage to know about your database), click on the System DSN tab. Figure 13.3 shows this tab.

Figure 13.3.

Publicly available data sources are listed in the System DSN tab. Unless you have set one up, or you have a program that created one, this list will be empty.

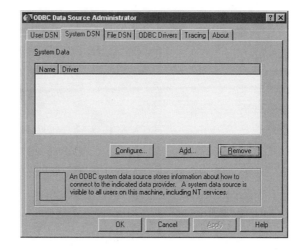

Click on the Add button to create a new System DSN. The system will ask you what type of driver you want to use (see Figure 13.4).

Figure 13.4.

Because Windows has many ODBC drivers installed, you must select the driver that is related to this data source.

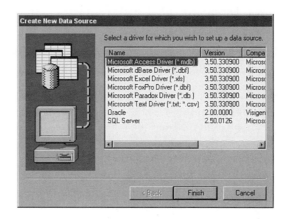

You may have many ODBC drivers installed. Selecting a driver for your data source is just another piece of information Windows needs to create your System DSN. For this example, you should select Microsoft Access Driver (*.mdb). When you have selected it, click on the Finished button.

Figure 13.5.

Give your data source a name and select the file that is associated with this name.

Finally, the new data source dialog is displayed (see Figure 13.5). Here is where you name your data source. Now that Windows knows what type of ODBC driver is associated with this data source, you must give it a name and a description. Call your data source name Guestbook. The description should be Guestbook Database.

 The last piece of information that the administrator needs is the location and name of the database file itself. This is a good time to copy the sample database from the CD-ROM to a folder on your hard disk. Once copied, you can select it as the database for your new data source.

Click on the Select button and the standard Windows open file dialog box is shown. Select the guestbook.mdb file from the folder to which it was copied. Once selected, the name is displayed above the Select button after the Database label. Click on OK to save your new data source.

Once saved, the System DSN tab is redisplayed and you should see your addition in the list (see Figure 13.6).

Figure 13.6.

The Guestbook data source is displayed.

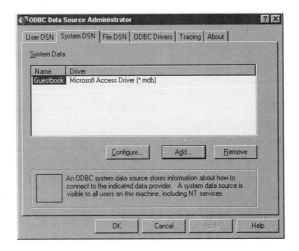

The IDC File

Now that the configuration is finished, it is time to create the first half of the database connectivity solution. This is the IDC file. Think of this file as a special program that your server runs for you. The server interprets the instructions in this file as a database query.

Inside this file is information about which database to use, which user and password to sign on with, how to display the results, and—most importantly—the query to execute against the database.

NOTE

> For the purposes of this discussion, a Web has been created in FrontPage Explorer. It is called Guestbook and is included on the CD-ROM for you to explore. However, if you'd like to work along with the examples in this chapter, you can create it yourself. It was created in FrontPage Explorer by creating a new Web from a wizard or template. You use the Normal Web template as your guide, which provides you with a single home page that you will build upon in the following examples.

Go ahead and create the sample Web (per the Note) or any other Web you might want to use. We're about to get our feet wet!

13

Creating a Scripts Folder

Before you can create IDC and HTX files, you must create a folder to hold these files. Let's call this your Scripts folder. To create this folder, go to FrontPage Explorer and switch to the folder view.

In this view, when you select your home page, you can create a new folder underneath it. Select your home page and then select from the File, New Folder option. This creates a folder called New Folder. Right-click on the new addition and select the Rename option on the menu that appears. Rename this folder scripts.

Once you rename this folder, you must tell FrontPage that it is where executable programs will be stored. You do this by changing the properties. Right-click on the folder and select Properties from the pop-up menu.

Simply check the checkbox on this page titled Allow scripts or programs to be run. Press the OK button and you are finished installing your new folder.

Creating the IDC File

Before you can display the results of a database query on your Web, you must create the query. This is done in the IDC file. To create an IDC file, you use the Database Connector Wizard.

Using the Database Connector Wizard

The Database Connector Wizard enables you to create and/or edit IDC files quickly without having to use a text editor and know the syntax of the file. The wizard automatically comes up when you attempt to edit an existing IDC file or when you create a new one. You're going to create a new IDC file now.

Creating IDC Files

To create an IDC file, go to the FrontPage Editor. Under the File menu, select New. Select the Database Connector Wizard from the list (see Figure 13.7).

13

Figure 13.7.

The list of available wizards and templates for creating new pages, with the Database Connector Wizard selected.

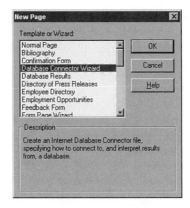

Once selected, the Database Connector Wizard is displayed (see Figure 13.8). This will be the interface to your database for all your queries.

Figure 13.8.

The Database Connector Wizard.

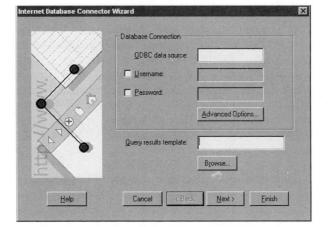

The first piece of information that the wizard needs is the name of your data source. This is the System DSN (data source name) that you created earlier in this chapter, and the name was Guestbook. Type Guestbook into the ODBC data source field.

Because the Access database is not restricted, there is no need for you to enter a user name or password. However, these are useful if you are accessing a database that has some level of security. For instance, if you were to access an Oracle database using ODBC, you would be required to enter a user name and password. Without these, you would be unable to connect to your database.

13

The last bit of information that is needed here is the name of the template that will hold the results of this query. This is actually created in the next step. However, you must specify the name of the template now. This template must be an HTML extension file, therefore ending with an htx extension. Let's call the results guestbook.htx because you are going to name your IDC file guestbook.idc.

 TIP

It is good practice to name your result template files the same as your IDC query files. This way you can always match them up.

Figure 13.9 shows the completed section.

Figure 13.9.

The completed name section of the Data-base Connector Wizard.

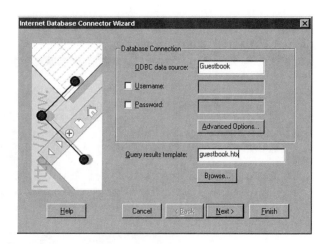

 WARNING

Any name that you give to your results file must be relative to the folder where the IDC file is stored. For example, if the guestbook.idc file is in the scripts folder, specifying scripts/guestbook.htx as a database results template will fail because the system is already in the scripts folder when it is looking for the results page.

Click on the Next button to proceed on to the next step.

The next step in creating the IDC file is to specify the query. This is the SQL statement that is executed by the database and produces a result set of data.

13

What Is SQL?

Structured Query Language (SQL) provides a standard method of querying data from different data sources.

SQL, usually pronounced like the word "sequel," was adopted as an industry standard in 1986. SQL was completely overhauled in 1992, and the new language was called SQL92, or SQL2. Work is currently ongoing to produce the next generation, SQL3.

For more information about SQL, check out these Web sites:

```
http://www./inquiry.com/techtips/thesqlpro
```

and

```
http://www.contrib.andrew.cmu.edu/~shadow/sql.html
```

First, create a simple query that returns the names and e-mail addresses of persons who have signed your guestbook:

```
SELECT GuestName, EmailAddress FROM Guests
```

`GuestName` and `EmailAddress` are the database columns that are returned. Guestbook is the table name from which to select the columns. Figure 13.10 shows this query entered.

Figure 13.10.

The company name query entered in the Database Connector Wizard.

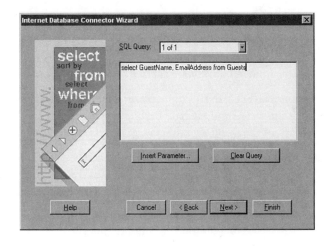

13

After you enter your query, you must save the IDC file. To do this, click on the Finish button. The standard Save As dialog box is displayed.

You must save the IDC file in the scripts folder that you created earlier. If you do not, the Web server will have no way of knowing that this IDC file should be executed instead of displayed.

Open the scripts folder, type the name guestbook.idc, and press the Save button (see Figure 13.11).

Figure 13.11.
Saving your IDC file.

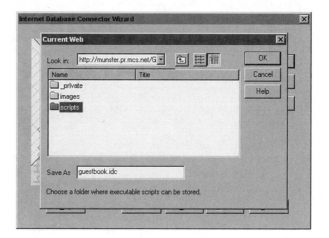

Creating the HTML Extension File

Now that you've created your query and your IDC file, you need to create the second half of your database connection, the HTX file. This file is used as a template by the Web server to display the results of your query to Web browsers.

Creating the HTX file is simple. From the FrontPage Editor, select File, New. From the list that is shown, select Database Results (see Figure 13.12).

You now have a blank results page. It's not quite blank; there are some comments about its use. You can delete them if you'd like. You add your results to this page by using the database directives. These are accessed under the Edit menu in the Database submenu. From this menu, you can add the following database content to your Web page:

☐ *Database Column Value.* These are columns returned by a query. For example, the query created returns the column GuestName. This is displayed a little later.

☐ *IDC Parameter Value.* You can specify parameters to your query to make your Web pages dynamic. This option enables you to display data based on information gathered from the reader of your Web page.

13

☐ *Detail Section.* A detail section, as you'll see, is a placeholder for multiple returned rows. It enables you to present much more data than a single row.

☐ *If-Then Conditional Section.* This denotes an area of HTML that is displayed if an expression or condition is true.

☐ *Else Conditional Section.* This adds an auxiliary control path to your conditional section.

Let's take a look at results of our query. To do this, you need to add a detail section to your results page.

Figure 13.12.

Creating a Database Results page.

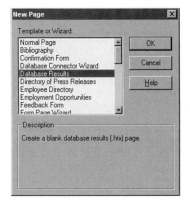

Detail Sections

When you make a database query, many times more than one record—or row—of data is returned. Usually, it will be tens of rows, but you can't be expected to know the number of rows returned at all times. That would require enormous mental capacity, in addition to some psychic powers. Because most of us don't have these abilities, the detail section comes in quite handy.

A detail section enables you to create a template or placeholder for a single row. Then, when each row is returned and merged with your results file, the template is copied for each one. This produces a nice, uniform set of output that not only looks nice, but also is quite useful.

To add a detail section to your results page, select Detail Section from the Edit, Database menu. This creates what appears to be brackets on the screen. Figure 13.13 shows the result of adding a detail section. Add this to the blank database results page that you created earlier.

13

Figure 13.13.

The results page with an empty detail section shown.

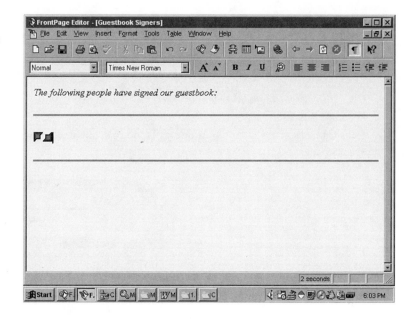

Now that you have your section, let's fill it in with the results of your query. To do this, position the caret (text cursor) between the two halves of the detail section graphic and press the Enter key. This will separate them enough for you to insert database columns. Next, insert a database column value. This is done from the Edit, Database submenu by selecting the Database Column Value item. The system will ask you for the name of the database column to display. Type GuestName (see Figure 13.14).

Figure 13.14.

Inserting GuestName *into the detail section.*

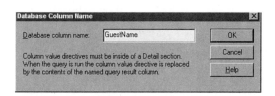

If you remember, GuestName was the column used in the SQL query. Figure 13.15 shows the page after you insert the database column.

Figure 13.15.

The database column is now inserted.

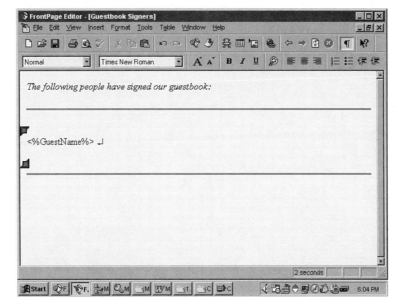

Getting the Ball Rolling

You've now created the two necessary halves of the database connection puzzle. The first half is the Internet Database Connector (IDC) file. This defines the query and the result template in which to display the results. The second half is the HTML extension, or HTX, file. This file is that template that displays the results.

By now you're probably wondering how to kick it all off and actually make the query happen and see the results. You need one more page to do that—the query page. This page can consist of anything you want, but it must somehow cause the query to be executed. You'll use an HTML form with a button to do the trick.

Go back to FrontPage Explorer and open the home page for the current Web. On this page, you will create a new form field.

From the Insert menu, select Form Field, then select Push Button. This creates a button on your page labeled Submit (see Figure 13.16).

13

Figure 13.16.

The Submit button placed on the page.

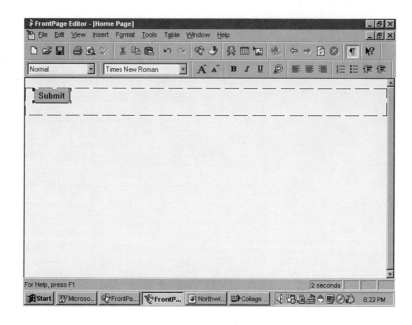

As you know, the dotted lines represent the HTML form area of this Web page. Right-click between the dotted lines and select Form Properties from the pop-up menu. This is where you tell this form that instead of executing a CGI script, you will be using the IDC.

When the form properties dialog box is displayed, select Internet Database Connector as the Form Handler from the drop-down listbox (see Figure 13.17).

Figure 13.17.

Selecting the Internet Database Connector Form Handler.

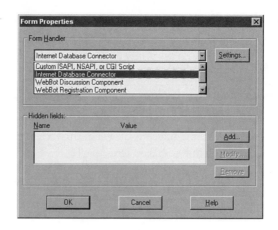

Finally, before you close the form properties dialog box, you must tell the form which IDC file to use when this button is pressed. This is done by pressing the Settings button on the Form Properties dialog. Figure 13.18 shows the Settings dialog box.

Figure 13.18.

The IDC file is chosen for this form handler in the Settings dialog box.

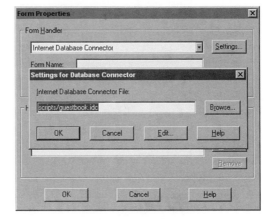

At this point, select the IDC file you want attached to this button. For now, just choose the guestbook.idc file that you made. From the root of the Web, the IDC file is in the scripts folder. Therefore, the full filename is scripts/guestbook.idc.

TIP

> If you feel uneasy putting in pathnames, or you are not sure, you can always use the Browse feature. This makes it easy to navigate through your folders to more easily find the name of the file.

Now you can try out your new Web pages. Select Preview in Browser from the File menu or press the corresponding toolbar button. You should see a button similar to the one shown in Figure 13.19.

13

Figure 13.19.

The Submit button is displayed for your approval.

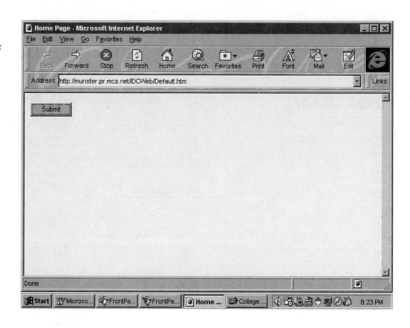

Press the button and if everything was done correctly and the database file can be read, the results of the query will be displayed (see Figure 13.20).

Figure 13.20.

The results of the SQL query are shown on a Web page.

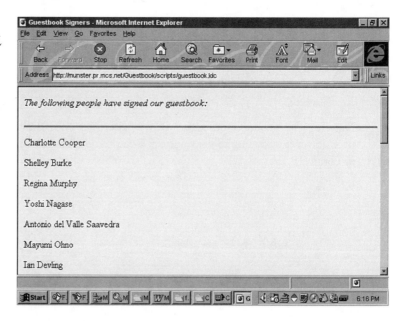

Now that you can see the fruits of your labor, you will start to realize the power of merging database data with your Web site.

Creating a Guestbook Web Page

The last thing to do in this chapter is enhance your submission page. You can set it up so that people can enter their own names into your guestbook for others to see. To do this, you must enable the form to take some input.

Create three text areas on your form: guest name, e-mail address, and comments. Each will hold a portion of the guestbook entry. Figure 13.21 shows the completed form.

Figure 13.21.
The guestbook form.

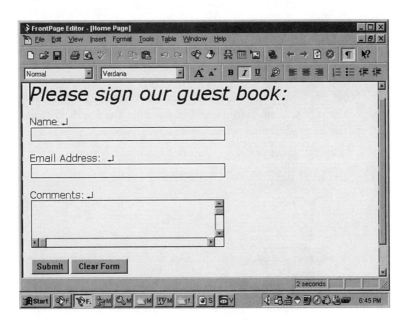

Make sure that you give each field a name. In the figure, they are named guestName, emailAddress, and comments. These names are important, as you will see.

Inserting Data into the Database

Now this form is a placeholder for the data entered by the user. You need to create a new IDC file. This file will be used to insert this data into the database. You do this in the same manner as before using the Database Connector Wizard. This is a new IDC, which will be an SQL INSERT statement rather than a SELECT statement.

Using Parameters

When you use the IDC to transfer data to and from your database, you surround the column names with percent signs (%). You must also surround your form fields with percent signs when going to the database. This is done for you by the Database Connector Wizard. Start

13

up the Database Connector Wizard by creating a new file of type Database Connector Wizard in the FrontPage Editor.

Type Guestbook for the ODBC data source. Remember, you're still using the same database. For a results filename, type signbook.htx. This is what you'll call your results page. Click on Next and you move to the query associated with this IDC file.

You want what the user typed to be placed into the database directly from the HTML form. You do this by using the Insert Parameter button under the query window. First, type the first half of the INSERT statement to put data into the database:

```
INSERT INTO GUESTS
    ( GUESTNAME, EMAILADDRESS, COMMENTS )
VALUES
    (
```

Now, when you press the Insert Parameter button, a pop-up window asks you for the name of the HTML form field to place to the database. For this particular query, you need three parameters: guestName, emailAddress, and comments. Your query now reads

```
INSERT INTO GUESTS
    (
        GUESTNAME,
        EMAILADDRESS,
        COMMENTS
    )
VALUES
    (
        %guestName%,
        %emailAddress%,
        %comments%
    )
```

You need to enter single quotation marks manually into your query at this point. The Database Connector Wizard helps you only so much. All columns that are text-based must be enclosed in single quotation marks. Make your query look like this:

```
INSERT INTO GUESTS
    (
        GUESTNAME,
        EMAILADDRESS,
        COMMENTS
    )
VALUES
    (
        '%guestName%',
        '%emailAddress%',
        '%comments%'
    )
```

13

NOTE

Some of the Database Connector Wizard's features (such as the Insert Parameter button) are not very good at figuring out what you are trying to do. You are much better off inserting parameters into your query by hand. Just remember to enclose your form field name in percent signs (%) and enclose all text-based columns in single quotes.

After you add single quotation marks to all text-based parameters, be sure to add the trailing closing parenthesis. Click on the Finish button; name this `signbook.idc` and place it in your scripts directory so it may be executed.

If you now run your main HTML page that submits the change to the database through your browser, you'll see Figure 13.22.

Figure 13.22.

This form enables you to enter the data, which is placed into the database.

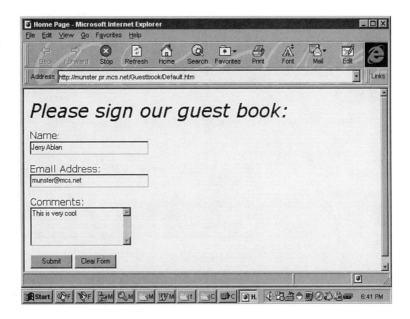

13

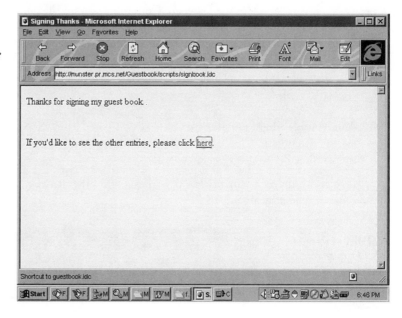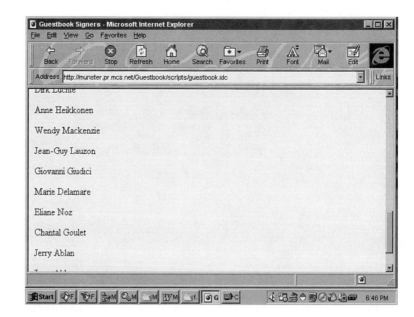

Figure 13.23 shows the results of your database insertion.

Figure 13.23.
By clicking on the link, you can cause the display page IDC to be executed.

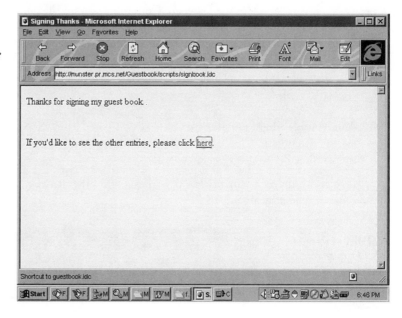

Finally in Figure 13.24, you see your insertion retrieved and displayed in the original display form.

Figure 13.24.
This is the form that displays all the rows returned by our original query.

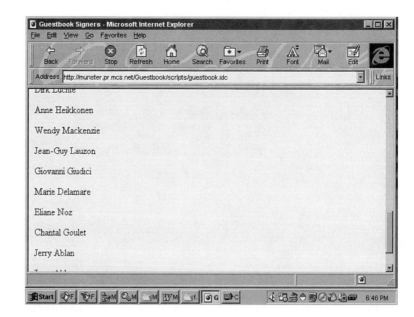

Summary

You've learned quite a bit in this chapter. You learned about Internet Database Connectors and ODBC and how to create ODBC data source names. In addition, you learned how to use FrontPage to add dynamic data from databases to your Web pages. You took this and created a small guestbook Web application. This application enables people to "sign" your Web guestbook and see who else has signed it. You can now build on this and create complex database queries and systems using FrontPage and your browser.

Q&A

Q Why use the Internet Database Connector over a static CGI program?

A Using the IDC instead of CGI programs gives you quite a bit of flexibility. Instead of having to change your program and reload it on the server each time your database changes, you can simply change the layout. This layout change can be done inside of FrontPage.

Q Can the Internet Database Connector work with database interfaces other than ODBC?

A Unfortunately at this time, the Internet Database Connector only works in conjunction with ODBC. On the bright side, however, you can find an ODBC driver for almost any database. Contact your database vendor for more information regarding where and how to purchase ODBC drivers.

Q Must I use FrontPage to edit IDC and HTX files?

A No. You can use the Windows Notepad or WordPad programs to edit these files. The formats are quite straightforward, and editing them outside of FrontPage seems to give you more control over the layout of the resultant data.

Workshop

Use the Database Connector Wizard to modify your guestbook queries. Try adding the e-mail address and comments fields to the display.

13

Quiz

1. What is one major benefit of using ODBC?
2. What does HTX stand for?
3. The Database Connector Wizard helps you manage what type of file?

Chapter 14

Using WebBots with an Extended Server

Because this is the last lesson of the last day, you explore some advanced topics. In particular, you learn about expanding the capabilities of FrontPage's Personal Web Server. FrontPage comes with the Personal Web Server, but it runs only on Windows 95 or Windows NT. This is not a problem for many small sites, but it can pose problems for large organizations. Chances are very good that at such places, you're already using some other Web server on some other operating system. You also learn about some useful tools that can help you in creating your Web pages.

In this chapter, you

- ☐ Install the Server Extensions
- ☐ Access WebBots
- ☐ Use the Confirmation Field
- ☐ Use Include, Scheduled Image, and Search
- ☐ Use the Substitute WebBot
- ☐ Create a Table of Contents
- ☐ Use the Timestamp and other WebBots

What Is the Extended Server?

A Personal Web Server becomes an extended server once the FrontPage Extensions are installed. The FrontPage Extensions are CGI programs that enable FrontPage features to be implemented on non-FrontPage machines. When FrontPage receives information directed to a server extension, it redirects the information to the appropriate server. This information is sent with HTTP using a Remote Procedure Call (RPC). The extensions server then takes the information and runs the appropriate script or CGI program. By default, these extensions implement a number of FrontPage features. Such features include uploading and downloading of documents, To Do lists, and browse-time WebBot components. A number of administration functions are also supported with Server Extensions.

> **NOTE**
>
> The FrontPage Extensions are not created by Microsoft. Rather, a third-party company, Ready-to-Run Software (http://www.rtr.com/) has done the real work.

Getting Server Extensions

You can get the FrontPage Server Extensions by pointing your Web browser to http://www.rtr.com/fpsupport/downl_reg.htm. Simply read and accept the end-user license at the top of the Web page. At the bottom of the Web page is a registration form where you fill in information about yourself. At the very least, you must enter your full name and e-mail address. After this, choose the platform that you want to get the Server Extensions for (see Figure 14.1). Finally, click on the I Accept button and you download the extension for the specified platform.

> **NOTE**
>
> The FrontPage Server Extensions are programs that work with an existing Web server. If you don't have a machine set up as a Web server, you won't be able to use the Server Extensions.

Installing the Server Extensions

Once you download the Server Extensions, you have to install them. This can be done by first logging into the remote system as root. Next, copy the file you downloaded to a temporary directory, such as /tmp. Now, you have to uncompress, and unpack, the distribution. This can easily be done by typing zcat /tmp/*filename*.tar.Z ¦ tar xvf -. The name of the file you downloaded is represented by *filename*.tar.Z. This creates a new directory, a FrontPage directory under the /usr/local hierarchy.

Figure 14.1.

You must specify the platform for which you want to get the Server Extensions.

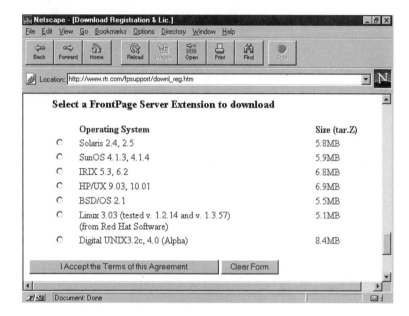

To install the FrontPage Server Extensions, you must type cd /usr/local/frontpage/ version2.0/bin and run fpsrvadm.exe. This brings up the FrontPage Extended Server Administrator (see Figure 14.2). This is the primary program you'll use to manage the Server Extensions for this machine. If you're using the Extended Server for multiple hosts, you need to install it for each machine.

When you start up the program, you're presented with a list of 10 options. To install the Server Extensions, select option 1. You are next asked for the existing Web server that is on the system on which you're installing the server. Next, you are asked to specify the absolute file path to the configuration file for the server for which you want to install the Extensions. Then, you are prompted for the hostname on which the Web server is listening for connections. For multihome-capable Web servers, you are asked to specify other possible hostnames of this system.

Once you answer all the questions, the necessary FrontPage files are copied to the Web server. A FrontPage configuration file is placed in the /usr/local/frontpage directory. Additionally, some Web server configuration files are modified by FrontPage. You are also prompted for the server administrator's login name and password.

14

Figure 14.2.

The FrontPage Server
Administration
program enables you
to manage your Server
Extensions.

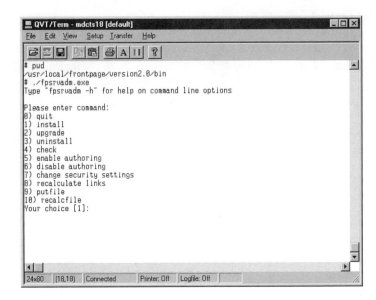

Where the Files Are

When you installed FrontPage on your Windows machine, you defined two directories. One directory specified where the FrontPage binaries are stored. The other one indicated where the content for the FrontPage Webs should be kept. Because you're installing an Extended Server on a non-FrontPage system, you may not necessarily know where the files are. As you might have guessed, there is no Extended Server equivalent to the FrontPage program directory.

Because the FrontPage Server Extensions can be used to create content, however, it has to be stored somewhere. On an Extended Server, the corresponding Web content is stored in the same place; the Web server stores the other Web content. Using the default NCSA server configuration, for example, the Web content is stored in /usr/local/etc/httpd/htdocs. This is the directory that the Server Extensions will use to store the FrontPage content.

Whenever you create a new Web with FrontPage with the Personal Web Server, it creates a new directory structure. That structure is placed under the directory you specified for the FrontPage Webs. Similarly, with a Server Extension installed, the new directory structure is also placed under the Web content directory.

14

What Are WebBots?

So far, all these lessons have taught you the basics of working with a Web server and creating a Web page. This information is easily transferred to almost any other Web environment. Many of the same basic concepts that you've learned so far are available in many other places. Until now.

FrontPage has a set of tools, known collectively as WebBots, that are available only with FrontPage. Some WebBots make it easy to automate some tasks; others are simply implementations of popular CGI scripts. This means that your work in creating, and maintaining, content for a Web site can be simplified with WebBots.

When Can I Use Them?

WebBots are simply special items that you can put into Web pages. They aren't, by themselves, individual Web pages, but they can refer to them. They are essentially special commands embedded in Web pages that FrontPage looks for. When one of these components is found, FrontPage interprets the commands. This means that if you try to publish a Web that has some WebBots, they might not all work. Some WebBots will work fine without needing FrontPage or an Extended Server. Others will completely fail without the Personal Web Server or an Extended Server. For these WebBots, you will likely have to implement your own CGI scripts to duplicate the WebBot's behavior. For example, you may have to create your own script to process form field inputs, if you're using the Confirmation WebBot.

How Are WebBots Affected by an Extended Server?

Because an Extended Server enables the Personal Web Server to communicate with other servers, you might expect some problems when using WebBots. In particular, you might think that inserting WebBot components into a Web page on an Extended Server would fail. Fortunately, that's not the case at all. All WebBots behave exactly the same on an Extended Server system as they do on the Personal Web Server.

14

Accessing WebBots

You can access most WebBots by starting up the FrontPage Editor with a Web page. Next, put your text cursor on the Web page where you want the WebBot to be placed. Click on **I**nsert, **W**ebBot Component, which brings up the Insert WebBot Component dialog box where you make your selection (see Figure 14.3). Most of the time, after you've made your choice, you are presented with a dialog box. You learn what each WebBot component in the dialog box does in the following sections.

Figure 14.3.

Simply choose which WebBot you want to insert.

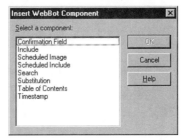

The only WebBot that isn't included in the WebBot selection dialog box is the Comment WebBot. This isn't really a WebBot in the usual sense of the term. It doesn't really perform any task; rather, it's an easy way for you to insert comments into a Web page. The purpose of the comments is left entirely up to you. You can use them to leave notes to yourself or to other Web authors. You can insert a comment anywhere in a Web page by inserting the component. To do so, bring up a Web page in the FrontPage Editor and select **I**nsert, Co**m**ment. This brings up an empty dialog box where you merely type in the comments you want to insert. When you're happy with what you've written, click on OK; to abort, click on the Cancel button.

Confirmation Field

As you learned in Chapter 1, "Building Your First Web," the Confirmation Field WebBot is used with forms. The Confirmation Field WebBot is one of the few form fields that can't work by itself. That is, this WebBot is used to process data submitted through form fields, so you actually need two Web pages before you can use the Confirmation Field WebBot.

Using the Confirmation Field

The first Web page you need is a page that contains a form field. This page can have anything at all, provided it has a form field in it. The second Web page is the page that will actually contain the WebBot Confirmation Field. You can put any descriptive text you want before the WebBot. All you have to do is click on **I**nsert, **W**ebBot Component, and select

14

Confirmation Field. It will ask you for the name of the field from which it should pull the results. Type its name and click on the OK button.

For example, suppose you wanted to get a person's name and age. The first page for this situation consists of a new blank Web page. Insert three one-line textboxes: one for the first name, one for the last name, and one for age. Select the entire form field and click the right mouse button. You also should create Submit and Reset form buttons. Select Form Properties and a new dialog box will appear. Choose the drop-down menu under the Form **H**andler heading and select the last entry, WebBot Save Results Component. Clicking on the **S**ettings button brings up another dialog box, used for defining the attributes of the WebBot. In the **F**ile for Results text field, type any name you want, such as save.htm. Click on the Confirm tab and type a new filename, such as results.htm, in the URL of **C**onfirmation Page text field. You are prompted that the results.htm file doesn't exist, to which you can answer **Y**es. Finally, click on the OK button to incorporate all the changes. Give the page any title and save it under the filename input.htm.

You may optionally want to find out the variable names for each textbox form field. This can be done by selecting the field, clicking the right mouse button, and selecting Form Field Properties. The value in the Name text field is the name for which the Confirm Field WebBot will be looking. Figure 14.4 shows a sample page in the FrontPage Editor where everything is set up.

Figure 14.4.

Before you can use the Confirmation Field WebBot, you must create a Web page from which it will interpret input.

Now you have to create a Web page where the data from the first page can be displayed. This can be done by creating another blank Web page. Type some descriptive text that introduces what the information you received is. Then type a heading for the person's first name. Next, click on Insert, WebBot Component and select Confirmation Field. A dialog box will show up asking you for the name of the form field from which you want the data processed. Assuming you didn't change any of the names from the first page, you can type T1. The text [T1] is inserted into the current Web page. Create a heading for the last name, insert another Confirmation Field WebBot, and use the name T2. Finally, repeat the same steps for the age field and use the form field name T3. You can now give the page any name you want and use the filename results.htm. Figure 14.5 shows a sample form acknowledgment page in the FrontPage Editor.

Figure 14.5.

To process the results, you need to create a Web page that uses the Confirmation Field WebBot.

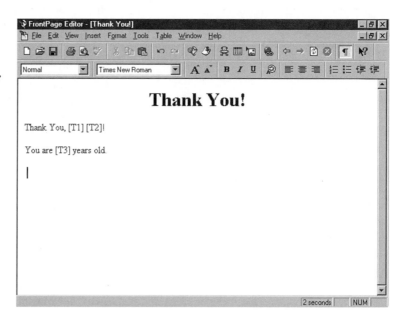

Once you have everything set up, it's time to test it. Bring up a Web browser and access the input.htm page that you created. Next, fill in all three fields and press Enter. After some processing, you are presented with the results the Confirmation Field WebBot returns.

You might be wondering about the purpose of the save.htm file that was defined in the first page. That file is created, and appended to, every time someone submits data to the input.htm file. It's usually stored in the same directory as the other files for wherever Web input.htm resides. The data can be stored in HTML format, the default, or a number of different text formats. This file is useful if you want to include it in another Web page automatically or just for logging purposes.

Confirmation Field Without an Extended Server

The Confirmation Field WebBot is perhaps the most sophisticated WebBot available. Usually, a CGI script has to be created to pass information from one Web page to another. However, with this WebBot, it uses the environment of FrontPage to its advantage. Consequently, this WebBot will work only under FrontPage or an Extended Server. If you publish a Web page that has this WebBot in it, the results from a form submission won't be properly displayed. Users see, instead of the form field values, the names of the form fields. In our example, the users will see T1, T2, and T3 in the Web page that has the three WebBots.

Why Use the Confirmation Field?

Because it works only under FrontPage, you might be wondering what the use of such a WebBot might be. It can be used as a way of debugging the "real" CGI script that will interpret the form field values. That is, using the preceding example, you could create a third Web page. This page would be a CGI script written in a non–platform-dependent language, such as Perl. The purpose of the script is to handle the form field input, just like the WebBot. So, with the example, you can have the first Web page point to the WebBot page and see what the results are. Then you can modify the first page to point to the CGI script and see the new results. You can then compare the values returned by the WebBot and your CGI script. Any differing values would indicate a possible flaw in your CGI script.

Include

One of the most important concepts in designing a Web site is to make pages consistent. This generally takes the appearance of giving all Web pages on the site a consistent look and feel. Same, or similar, colors and font sizes are used, along with a consistent interface. An easy approach to making your Web pages consistent is to include other Web pages. There are some Web servers, and some CGI scripts, that enable you to include other Web pages. With FrontPage, such include capability is easily accomplished with the Include WebBot.

14

Using Include

To use the Include WebBot, simply bring up a Web page in the FrontPage Editor. Put your text cursor wherever you want the include text to be inserted. Click on **I**nsert, **W**ebBot Component and select Include, where you are presented with a dialog box (see Figure 14.6). Even though the dialog box is asking for a URL, it's not entirely accurate. You can enter a URL that points to a file only on your Web site, not the entire World Wide Web. FrontPage will insert the first few lines of the Web page you want to include. Whenever the included file is updated, the WebBot will also automatically be updated. If you try to include a page from another Web site, it will appear fine in the Editor. However, this included page won't show up when the page is actually accessed.

Figure 14.6.

*You can include any
Web page on your site
in the current page.*

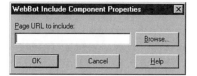

If you want to include another Web page from the current Web, you can click on the **B**rowse button. You are shown the top level of the current Web that lists files and directories that are immediately accessible. That is, you are shown only files that are directly referenced by Web pages. If you have an HTML file, such as the results from a Confirmation Field WebBot, it won't be listed. To include such a file, don't use the **B**rowse button; rather, type the relative pathname for it.

Include Without an Extended Server

When you insert the Include WebBot, the page to include is referred to twice. The first time it's referenced is to get the content to be inserted into the current Web page. The second time the included file is referred to is for future updates. It's important to know about both file references, especially for non-FrontPage Web servers. While the Web page with the Include WebBot is on a Personal Web Server, or an Extended Server, it will behave properly. However, if the Web page is published to a non-Extended Server, only the first reference will be kept. That is, the content for the included Web page will be published. That means that any changes to the included file won't be updated in the published Web page.

Scheduled Image

On Day 3, you learned how to include images in your Web page. A useful application of this information is the Scheduled Image WebBot. With most traditional Web servers, it's up to the Web author to update all aspects of a Web site manually. If a new section is added to the site, therefore, its presence must be deliberately noted. This can be quite a bit of work, especially for busy Web sites that are constantly adding content.

Using the Scheduled Image

The Scheduled Image WebBot is intended to help make such situations more manageable. It enables you to have an image displayed for a specified amount of time. You can use this WebBot by opening a Web page in the FrontPage Editor. Then click on Insert, WebBot Component, and select Scheduled Image from the resulting dialog box. You are presented with a new dialog box where you enter the specifics (see Figure 14.7).

Figure 14.7.

Use this dialog box to control when an image will be displayed.

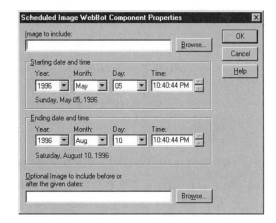

Although the dialog box might appear intimidating, it really isn't. Use the Image to Include text field to specify the relative URL path for a picture. Use the two date and time sections in the middle of the dialog box to precisely specify the timeframe. When the date and time are between the starting and ending times, the image will be displayed. If you want an image to be displayed when the timeframe isn't in effect, enter the relative URL path to a different file. If no file is specified, when the date and time aren't within the timeframe, no image will be displayed.

Scheduled Image Without an Extended Server

If you publish a Web page that uses the Scheduled Image WebBot, its behavior will be somewhat different. When the Web page is stored on a non-Extended Server, the timeframe that you specified will always be in effect. That means that if you've specified an image to be used, when not inside the timeframe, it won't be displayed.

14

Scheduled Include

Very similar to the Scheduled Image WebBot is the Scheduled Include WebBot. The only difference is that the Scheduled Include WebBot is used on any type of file instead of images. Aside from that, the dialog box, usage, and restrictions are identical to the previously discussed WebBot.

Search

A common element in many Web sites is the capability of searching the contents. Keywords are specified and searched for, and matching Web pages are returned to the user. Some of the sites that have this capability implement their own simple search engines. For many small businesses or intranets that don't have time to implement their own search engine, there's the Search WebBot.

Using Search in Your Web Page

As you might have guessed by its name, the Search WebBot implements a simple searching mechanism. You can insert it into any Web page by opening up a Web page in the FrontPage Editor. Click on Insert, WebBot Component and select Search to bring up a new dialog box (see Figure 14.8). This dialog box is pretty easy to understand; you basically specify the prompts to be used. You can also control the data to be returned for matched search results with the checkboxes at the bottom of the dialog box.

Figure 14.8.

There's not a lot to control when you're using the Search WebBot.

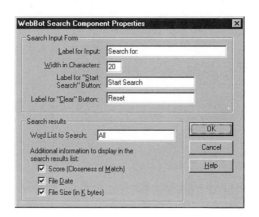

14

The User Interface for Search

Using this WebBot is a simple matter of typing a keyword to search and clicking on the search button. To search for multiple keywords, users can use Boolean text, such as AND, NOT, and OR. Additionally, keywords with Boolean operations can be grouped together using parentheses. Even though this sounds like a rather sophisticated search engine, it really isn't. It will sometimes fail to find a keyword, and there seems to be no way to get around the problem.

Search Without an Extended Server

Because the Search capability is implemented through a WebBot, it depends on some FrontPage files. Consequently, if you create a Web page using the WebBot, it probably won't work if the page is published. That means that you should really use the Search WebBot only if you know your Web page won't be moved away from FrontPage. If you must have a search engine, you should implement your own searching scheme.

Substitution

Another useful WebBot is Substitute, which is used to insert variables. By default, there are four variables that every Web created by FrontPage has: Author, ModifiedBy, Description, and Page-URL. The Author variable is the name of the author who first created the page. The ModifiedBy variable specifies the name of the person who most recently made changes to this page. The description of a particular Web page is the contents of the Description variable. Finally, there's the Page-URL variable, which is the complete URL for a particular page. You can see the values of each of these variables by opening a Web with FrontPage Explorer and selecting a Web page. Clicking on **E**dit, **P**roperties brings up a dialog box that will show you the values of the variables. By default, the General tab is selected, which shows you the Page-URL variable in the Location field. If you click on the Summary tab, a new set of variables is shown. The Created field is the value for the Author field, and the Modified By field is the ModifiedBy variable. Finally, the scrollable text at the bottom of the dialog box, the Comments section, is the Description variable.

Defining New Variables

The four basic variables are simply informational, without much use for actual Web pages. Fortunately, you can define your own variables, on a Web-by-Web basis. To define a variable for the currently selected Web, go to FrontPage Explorer. Click on Tools, Web Settings to bring up the FrontPage Web Settings dialog box. Click on the Parameters tab to see all the custom-defined Web variables. To add a new variable, click on the **Ad**d button where you

14

are shown a new dialog box (see Figure 14.9). Specify the variable name in the Name text field and its value in the Value text field. To change a defined variable, select it from the list and click on the **M**odify button. Finally, you can get rid of a variable by selecting it and clicking on the **R**emove button.

Figure 14.9.

When you want to create a user-defined variable, you have to give it a name and a value.

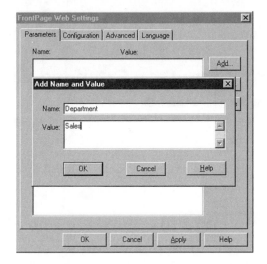

Using the Substitute WebBot

The Substitute WebBot enables you to insert the raw value of any Web variable, basic or user-defined. This is useful if you're working on a large Web site and each department has its own value. Generic Web pages could be created, such as for contact information, in which only the department name is changed.

To insert a Substitute WebBot, simply open up a Web page in the FrontPage Editor. Click on **I**nsert, **W**ebBot Component and select Substitute from the dialog box. You are presented with a simple dialog box, asking for the name of the variable to substitute. If you're not sure what the variable name is, click on the blank drop-down list and locate the variable. Once you've found the variable you want to use, click on the OK button.

Substitute Without an Extended Server

Because the Substitute WebBot can be used in a large number of Web pages, its behavior outside FrontPage is important. When a Web page makes use of Substitute, the specified value will automatically be updated. However, when the entire Web is published, the variable has to become a constant. The constant value that is taken is the last assigned value for that Web before it was published.

14

Table of Contents

Many complicated Web sites, with lots of Web pages, have an index of its Web pages. You can create a similar index by using the Table of Contents WebBot. This can be done by bringing up a Web page in FrontPage Explorer. Click on **I**nsert, **W**ebBot Component, and select Table of Contents. This brings up a simple dialog box that enables you to control the look and behavior of the Table of Contents (see Figure 14.10).

Figure 14.10.

Just tell the Table of Contents WebBot where to start and how the entries should be formatted.

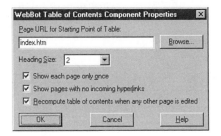

Perhaps the most important part of the dialog box is the text field at the top. You use this field to specify the Web page for which the Table of Contents should be created. The WebBot bases its Table of Contents on all the links that are attached to this page. By default, the WebBot will create a Table of Contents for all the Web pages in the current Web.

The Table of Contents WebBot is accessed only when you first save the Web page or the Web content is modified. When either of these two events occur, FrontPage goes through the Web and creates the Table of Contents. That means that if you publish a Web page to a non-Extended Server, the contents may not be up-to-date. If in the future you add more Web pages, the published Table of Contents will not be updated. To insure that the Table of Contents is always current, you should execute two steps. The first is to access FrontPage Explorer and click on **T**ools, **R**ecalculate Hyperlinks. This automatically updates all links, including any Table of Contents WebBots. The second step is to publish the Web page with the Table of Contents WebBot. If you don't do the second step and you've added more content, the Table of Contents won't be up-to-date.

Timestamp

The last WebBot available to you is the Timestamp WebBot. This WebBot is used to automatically insert the time and date that this page was changed. You can control under what conditions the WebBot is updated and the format of the date and time. To use this WebBot, bring up a Web page in the FrontPage Editor. Click on **I**nsert, **W**ebBot Component, and choose Timestamp.

14

The Timestamp WebBot is always in effect while the Web page is under an Extended Server. However, once the Web page using this WebBot is published to a non-Extended Server, its value won't be automatically updated. The time of the last modification made on each Web page using the Timestamp WebBot will be stored in each Web page.

Other WebBots

Not all the WebBots that are available in FrontPage are accessed through **I**nsert, **W**ebBot Component. There are three other WebBots that you can use, but they are menu items of their own: Comments, Scripts, and HTML Markups.

Comment

The Comment WebBot is available in the FrontPage Editor by clicking on **I**nsert, **C**omment. You are presented with a simple dialog box where you can type whatever text you want. When you're finished, just click on the OK button to accept the comments. The comments will never appear on any Web page, whether it's on an Extended Server or not. They will be shown by the FrontPage Editor when you load a page that uses this WebBot.

Script

On Day 10, you learned about creating VBScripts and JavaScripts. When you embed a script in any language through the FrontPage editor into the current Web page, the script is represented by a WebBot. This is done to make you, the Web author, aware of its existence. Because most scripting languages that are embedded in Web pages are interpreted by the user's Web browser, FrontPage does no interpretation. Consequently, it's possible for you to create invalid, and possibly harmful, scripts. Because FrontPage doesn't modify any embedded scripts, their behavior won't change when you publish such a Web page.

HTML Markup

Like the script WebBot, the HTML Markup WebBot is more of a placeholder than a WebBot. Although FrontPage provides support for many HTML tags, it can't cover all of them. In particular, if new HTML tags are created, FrontPage won't know or be able to validate them. As a result, if you want to use HTML tags that FrontPage doesn't know about, you use the HTML Markup WebBot.

14

To do so, open a Web page in the FrontPage Editor and click on **I**nsert, **H**TML Markup. This brings up a basic scrollable text dialog box (see Figure 14.11). Type the HTML code you want inserted and then click on the OK button. You don't have to specify the beginning and ending tags in the dialog box, because its contents are never checked. Because HTML Markups aren't checked, they also aren't affected by what Web server the pages reside on.

Figure 14.11.

The HTML Markup WebBot enables you to insert HTML codes that FrontPage doesn't know about.

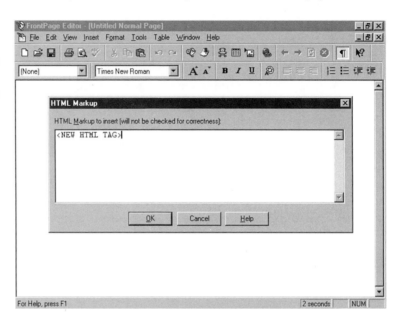

Summary

When using FrontPage as a Web page development platform, it's very important to look at the Web server being used. If you just stick with the Personal Web Server, all the features of FrontPage will work fine. However, for many large companies, having a single PC as their development machine is unworkable. It would be better to distribute FrontPage's capabilities across multiple computers. The FrontPage Server Extensions provide such a feature. The Server Extensions are installed on each machine where you want to use FrontPage's features. When installed, any FrontPage administrator can add, delete, or modify Webs on that machine.

Because FrontPage is probably being used as a Web page design platform, it's important to understand how its features behave. Most of FrontPage's features deal with HTML layout and controlling how the Web page looks. However, WebBots are special components that can do a number of different tasks. Many such tasks are those that are often implemented with CGI scripts, written by Web authors. When a Web page with a WebBot is published to a

14

non-Extended Server, the WebBots often stop working. In particular, many WebBots simply lose the capability of being updated dynamically when on a non-Extended Server system. A handful of WebBots are meaningful only when used with the Personal Web Server or an Extended Server. As a result, if you use them, you may have to substitute their behavior with CGI scripts.

Q&A

Q What is an Extended Server?

A An Extended Server is a Web server that isn't the Personal Web Server, with the FrontPage Extensions installed on it.

Q What are WebBots?

A WebBots are dynamic objects on a Web page that are evaluated, or executed, when the page is saved, and sometimes when it's accessed.

Q What happens to most WebBots when they're taken off an Extended Server?

A Most of the time, the WebBot's value will be frozen to when the Web page using that WebBot was last updated.

Workshop

Create a Web site with three Web pages and add some generic content. Get some information about the user and make it possible to go to any page in the site. Allow the user to be able to search the site for keywords. After you have everything working, bring up a Web browser and access the files directly off the hard drive. This will give you an idea of how each WebBot functions outside an Extended Server.

Quiz

1. Which two WebBots are most dependent on the Personal Web Server or an Extended Server? Why?

2. How many other WebBots are there, aside from those in the WebBot selection dialog box?

3. How do these WebBots function without an Extended Server?

14

APPENDIXES

G Quiz Answers

H What's on the CD-ROM

APPENDIX

A

Installing FrontPage

FrontPage isn't just a program that you use to create and publish Web pages. It's a suite of Web publishing tools that are extremely useful for Web authors. In particular, you can use Microsoft Image Composer, a powerful image editing program. You can easily apply professional-looking effects to customize your images. For Web authors on the Internet and intranets, there's also the Web Publishing Wizard. This program automates the usually repetitive task of copying your Web content between systems.

Installing the FrontPage Program

The most important part of the FrontPage set of programs is, of course, FrontPage. Before installing Microsoft FrontPage 97, you have to make sure you have enough disk space. The FrontPage installation is made up of two principal components: the program and its Webs. When doing a full install of FrontPage 97, the program portion can take up a significant amount of disk space. This portion, made up of the Personal Web server, FrontPage Explorer, and the FrontPage Editor takes up to 14.4MB of disk space. The Web content can change sizes as you change the content. By default, with no existing Web content, the content directory will take up about 630KB. This space is made up primarily of support programs and configuration information for each Web. Unless you're managing a small Web site, you should consider installing the two components into separate drive letters.

By default, FrontPage will install both the content and Web server on the same drive. This isn't always the best option for all situations. For example, except for FrontPage extensions, most of the content is transportable to other Web servers. That means that if your Web server drive fails, you can always use another Web server temporarily. Another advantage of putting the server and content on separate drives is for intranets. In such situations, it's possible to have existing Web content. Usually, the content is on a network-accessible drive so that many people can add content. For this case, you'll definitely want to install the content on a separate drive.

Installing FrontPage 97 is a simple matter of following its installation wizard. For most of the wizard's dialog boxes, if you make a mistake, you can click on the **B**ack button. The first screen of this program presents some introductory information, which you can bypass by clicking on **N**ext. You are next presented with a dialog box asking for your personal name and company name. You have to fill in *both* fields before proceeding with the installation (see Figure A.1). After you identify yourself, click on the **N**ext button. FrontPage asks for confirmation of the information, which you do by clicking on **Y**es.

Figure A.1.

When identifying yourself to FrontPage, you have to fill in the fields.

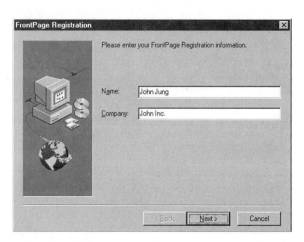

Now you are asked where you want to install the FrontPage program components. By default, FrontPage installs to the C:\Program Files\Microsoft FrontPage directory (see Figure A.2). To change the directory, simply click on the Browse button, where you are presented with a file selection dialog box. You can use the dialog box to specify the location of an existing directory. To install it to a new directory, simply type its name. If you specify a new directory that doesn't exist, you are prompted to create it. After you specify the target directory, click on the Next button to continue.

Figure A.2.

You get to specify the destination directory for the FrontPage program components.

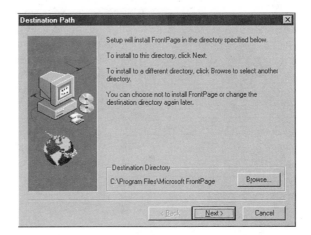

You're now prompted to specify what type of installation you want, **T**ypical or **C**ustom (see Figure A.3). The Typical installation is ideal for most situations, because it will install everything. That is, you'll be installing FrontPage's client software, the Personal Web server, and the server extensions. If you want to specify what parts of FrontPage to install, choose the **C**ustom installation. Additionally, you can change FrontPage's installation directory by clicking on the **B**rowse button. Once you select your installation type, click on the **N**ext button.

If you select a **C**ustom installation, you are presented with a list of components that you want installed on your system (see Figure A.4). Simply click on the parts that you do—and don't—want installed. If this is a new installation, the Server **E**xtensions will automatically be installed. Otherwise, for upgrades of an existing FrontPage installation, you can choose not to have the extensions installed. Here, too, you can change where FrontPage is installed by clicking on the **B**rowse button. Once you make your selection, click on the **N**ext button.

The next dialog box presented asks where you want the FrontPage Webs to be installed (see Figure A.5). The Webs are the actual content of the Web site that you'll be administering. By default, the installation directory is set to C:\FrontPage Webs. As with the program component selection part, you can change the directory to which to install. You should be careful about where you want your Webs to reside, because they can take up a lot of disk space. If you're running a large Web site, you should specify a drive letter with a great deal of free space. After you select the directory where you want the Webs to be stored, click on the Next button.

Figure A.3.

You can customize your FrontPage installation with the Custom setup.

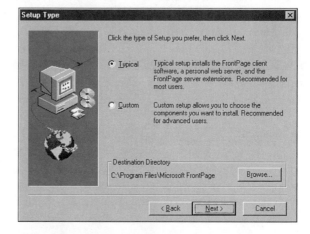

Figure A.4.

With the Custom installation, you can choose what FrontPage components you want installed.

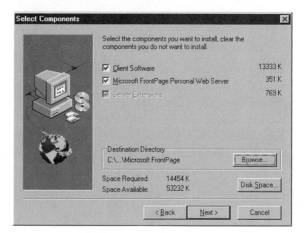

You are now presented with a dialog box summarizing what the installation wizard will do. This is your last chance to make any modifications to your FrontPage installation (see Figure A.6). To make any changes, click on the **B**ack button to go back to the last previous configurable option. Keep hitting that button until you arrive at the option you want to change.

Figure A.5.

You should be careful about where you want your FrontPage Webs installed.

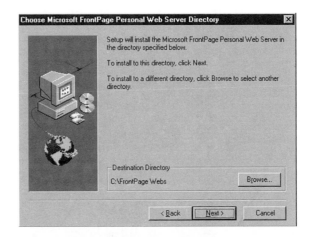

Figure A.6.

FrontPage gives you a final look at your FrontPage installation.

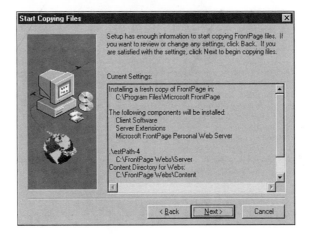

If you're happy with your configuration, click on the **N**ext button. FrontPage now proceeds to install all specified components in the appropriate directories. You are shown a status dialog box displaying how far along the installation is proceeding (see Figure A.7). It shows you what file is currently being installed, along with the overall progress. After it finishes copying everything, you are given the option of starting up FrontPage Explorer. This option, if selected, takes effect only after FrontPage is installed. Whichever choice you make, click on the Finish button to complete the FrontPage installation.

Even though you've completed the installation, you still have some minor configuration to do. This is first done after you click on the Finish button upon copying the FrontPage program files. You are presented with a dialog box (see Figure A.8). Simply type the name you want to use as the Webmaster and the password to be used. After you type everything, you can hit the OK button.

Figure A.7.

The FrontPage installation wizard gives you a status of how much of FrontPage is installed.

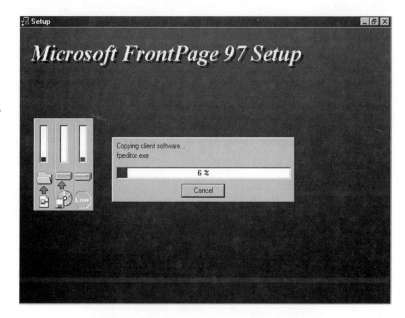

Figure A.8.

After you've installed FrontPage, you have to specify information for the administrator.

Even though you've finished installing and configuring FrontPage, you're still not quite finished. The first time you start up FrontPage, you are told that it needs to get your hostname and TCP/IP address. After clicking on the OK button, FrontPage searches your system for the appropriate information. It then returns with the hostname that it found for your system. You may now use FrontPage.

Installing Microsoft Image Composer

The Microsoft Image Composer is a very powerful and versatile program. Although you might expect the installation process to be difficult, and laborious, it really isn't. To install the Image Composer, simply start up its installation wizard. The first dialog box presented is simply informational, which you can bypass by clicking on the Continue button. The next screen asks for your full name and company name. After you've specified it, click on the OK button. After confirming your information, you're presented with the license agreement (see Figure A.9).

Figure A.9.

You should read over the license agreement carefully to see what rights you have.

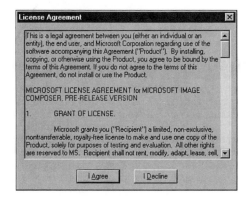

If you agree to the terms of the license agreement, click on the I **A**gree button. The installation wizard will fetch some information about your system. You'll now be presented with a dialog box asking you for installation information (see Figure A.10). If you want to abort the installation, click on the E**x**it Setup button. By default, the Image Composer is installed into C:\Program Files\Microsoft Image Composer. You can change this by clicking on the Change **F**older button and choosing a new directory. Once you've selected your target installation directory, click on the **C**omplete Install button. This will proceed with the installation of the complete distribution of Microsoft Image Composer.

Figure A.10.

You can choose where you want the Image Composer installed to, or quit without installing anything.

Because you want to install the Image Composer, the wizard will ask for a group name. The group name will appear under the **P**rograms menu heading of the Windows 95 Start button. By default, the name will be Microsoft Image Composer, but you can change this simply by typing whatever name you want. By clicking on OK, you start the actual installation of Image Composer. During the installation, you're shown what file the wizard is currently installing. An indicator of the overall installation progress is also displayed (see Figure A.11).

Figure A.11.

While the files are being installed, you're told where they're being installed.

Installing the Web Publishing Wizard

The Microsoft Web Publishing Wizard enables you to publish your Web pages easily. That is, you can do all your Web site development under FrontPage, and then "publish" the results to the destination Web server. This usually happens with Internet Service Providers, or intranets. In these situations, Web pages are created on a "staging area," where all the bugs are shaken out. When a page is ready to be made public, it's published to the primary Web server. The Web Publishing Wizard automates the publishing of the Web pages, from the staging area to the primary Web server.

To install the Web Publishing Wizard, start its installation program. You'll be presented with the license agreement for the program (see Figure A.12). If you don't agree with the terms of the agreement, simply click on the **N**o button. Clicking on **Y**es will install the entire Web Publishing Wizard program. During the installation process, you'll be shown the overall progress of the installation. Additionally, you'll be told which files are being installed and the directories to which they are being installed.

Figure A.12.

Installing the Web Publishing Wizard is simply done by agreeing to the license agreement.

APPENDIX B

Wizards and Templates

Because many of the tasks and Web pages are so common, FrontPage tries to be helpful. It comes with a number of wizards and templates that can simplify how to create content for your new Web. Some of these are accessible from FrontPage Explorer, and others from the FrontPage Editor. This appendix lists all the wizards and templates that are available. For templates, you learn the name of the template, when it's accessible, and why it's used. For wizards, you learn the same information along with some descriptions on important dialog boxes.

FrontPage Explorer

FrontPage Explorer is intended to give you a broad overview of your entire Web site. Consequently, the templates and wizards that are available from it are intended as starting points for new Webs. Although you can certainly add them to existing Webs, that task is primarily aimed at the FrontPage Editor.

Normal Web

The Normal Web template is a good starting point for most Web pages. It creates a single, blank Web page with no content. You have to add the content to the page manually with the FrontPage Editor.

Corporate Presence Web Wizard

The Corporate Presence Web wizard offers a quick and easy approach to creating a Web page for your corporation. It presents you with up to 16 dialog boxes in which you fill in whatever information is asked of you. You go forward through the dialog boxes by clicking on the **N**ext button and go to the previous one by clicking on the **B**ack button. Once you've filled in as much information as you like, simply click on the **F**inish button. The wizard takes the default values for the remaining dialog boxes and creates your Web page. You can quit this wizard at any time by clicking on the Cancel button.

The first dialog box of the wizard offers basic introduction about itself. The next one is far more important, enabling you to choose which components of the corporate Web page you want to use (see Figure B.1). The listed components include What's New, Products/Services, Table of Contents, Feedback Form, and Search Form. Of the five, What's New and Feedback Form are enabled by default. Additionally, a home page for this set of Web pages is created by default if this is a new Web.

Figure B.1.

You decide immediately what Web pages you want to create for your company's Web site.

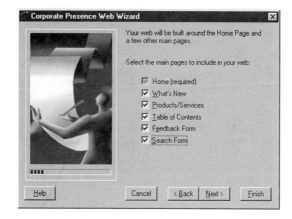

The next dialog box enables you to choose which topics you want to appear in the home page for the new Web (see Figure B.2). Your options include Introduction, Mission Statement, Company Profile, and Contact Information. By default, the Mission Statement and Contact Information are selected for creation.

Figure B.2.

You can choose what to include in the main Web page for your company.

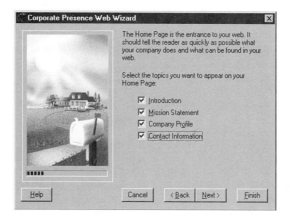

If you select to create a What's New section, the next dialog box enables you to specify its contents (see Figure B.3). There are four options for which the wizard can create templates: Web Changes, Press Releases, Articles, and Reviews. The Web Changes option is the only one set to be created by default.

Figure B.3.

*You can specify how
many sections you
want for your What's
New section.*

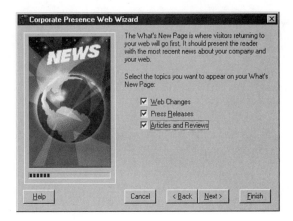

For those who select the Product/Services option, the next two dialog boxes are important. The first dialog box of this set enables you to determine how many links to products/services should be created. The wizard creates three links for products and three links for services by default. The second dialog box asks you to specify the template information for the products and services (see Figure B.4). For products, you can choose to include Product image, Pricing information, and Information request form. Of the three, only the Pricing information option isn't set. For services, you can choose to include Capabilities list, Reference accounts, and Information request form. Only the Information request form option is set to be created.

Figure B.4.

*For your Products and
Services section, you
can control what
information to
present.*

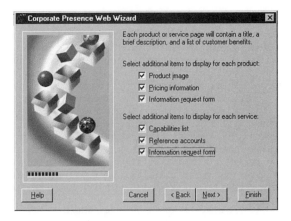

If you want the wizard to create placeholder documents for the Feedback Form, you have to work with two dialog boxes. The first dialog box enables you to specify the information that you want to collect from each user (see Figure B.5). You can ask for the Full Name, Job Title, Company Affiliation, Mailing Address, Telephone Number, FAX Number, and E-mail Address. The user's name, company, both phone numbers, and e-mail address are set to be created by default. After specifying the information to be retrieved, you get to determine how the data is returned. By default, all data will be returned in tab-delimited format, appropriate for integrating into databases. If this isn't what you're looking for, the wizard can return form data in Web format.

Figure B.5.

When getting information from the feedback form, you specify what information to request.

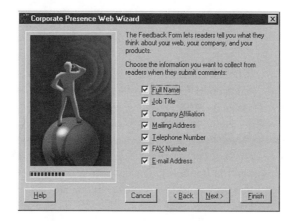

When you want a Table of Contents to be created for your Web page, you only have to deal with one dialog box. You can choose to create any number of the three options: Automatically Update Web Pages, Show Pages Not Linked Into Webs, and whether to Use Bullets for Top-Level Pages. By default, only the bulleted option is set to be used.

The next four dialog boxes of the wizard enable you to control the general look and feel of your Web pages. The first one enables you to specify the default headers and footers (see Figure B.6). For the headers, you can use Your company's logo, the Page title, and Links to your main web pages. For the headers, you can include Links to your main web pages, E-mail address of your webmaster, Copyright notice, and Date page was last modified. Of these various options, by default, all of them are set to be created except Links to your main web pages and the Copyright notice.

Figure B.6.

Because consistency in Web pages is important, you can determine what appears at the top and bottom of every Web page.

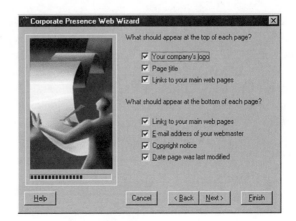

The second and third dialog boxes enable you to control the general look and feel of all Web pages. The second dialog box enables you to control the graphical presentation of all Web pages. The four options are Plain, Conservative (the default), Flashy, and Cool. You can see what each of these options will look like with the preview on the left side of the dialog box. The third dialog box enables you to control the color settings for all Web pages (see Figure B.7). By default, the wizard enables you to specify your own custom color configuration with the top-level drop-down list. The drop-down list in the middle of the dialog box enables you to specify the background. This drop-down list enables you to use brown, blue, gray, and white patterns or none at all. If you've selected no background pattern, the Solid Color button becomes enabled. When used, this button specifies the solid background color. The last group of color components that you can control are those for the text. You can specify the colors for the Normal text, Visited Links, Unvisited Link, and Active Link. Each has its own color button, which, when clicked on, enables you to choose the color to be used. As before, a preview of what each page will look like appears on the left side of the dialog box.

The next dialog box enables you to specify whether or not to use the Men At Work icon for unfinished Web pages. By default, the wizard will do so.

The next two dialog boxes enable you to specify various information for the wizard to use. The first dialog box asks for your Company Full Name, a One Word Version, and the Street Address. All these text fields are defaulted to a mythical company. The next dialog box asks for contact information to be placed at various parts of the Web: Company Telephone Number, FAX Number, E-mail Address for the Webmaster, and E-mail Address for General Information. Again, all these fields are set to generic values.

The final dialog box of this wizard is a simple one. It asks whether you want the To Do list to appear after the wizard is finished creating this Web. By default, this option is enabled. To create the entire Web, with your specified values and options, click on the Finish button. To change any of the values, keep clicking on the Back button until you get to the dialog box you want to change.

Figure B.7.

FrontPage lets you completely determine your corporate Web pages' color schemes.

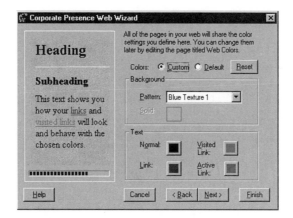

Customer Support Web

For companies that want to offer a customer support area on their Web site, the Customer Support Web is a good start (see Figure B.8). Even though it's simply a template, this Web is incredibly tightly integrated with itself. It creates a discussion area, complete with the capability of searching it. Additionally, this template also provides support for Web-wide search capabilities. Further, it has generic Web pages for customer support FAQ, download area, and What's New. This template also provides for bug reports and suggestions from customers.

Figure B.8.

The Customer Support template comes prepackaged with features people want in a support child Web.

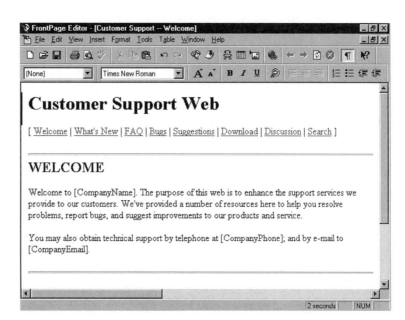

Discussion Web Wizard

The Discussion Web Wizard creates a discussion area that suits your taste. You enter data into a series of dialog boxes, and when you're finished, FrontPage creates all the components for you. Of the eleven dialog boxes you have to respond to, the first and last ones are simply informational. The last dialog box exists to give you one last chance at changing your entered values.

Following the first dialog box is one that asks you what components of a discussion area you want to include (see Figure B.9). The options you have to choose from include Submission Form, Table of Contents, Search Form, Threaded Replies, and Confirmation Page. All five options are enabled by default.

Figure B.9.

Choose the features of the Discussion Web Wizard that you want to include.

After choosing what you want to include, the next dialog box asks you for two names. The first name is the name of the discussion area, which by default is Discussion. This name is meaningful only during the creation of the Web, because it uses the name for a number of Web pages. The second name that FrontPage wants is the name of the discussion folder. This folder holds the table of contents and all the messages for the discussion forum that's being created.

The fourth dialog box in this wizard enables you to control the searching mechanism for the discussion forum (see Figure B.10). You can give users three search options: Subject and Comments; Subject, Category, and Comments; or Subject, Product, and Comments. Of the three options, the first one, Subject and Comments, is the one selected by default.

The next dialog box asks the simple question of who can post to this new forum. By default, this option is set to No so that anybody can participate. However, if you want only registered users to be able to post, you can change the option. When set to allow posting only for registered users, FrontPage automatically extracts the person's name.

Figure B.10.

You get to decide what information you want to request from each user who wants to post to the discussion Web.

The next two dialog boxes deal with the specifics of the Table of Contents. The first one enables you to specify how articles in the table of contents are sorted. You can choose from sorting Oldest to Newest, the default, or Newest to Oldest. The second dialog box of this pair asks whether you want the table of contents to be the home page for this Web. If you're creating a new Web that is only for this discussion forum, the default Yes is applicable.

The eighth dialog box of this wizard is actually related to the fourth dialog box. This one asks you what information the search form should return (see Figure B.11). In particular, FrontPage can return: the Subject; the Subject and Size of matches; Subject, Size, and Date; and Subject, Size, Date, and Score. The Score is how closely the matched article met your search words. The closer the match, the higher the Score. By default, the Subject, Size, and Date will be returned with each search result.

Figure B.11.

You can control the information returned by searches on the discussion Web.

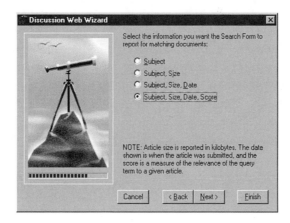

The ninth dialog box enables you to control the color scheme for all the Web pages in the discussion Web. You can choose to use either the default color scheme or your own custom configuration. You can use the Background group of controls to control the background pattern. Simply use the drop-down list to choose from either brown, blue, gray, or white patterns. You can also choose to have no colored pattern, preferring a solid color, which you also can choose. Additionally, you can control the various text colors by clicking on the button next to each text. To help you figure out what each of the pages will look like, there's a minipreview on the left side of the dialog box. As you make your selections, the appropriate attribute in the preview also changes.

The next-to-last dialog box asks whether you want the discussion Web to use frames or not (see Figure B.12). Frames are a new Web page design mechanism for segmenting information. As the Web author, you can determine the size, shape, and location of each frame. When a user clicks on a link in one of the frames, the data in another frame can be updated. The biggest drawback with using frames is that some older browsers can't handle them properly. Because of their usefulness, FrontPage enables you to decide whether you want to use frames. You can either choose to use No Frames, Dual Interface, Contents Above Current Article, or Contents Beside Current Article. The first option, no use of frames at all, is the most obvious, making the area as compatible as possible. The second option, the default Dual Interface, uses frames when possible; otherwise, it resorts to a nonframe setup. The last two options are three-pane configurations. The only difference between the two is what each one is used for and where the panes are located. A preview of what the discussion home page will look like appears on the left of the dialog box. For options that use frames, you can change the size of the frames. This can be done by clicking and dragging on the edge of each frame.

Figure B.12.

You may want to use frames for your discussion Web to make it easier for people to read the articles.

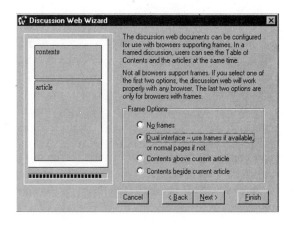

Empty Web

This is the most basic of all templates available from FrontPage Explorer. The Empty Web simply creates a Web with a certain name and creates no content. This gives you the most flexibility, allowing you to put in exactly the content you want. This Web doesn't even have a blank Web page.

Import Web Wizard

The Import Web Wizard is a simple wizard that takes existing content and puts it into FrontPage. This wizard is made up of three simple dialog boxes. The first dialog box asks you for the hard drive location of the existing Web content. The second dialog box lists all the files found in the specified directory (see Figure B.13). You can choose which file you don't want to be converted by clicking on its entry and clicking on the Exclude button. The last one is simply a confirmation that you want to convert the content. This gives you the ability to go back and change your selection before the Web is created.

Figure B.13.

When importing an existing Web, you can determine what files to carry over.

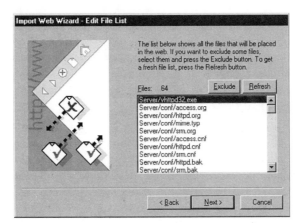

Personal Web

The Personal Web creates a Web with a single Web page. This page contains a lot of external links to a number of different locations (see Figure B.14). All the text and links are generic, so you should modify them to reflect your own tastes. The links that are created include links to your department's server, your manager's Web page, and a link to your corporate Web page. Additionally, it has links to three people who report to you, three hot sites, and an e-mail link to yourself. Finally the bottom of the page contains fill-out form fields for user comments and suggestions. Obviously, because this is a template, there are no restrictions on any of the predefined links. You can completely remove the links to people who report to you or you can add more hot sites, also known as "cool links," if you want.

Figure B.14.

The Personal Web template is a good starting point for many people.

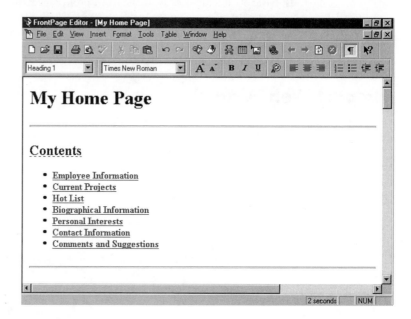

Project Web

The last template available from FrontPage Explorer is the Project Web. This template is similar to the Customer Support Web—everything is tightly integrated. To be precise, this template creates generic links for project members, the schedule for the project, and the capability of searching the Web (see Figure B.15). Additionally, this template creates two discussion forums for your use. The first, the Requirements Discussion, is intended for people to provide feedback for the project. The second, the Knowledge Base forum, is intended to record common questions asked by users.

Figure B.15.

*For groups within
organizations, the
Project Web enables
an immediate Web
presence.*

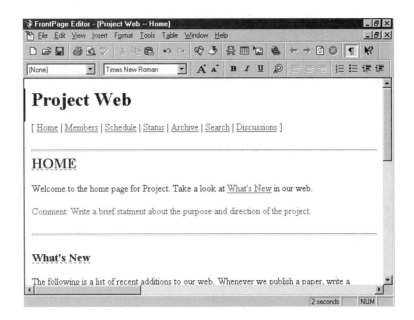

The FrontPage Editor

The FrontPage Editor is intended to be where most of the Web content is created. As a result, more templates and wizards are available from it. The primary difference between what's available with FrontPage Explorer and the Editor is the scope. The available FrontPage Explorer content is far reaching, offering tightly integrated Webs. This is different from the FrontPage Editor, which primarily offers individual HTML documents.

Normal Page

The first template available from the FrontPage Editor is the Normal Web page. This page is identical to the page created by FrontPage Explorer. The only difference between the two is that FrontPage Explorer's Normal page is created when a new Web is created. The FrontPage Editor's Normal page is intended to be used in an existing Web.

Bibliography

The Bibliography template in the FrontPage Editor is used to create an online bibliography. The template comes with generic text that you have to modify to suit your needs (see Figure B.16). The predefined text has space for up to three bibliographical entries, but you can obviously change it.

Figure B.16.

When you want to refer to books or magazine articles, you should use the Bibliography template.

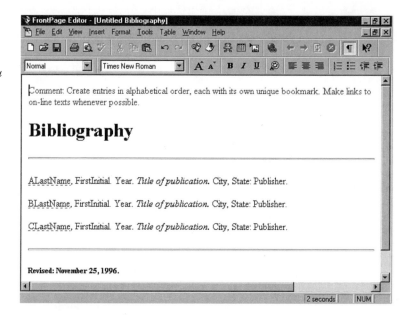

Confirmation Form

If you're creating a custom Web page with your own form fields, you'll probably also want to use the Confirmation Form template (see Figure B.17). When accessed, this creates a page that is suitable for acknowledging user input. It can be made to recognize input from Discussion, FormResult, or Registration forms. As with any other templates, you have to change the actual body of the text to match your Web.

Figure B.17.

The Confirmation Form template can be used to acknowledge any sort of user input.

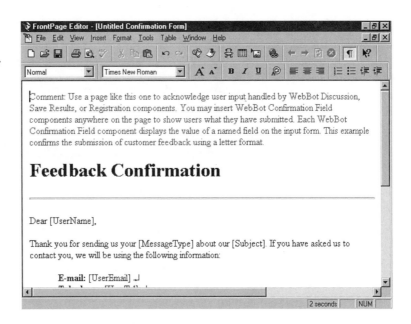

Database Connector Wizard

Many companies keep some, or most, of their data in a database. To make it easier to make some of this information available to a Web, you should use the Database Connector Wizard. This wizard, made up of three dialog boxes, will create all the necessary files to access, and return, information from a database.

The first dialog box of the wizard enables you to specify some introductory information about the database (see Figure B.18). In particular, you have to specify the ODBC data source. You also have to specify a filename that will format, and display, the query results (an IDC file). You can optionally specify the username and password for connecting to the database.

The second dialog box enables you to enter a sequence of Structured Query Language (SQL) commands. These commands are used by the IDC file specified in the first dialog box. The drop-down list at the top of the dialog box is used to list each of the SQL commands. The last entry in the drop-down list enables you to add more SQL commands. The SQL commands themselves go into the textbox in the middle of the dialog box. You also can add a parameter for the IDC file to interpret by clicking on the Insert Parameter button. You must specify at least one SQL query before continuing.

Figure B.18.

At the very least, you must specify a data source and the query results file for the Database Connector Wizard.

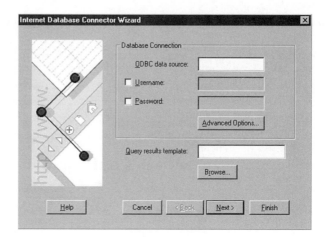

After you specify all the SQL commands you want to run, you'll be presented with the third dialog box. This one enables you to define the default values for any parameters used by the IDC file. To specify these values, simply click on the Add button and type the name of the parameter and its default value. You don't need to specify any default parameters, but if you want to, you can. After you specify all the appropriate values, click on the Finish button. You'll be asked one last question from the wizard. You must specify the folder name where you want all the database connection scripts to be stored.

Once FrontPage has created all the files it needs, you'll be returned to the Editor. No physical Web page was created, but if you go to FrontPage Explorer, you'll see a new element in the Web. This element has the filename you specified in the first dialog box. It can't be edited, but its results can be displayed in a Web page. This can be done by using the Database Results template.

Database Results

After you've used the Database Connection Wizard, you'll want to store the results somewhere. That's what the Database Results template is used for—to store all the data returned from a database query.

Directory of Press Releases

When selected, the Directory of Press Releases template creates a single Web page. The purpose of this page is to have a list of press releases by your company (see Figure B.19). The created page is divided into three distinct sections where you can put the titles of your press releases: this month's press releases, last month's press releases, and previous press releases. It is up to you, the Webmaster, to move the press releases manually from month to month. Additionally, by default, there are no links for any online press releases, so you also have to add those yourself.

B

Figure B.19.

Just change the template text with your own press releases.

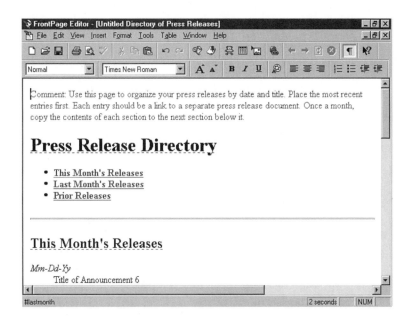

Employee Directory

The Employee Directory template is a single Web page where you can put an alphabetical list of your employees (see Figure B.20). By default, this template has all the names in alphabetical order, based on their last name. There are three predefined, generic entries, which include space for numerous personal information. Additionally, there are placeholders for each person to put a picture of themselves. The actual content of the page, as it relates to your company, has to be modified.

Figure B.20.

The Employee Directory template makes it easy for your workers to find each other.

Employment Opportunities

If you're working on a Web for a large company, there's a good chance that you'll always have job openings. It's not because your company is losing business, but just that there is always something open. For such companies, the Employment Opportunities template is perfect (see Figure B.21). It comes with five generic positions as placeholders for the actual jobs available at your company. Each position has space for job description, job requirements, and contact information. At the bottom of the page are some form fields. This is intended to be used by people who don't meet any of the job openings, but they want their name to be kept on file.

Figure B.21.

The Employment Opportunities template comes with five generic positions, which you should change.

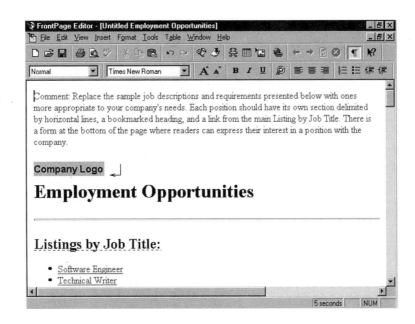

Feedback Form

The Feedback Form template is a single HTML page that is used to return comments from users. These comments can be about anything at all, such as your company, the Web site, or an employee.

Form Page Wizard

For those looking to create Web pages with complicated form fields, the Form Page Wizard is great to use. It is made up of essentially eight dialog boxes, the first and last being purely informational. You simply answer a few questions and make a few selections, and the wizard will create a page. The second dialog box, after the introductory one, asks for the URL for the new page and its title.

The next dialog box lists all the form fields that you've decided you want to use (see Figure B.22). To remove or edit a form field, simply select the field you want and click on the Remove or Modify button. You can also move the placement of form fields around by clicking on a form field and using the Move Up and Move Down buttons. To add a new form field, just click on the Add button, which will modify the current dialog box. At the top is a list of information that you're seeking. Once you've make a selection, the textual prompt that goes with that information is displayed on the bottom. You can edit the prompt by putting your text cursor in the bottom textbox and editing the text.

Figure B.22.

You can see exactly what forms will be placed, and in what order.

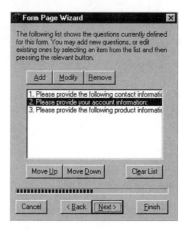

The fourth dialog box looks different from the previous dialog box, depending on the information you're seeking. The wizard gives you a list of nine items you can ask for—for example, if you're asking for contact information. However, if you're asking for a certain date, you can only specify the format of acceptable entries. Whatever piece of information you're looking for, however, you must specify a variable name. This name is used to store the information passed by the user.

After specifying technical information for the form field, you'll be taken back to the third dialog box. This enables you to use as many form fields on a Web page as you like. If you want to stop adding form fields, just don't click on the Next button without adding a form field.

Once you've selected all the information you want to ask the user, you have to control how the questions will be asked (see Figure B.23). These questions can be presented as a Normal Paragraph, a Numbered List, a Bulleted List, or a Definition List. By default, the wizard will use HTML paragraph tags to separate each question. In the middle of this dialog box, you can choose to specify whether to create a table of contents. By default, the wizard will create a table contents. The table of contents is only used for this single page, not for any other pages in the Web. The final set of options you can set enables you to decide whether you want to use tables to align the form fields. All but the oldest Web browsers support tables, and consequently, the option is enabled by default.

Figure B.23.

After deciding what questions to ask the user, you can specify how the questions should appear.

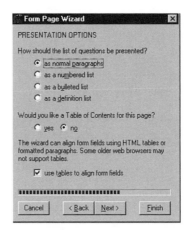

The next-to-last dialog box in the wizard enables you to control how the input data is returned. You can have FrontPage Save Results to a Web Page, Save Results to a Text File, or Use a Custom CGI script. By default, all data from the Form Page Wizard will be returned to a Web page.

Frames Wizard

Frames are a useful method of keeping information distinct and separate. However, they can be burdensome to create and specify. The Frames Wizard enables an easy method of creating, and controlling, frames. This wizard can take up to five dialog boxes to create all the necessary information. The first dialog box enables you to choose the frame layout to be used (see Figure B.24). You can either choose from a list of templates or define a custom frame layout.

Figure B.24.

You can choose from a predefined set of frame layouts or design your own.

If you choose to use a template layout, the second dialog box is made up of six possible choices (see Figure B.25). Each selection changes the number, size, and positions of the frames. On the left of the dialog box is a preview pane that shows you what each selection will look like. You can further change the sizes and shapes of the frames with the preview pane. Simply put your mouse cursor over one of the frames, click, and drag it to its new desired location.

Figure B.25.

You get to see what your frame layout will look like, as well as control where the frames belong.

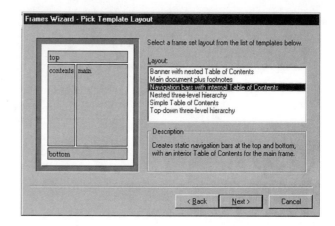

If you chose a custom layout frame, the second dialog box merely asks you for the number of rows and columns it should have. Here, too, the left of the dialog box is made up of a preview pane. However, along with resizing the frames, this pane enables you to split and merge frames together. To split a frame, hold down the Shift key, choose the frame to split, and click on the Split button.

The third dialog box also differs, depending on the frame type you've selected. If you're going with a template frame, you are presented with an alternate URL. This Web page will be used by FrontPage if it determines that the user's Web browser can't handle frames. For a custom frame configuration, the dialog box is a little different. You're shown your frame pattern, which you have to select for each frame, and you type in the URL to which each frame points (see Figure B.26).

As with the other dialog boxes before it, the fourth dialog box differs, depending on the frame configuration of your choice. If you're using a template frame configuration, you're asked to give the name of the Web page with the frames as well as its filename. This is the last dialog box if you went with a template frame layout. If you're using a custom configuration, you have to specify an alternate Web page for Web browsers that can't handle frames.

The fifth dialog box is seen only by users who choose to use a custom frame layout. It simply asks for the title and filename of the Web page that will hold the frames. After you type in both names, the Finish button ends the wizard.

Figure B.26.

You can easily specify which URL belongs in which frame.

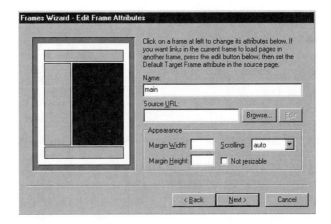

Frequently Asked Questions

The Frequently Asked Questions template is used to create a Web page to holding FAQs. As the name implies, FAQs are questions that many people ask. The page can be pointed to by other pages in your Web to try and minimize the questions which you have to consider (see Figure B.27). The created page comes with links to generic questions and their corresponding answers. You have to modify the text to suit your own questions and answers.

Figure B.27.

The Frequently Asked Questions template is a good start in reducing the number of support calls you may have to deal with.

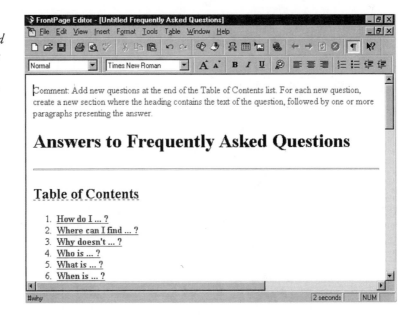

Glossary of Terms

The Glossary of Terms template is perfect for Web sites that use a lot of technical terms. Rather than defining each of the terms as they appear, and possibly defining it multiple times, you can use this template. It comes as a single Web page with a default set of links to, and placeholders for, generic terms.

Guest Book

Many Web sites, small and large, have a place where people can sign in. This is commonly known as a guest book and often requires a fair amount of Web authoring. The Guest Book template takes much of the work out of adding such a page to your Web site. It includes a form field at the bottom where people can give your their comments.

Hot List

A lot of individuals, as well as companies, have links to "cool sites." These are often just pointers to the Webmaster's frequent haunts. Unfortunately, some of these cool sites pages are disorganized, with all links thrown into a single page. The Hot List template creates a hot links—or cool sites—Web page that is broken up into five categories. You can modify the categories and links as you see fit.

HyperDocument Page

For those people working on large research papers or the like, the HyperDocument Page template is invaluable. It creates a single Web page that is intended to be part of a larger document. The top of the document enables you to specify the document name and the section to which it belongs. You can further subdivide this document by using its predefined subsections. Along with the usual placeholder text, this template also has room for icons representing each section or subsection.

Lecture Abstract

The Lecture Abstract template is meant to be used for lectures or seminars. It's intended to describe an upcoming event, enabling you to specify the name of the lecturer, the topics, and the date and time.

Meeting Agenda

For those who wish to announce upcoming meetings, the Meeting Agenda template is useful. It creates a generic meeting agenda Web page that includes the agenda, date, time, location, purpose, topics of discussion, and attendees. Although it could be used as a means of scheduling meetings, it should probably be used as a reference about meetings.

Office Directory

Large companies often have many offices in many different parts of the country, even the world. For such companies, the Office Directory template should be used (see Figure B.28). It creates a Web page with links for all fifty states in the United States. Additionally, it has links for Canadian provinces and a handful of foreign countries. Obviously, the information about each office is meant to be filled in by the Webmaster.

Figure B.28.

For corporations, the Office Directory template is useful.

Personal Home Page Wizard

For those people who are short on time, but still want to have a Web page, the Personal Home Page Wizard is invaluable. This wizard will present you with up to eleven dialog boxes asking you a variety of information. The last dialog box is purely informational and only there to give you the chance to change your answers.

The first dialog box asks you what sections you want to include in your personal home page (see Figure B.29). You can choose to use Employee Information, Current Projects, Hot List, Biography, a list of Personal Interests, Contact Information, and Comments and Suggestions. By default, the Current Projects, Biography, and Personal Interests are not enabled. The next dialog box merely asks you for the title for the new Web page and the URL to use.

Figure B.29.

*You can decide what
you want in your
personal home page.*

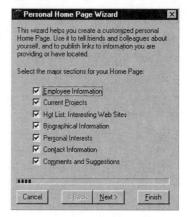

The third dialog box pertains to Employee Information. It can be set to include information such as Job Title, Responsibilities, Department or Workgroup, Manager, and Direct Reports. Of the five options available, the last two are the only ones disabled by default.

The fourth dialog box relates to the Current Projects option. You can type which projects you're currently working on in the textbox. You also can specify how the list of projects will be presented. You can choose from either bulleted list, the default, numbered list, or definition list.

The fifth dialog box concerns the presentation for the hot list. You can choose how the hot list entries will be presented: bulleted list, numbered list, definition list, or import an existing list. The last option will ask you to specify the full path Glossary of Terms of the file that has all the links you want to use, such as a bookmark file. The default option is to create a definition list.

The sixth dialog box in the wizard will ask about the layout of your biography. You can choose which type of information to include: Academic, Professional, or Personal. Regardless of which option you choose, generic text will be put in for you. By default, the wizard will create a biography for your Professional life.

The next dialog box deals with your Personal Interests (see Figure B.30). As with the Current Projects dialog box, the list is rather free-form. Type the items for your Personal Interests in the textbox. Once again, you can control how the list will be presented: bulleted list, numbered list, or definition list. By default, FrontPage will create a definition list of your personal interests.

Figure B.30.

Type in whatever you want for your personal interests.

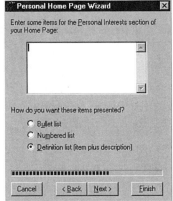

Your contact information makes up the entirety of the eighth dialog box. You're asked to provide your postal address, e-mail address, URL address, Office Phone number, FAX number, and home phone number. Only your e-mail address, URL address, and office phone are asked for by default.

The ninth dialog box enables you to control how Comments and Suggestions are returned to you. You can either have FrontPage Use the Form and Store the Results in a Data file, Use the Form and Store the Results in a Web page, or e-mail you the results. If you choose the last option, you must specify a valid e-mail address in the space provided. The default option is to store the results in a data file.

The next-to-last dialog box enables you to specify in which order the sections will appear. The default order is the order in which you entered the information. This can easily be changed by clicking on an entry and using the Up and Down buttons. When you're happy with the order, click on the Next button to go to the last dialog box.

Press Release

If you've used the Directory of Press Releases template, you'll obviously need press releases. That's why the Press Release template is meant to be used. It provides placeholder text for various information important for a press release.

Product Description

The Product Description template creates a page that describes the various aspects of a product. It has sections for product description, benefits of the product, and its specifications. Further, it also has room for a product summary and a list of key features.

Product or Event Registration

The Product or Event Registration template creates a page where people can register for a product or upcoming event. The default includes a set of form fields for various information (name, company, address, and so forth). A drop-down list provides options that apply to the product or event, and there are twelve radio buttons for nonexclusive options. Space is provided for the registration and serial numbers.

Search Page

The Search Page template should be used when you want to attach a search engine to your Web site. It creates a Web page with two search form fields: one for simple text and one for conditional text. The conditional text search engine lets the user use words such as AND, OR, and NOT. The template comes with numerous examples of using the conditional search engine.

Seminar Schedule

The Seminar Schedule template is similar to the Lecture Abstract template. It creates a Web page for an upcoming seminar event. The template enables the seminar to be broken up into sessions, or tracks, if it's appropriate.

Software Data Sheet

The Software Data Sheet template is similar to the Product Description template. The only difference is that this template is aimed primarily at a piece of software. It has space for including a screen shot, a list of benefits, a list of features, system requirements, and the pricing and availability.

Survey Form

The Survey Form template creates a Web page that's intended to ask the user for information. By default, it's broken up into three sections, each of which can be changed to your specifications. It has numerous form fields for a generic set of questions and possible answers. You may need to adjust the Save Results component settings to save the results to a text or HTML file.

Table of Contents

A good starting point for large Web sites is the Table of Contents template. It comes as a hierarchical list to major links in your Web. By default, it has three such links, but that can obviously be expanded.

User Registration

The User Registration template is meant as a place where users can self-register for a particular Web page. With some slight modification, this template can be converted to a registration area for a product. By default, it has space for the username, password, password confirmation, and e-mail address.

What's New

The What's New template should be used when you want to talk about something new. Because it's just a template, you don't have to mention what's new with the Web site. You can mention what's new with your company—or your family, if it's a personal Web page.

B

APPENDIX

C

VBScript Reference

Calculate, manipulate text, and perform other operations, using VBScript's operators and built-in functions. This appendix is a reference to VBScript's operators and built-in functions and an overview of how VBScript handles variables and constants.

Variables

You don't need to declare variables or their data types in VBScript. The VBScript interpreter automatically creates a `Variant` type variable when it encounters a new variable name. The `Variant` data type is the only type of variable VBScript supports.

`Variant` variables can hold integers, floating-point numbers, strings, and other objects listed in Table C.1. These are known as subtypes. The VBScript interpreter automatically assigns the variable's subtype based on the context of the operation performed (see Table C.1).

Table C.1. Variant subtypes.

Subtype	Description
Empty	No value assigned to the variable
Null	Variable contains no valid data
Boolean	Either true or false
Byte	An integer value in the range 0 through 255
Integer	An integer value in the range –32,768 through 32,767
Long	An integer value in the range –2,147,483,648 through 2,147,483,647
Single	A single-precision floating-point number in the range –3.402823E38 through –1.401298E–45 for negative values or 1.401298E–45 through 3.402823E38 for positive values
Double	A double-precision floating-point number in the range –1.79769313486232E308 through –4.94065645841247E–324 for negative values or 4.94065645841247E–324 through 1.79769313486232E308 for positive values
Date (Time)	A date and/or time value in the range January 1, 100 through December 31, 9999
String	A variable length string
Object	Any object reference
Error	An error number

When a variable is automatically assigned a data type, it is known as an *implicitly declared variable*. Implicitly declared variables are handy, but they can result in difficult-to-find bugs in your script. If you misspell a variable once anywhere in your script, for example, it is simply recognized as a new variable rather than as the old variable misspelled. You can avoid this sort of bug by forcing your scripts to allow only *explicitly declared variables*.

Force your script to allow only explicitly declared variables by placing the Option Explicit statement at the beginning of the script. Explicitly declared variables are declared using either the Dim or the Set statement. Almost all VBScript variables are declared using Dim. Use Set when you assign an object to a variable. An error message is generated if you forget to explicitly declare a variable when the Option Explicit statement is set. Typos and misspelled variables also generate error messages, making it much easier for you to debug the script.

Constants

Declare constants with Const. If you're declaring an approximation to the mathematical constant pi, for example, you add the following line to your script:

```
Const Pi = 3.14159
```

Operators

VBScript provides several built-in operators. Operators are used to manipulate data in some fashion. Tables of the operators are listed in the following sections, grouped by category.

Table C.2. Math operators.

Operator	Description
+	Addition
-	Subtraction or negation
/	Division
\	Integer division
Mod	Modulus
^	Exponentiation
*	Multiplication

Table C.3. Logical operators.

Object	Event Handler
And	Conjugation
Eqv	Equivalence
Imp	Implication
Or	Disjunction
Xor	Exclusion
Not	Negation

Table C.4. String operators.

Operator	Description
&	Concatenation
+	String concatenation (there are certain situations where this operator may become ambiguous)

Table C.5. Comparison operators.

Object	Description
<	Less than
<=	Less than or equal to
>	Greater than
>=	Greater than or equal to
<>	Not equal
=	Equal

Statements

Table C.6. Miscellaneous statements.

Statement	Description
Dim	Declare variables.
End Function	Mark the end of a function declared using the Function statement.

Statement	Description
End Sub	Mark the end of a procedure declared using the Sub statement.
Erase	Reinitialize fixed-size arrays and deallocate dynamic array memory.
Exit	Exit control blocks.
Function	Declare a function that ends with the End Function statement.
ReDim	Declare dynamic-array variables and allocate or reallocate storage space.
Rem	Comment or "Remark" that you add that is ignored by the VBScript interpreter. The ' is also used for comments.
Set	Assign an object to a property or variable.
Sub	Declare a procedure (subroutine) that ends with the End Sub statement.

Table C.7. Program control statements.

Statement	Description
Call	Transfer control to a procedure.
Do...Loop	Repeat a block of statements while a condition is True or until a condition becomes True.
For...Next	Repeat a block of statements a specified number of times.
If...Else ...End If	Decide between executing different blocks of statements depending on the value of an expression. The Else is optional.
On Error	Enable or disable an error handling routine.
Select Case	Select one of several statements based on the value of an expression.
While...Wend	Execute a block of statements as long as a given condition is True.

Functions

VBScript provides several built-in functions. Tables of the functions are listed in the following sections, grouped into specific categories.

Dialog Boxes

Table C.8. Dialog box functions.

Function	Description
InputBox	Displays a dialog box with a textbox. The user can input text, then choose a button. InputBox returns the contents of the textbox.
MsgBox	Displays a message in a dialog box. The dialog box closes when the user chooses a button.

Math

Table C.9. Math functions.

Function	Description
Abs	Returns the absolute value of a number
Atn	Returns the arctangent of a number
Cos	Returns the cosine of an angle, expressed in radians
Exp	Returns e raised to a power
Fix	Returns the integer portion of a number
Hex	Returns the hexadecimal value of a number
Int	Returns the integer portion of a number
Log	Returns the natural logarithm of a number
Oct	Returns the octal value of a number
Rnd	Returns a random number
Sgn	Returns an integer indicating the sign of a number
Sin	Returns the sine of an angle, expressed in radians
Sqr	Returns the square root of a number
Tan	Returns the tangent of an angle, expressed in radians

Date and Time

Table C.10. Date and time functions.

Function	Description
Date	Returns the current date
DateSerial	Returns the variant representation of the Date subtype for a given year, month, and day
DateValue	Returns the variant representation of the Date subtype
Day	Returns the day of the month
Hour	Returns the hour of the day
Minute	Returns the minute of the hour
Month	Returns the (numeric) month of the year
Now	Returns the current date and time
Second	Returns the second of the minute
Time	Returns the variant representation of the Date subtype of the current time
TimeSerial	Returns the variant representation of the Date subtype for a given hour, minute, and second
TimeValue	Returns the variant representation of the Date subtype containing the time
Weekday	Returns a number representing the day of the week
Year	Returns the year

Conversion

Table C.11. Conversion functions.

Function	Description
CBool	Returns a Variant expression converted to the Boolean subtype
CByte	Returns a Variant expression converted to the Byte subtype

continues

Table C.11. continued

Function	Description
CDate	Returns a Variant expression converted to the Date subtype
CDbl	Returns a Variant expression converted to the Double subtype
CInt	Returns a Variant expression converted to the Integer subtype
CLng	Returns a Variant expression converted to the Long subtype
CSng	Returns a Variant expression converted to the Single subtype
CStr	Returns a Variant expression converted to the String subtype

Text

Table C.12. Text functions.

Function	Description
Asc	Returns the ANSI character code for the first letter of a string
Chr	Returns the character associated with the given ANSI code
InStr	Returns the character position of the first occurrence of one string within another
InStr	Returns the byte position of the first occurrence of one string within another
LCase	Returns a string converted to all lowercase letters
Left	Returns a specified number of letters from the left side of a string
Len	Returns the number of letters in a string or the number of bytes required to store a variable
LTrim	Returns a string without leading spaces
Mid	Returns a specified number of characters from a string
Right	Returns a specified number of characters from the right side of a string
RTrim	Returns a string without trailing spaces
StrComp	Returns a value indicating the results of a string comparison
String	Returns a repeating character string of the specified length
Trim	Returns a string without both leading and trailing spaces
UCase	Returns a string converted to all uppercase letters

Variable

Table C.13. Functions for testing variables.

Function	Description
IsArray	Returns a Boolean value that indicates whether the variable is an array
IsDate	Returns a Boolean value that indicates whether the expression can be converted to a date
IsError	Returns a Boolean value that indicates whether the expression is an error value
IsEmpty	Returns a Boolean value that indicates whether the variable is initialized
IsNull	Returns a Boolean value that indicates whether the expression contains no valid data
IsNumeric	Returns a Boolean value that indicates whether the expression can be evaluated as a number
IsObject	Returns a Boolean value that indicates whether the expression references a valid OLE Automation object
VarType	Returns a number that indicates the variable's subtype

Array

Table C.14. Array functions.

Function	Description
LBound	Returns the lower boundary of an array
UBound	Returns the upper boundary of an array

APPENDIX

D

JavaScript Reference

You can calculate, manipulate text, and perform other procedures using JavaScript's operators and built-in functions. This appendix is a reference to JavaScript's operators and built-in functions. JavaScript also has about 23 built-in objects. Most of the objects are beyond the scope of this book. However, refer to a JavaScript reference to learn about the String, Math, and Date objects.

Operators

Tables D.1 through D.8 summarize the operators.

Table D.1. Unary operators.

Operator	Description
-	Negation
++	Increment
—	Decrement
~	Bitwise complement
!	Not

Table D.2. Arithmetic operators.

Operator	Description
+	Addition
-	Subtraction
/	Division
%	Modulo
^	Exponentiation
*	Multiplication

Table D.3. Assignment operators.

Object	Description
=	Assign
+=	Add, then assign
-=	Subtract, then assign

Object	Description
*=	Multiply, then assign
/=	Divide, then assign
%=	Modulus, then assign
&=	Bitwise AND, then assign
¦=	Bitwise OR, then assign
^=	Bitwise exclusive OR, then assign
<<=	Bitwise shift left, then assign
>>=	Bitwise shift right, then assign
>>>=	Bitwise unsigned shift right, then assign

Table D.4. Bitwise logical operators.

Object	Event Handler
&	Conjugation (AND)
¦	Disjunction (OR)
^	Exclusion (XOR)
~	Negation (NOT)

Table D.5. Bitwise shift operators.

Object	Event Handler
<<	Left shift
>>	Sign-propagating right shift
>>>	Zero-fill right shift

Table D.6. Logical operators.

Object	Event Handler
&&	Conjugation (AND)
¦¦	Disjunction (OR)
!	Negation (NOT)

Table D.7. String operators.

Operator	Description
+	Concatenation

Table D.8. Comparison operators.

Object	Description
<	Less than
<=	Less than or equal to
>	Greater than
>=	Greater than or equal to
!=	Not equal
==	Equal

Statements

Table D.9. Miscellaneous statements.

Statement	Description
break	Terminate execution of the current `for` or `while` loop and pass control to the first statement after the loop.
comment	Comment you add that is ignored by the JavaScript interpreter.
continue	Pass control to the condition in a `while` loop and to the update expression in a `for` loop.
function	Declare a function.
return	Specify a value to be returned by a function.
var	Declare a variable.
with	Establish a default object for a set of statements.

Table D.10. Program control statements.

Statement	Description
for	Repeat a block of statements a specified number of times.
if...else	Decide between executing different blocks of statements, depending on the value of an expression.
while	Execute a block of statements as long as a given condition is true.

Functions

In contrast to VBScript, JavaScript has a very small set of built-in functions (see Table D.11). However, several of the functions found in VBScript are found as methods of three objects built into JavaScript: the String, Math, and Date objects. The objects are beyond the scope of this book. Find information on these objects in any good JavaScript reference.

Table D.11. JavaScript built-in functions.

Function	Description
escape	Convert to the HTML escape code convention.
unEscape	Convert from the HTML escape code convention.
eval	Evaluate a string as a JavaScript expression and return the expression's result.
parseFloat	Parse a string as a floating-point number.
parseInt	Parse a string as an integer.

APPENDIX

E

HTML Quick Reference

This appendix is a reference to the HTML tags you can use in your documents. Unless otherwise noted, all the tags listed here are supported by both Microsoft Explorer 3.0 and Netscape Navigator 3.0. Note that some other browsers do not support all the tags listed, and some of the tags, listed as (MS), may also be supported in the final shipping version of Netscape 3.0.

The proposed HTML style sheet specification is not covered here. Refer to the Netscape (http://home.netscape.com/) or Microsoft (http://www.microsoft.com/) Web sites for details on this and other late-breaking changes to the new HTML 3.2 standard.

HTML Tags

These tags are used to create a basic HTML page with text, headings, and lists. An (MS) beside the attribute indicates Microsoft.

Comments

`<! ... >`	Creates a comment. Can also be used to hide JavaScript from browsers that do not support it.
`<COMMENT>...</COMMENT>`	The new official way of specifying comments.

Structure Tags

`<HTML>...</HTML>`	Encloses the entire HTML document.
`<HEAD>...</HEAD>`	Encloses the head of the HTML document.
`<BODY>...</BODY>`	Encloses the body (text and tags) of the HTML document.

Attributes:

`BACKGROUND="..."`	The name or URL of the image to tile on the page background.
`BGCOLOR="..."`	The color of the page background.
`TEXT="..."`	The color of the page's text.
`LINK="..."`	The color of unfollowed links.
`ALINK="..."`	The color of activated links.
`VLINK="..."`	The color of followed links.
`BGPROPERTIES="..."` (MS)	Properties of background image. Currently allows only the value FIXED, which prevents the background image from scrolling.
`TOPMARGIN="..."` (MS)	Top margin of the page, in pixels.
`BOTTOMMARGIN="..."` (MS)	Bottom margin of the page, in pixels.
`<BASE>`	Indicates the full URL of the current document. This optional tag is used within `<HEAD>`.

Attributes:

`HREF="..."`	The full URL of this document.
`<ISINDEX>`	Indicates that this document is a gateway script that allows searches.

Attributes:

`PROMPT="..."`	The prompt for the search field.
`ACTION="..."`	Gateway program to which the search string should be passed.
`<LINK>`	Indicates a link between this document and some other document. Generally used only by HTML-generating tools. `<LINK>` represents a link from this entire document to another, as opposed to `<A>`, which can create multiple links in the document. Not commonly used.

Attributes:

`HREF="..."`	The URL of the document to call when the link is activated.
`NAME="..."`	If the document is to be considered an anchor, the name of that anchor.
`REL="..."`	The relationship between the linked-to document and the current document—for example, `"TOC"` or `"Glossary"`.
`REV="..."`	A reverse relationship between the current document and the linked-to document.
`URN="..."`	A Uniform Resource Number (URN), a unique identifier different from the URL in HREF.
`TITLE="..."`	The title of the linked-to document.
`METHODS="..."`	The method with which the document is to be retrieved—for example, FTP, Gopher, and so on.
`<META>`	Indicates meta-information about this document (information about the document itself)—for example, keywords for search engines, special HTTP headers to be used for retrieving this document, expiration date, and so on. Meta-information is usually in a key/value pair form. Used in the document `<HEAD>`.

Attributes:

`HTTP-EQUIV="..."`	Creates a new HTTP header field with the same name as the attribute's value—for

	example, HTTP-EQUIV="Expires". The value of that header is specified by the CONTENT attribute.
NAME="..."	If meta data is usually in the form of key/value pairs, NAME indicates the key—for example, Author or ID.
CONTENT="..."	The content of the key/value pair (or of the HTTP header indicated by HTTP-EQUIV).
<NEXTID>	Indicates the "next" document to this one (as might be defined by a tool to manage HTML documents in series). <NEXTID> is considered obsolete.
<H1>...</H1>	A first-level heading.
<H2>...</H2>	A second-level heading.
<H3>...</H3>	A third-level heading.
<H4>...</H4>	A fourth-level heading.
<H5>...</H5>	A fifth-level heading.
<H6>...</H6>	A sixth-level heading.
<TITLE>...</TITLE>	Indicates the title of the document. Used within <HEAD>.

All heading tags accept the following attributes:

Attributes:

ALIGN="..."	Possible values are CENTER, LEFT, and RIGHT.
<P>...</P>	A plain paragraph. The closing tag (</P>) is optional.

Attributes:

ALIGN="..."	Align text to CENTER, LEFT, or RIGHT.
<DIV>...</DIV>	A region of text to be formatted.

Attributes:

ALIGN="..."	Align text to CENTER, LEFT, or RIGHT.
<A>...</A>	With the HREF attribute, this creates a link to another document or anchor; with the NAME attribute, it creates an anchor that can be linked to.

Attributes:

HREF="..."	The URL of the document to be called when the link is activated.

NAME="..."	The name of the anchor.
REL="..."	The relationship between the linked-to document and the current document—for example, "TOC" or "Glossary" (not commonly used).
REV="..."	A reverse relationship between the current document and the linked-to document (not commonly used).
URN="..."	A Uniform Resource Number (URN), a unique identifier different from the URL in HREF (not commonly used).
TITLE="..."	The title of the linked-to document (not commonly used).
METHODS="..."	The method with which the document is to be retrieved—for example, FTP, Gopher, and so on (not commonly used).
TARGET="..."	The name of a frame in which the linked document should appear.

Lists

<OL>...</OL>	An ordered (numbered) list.

Attributes:

TYPE="..."	The type of numerals to label the list. Possible values are A, a, I, i, 1.
START="..."	The value with which to start this list.
...</UL>	An unordered (bulleted) list.

Attributes:

TYPE="..."	The bullet dingbat to use to mark list items. Possible values are DISC, CIRCLE (or ROUND), and SQUARE.
<MENU>...</MENU>	A menu list of items.
<DIR>...</DIR>	A directory listing; items are generally smaller than 20 characters.
<LI>	A list item for use with <OL>, <MENU>, or <DIR>.

Attributes:

TYPE="..."	The type of bullet or number with which to label this item. Possible values are DISC, CIRCLE (or ROUND), SQUARE, A, a, I, i, 1.

`VALUE="..."`	The numeric value this list item should have (affects this item and all below it in `<OL>` lists).
`<DL>...</DL>`	A definition or glossary list.

Attributes:

`COMPACT`	The `COMPACT` attribute specifies a formatting that takes less whitespace to present.
`<DT>`	A definition term, as part of a definition list.
`<DD>`	The corresponding definition to a definition term, as part of a definition list.

Character Formatting

`<EM>...</EM>`	Emphasis (usually italic).
`<STRONG>...</STRONG>`	Stronger emphasis (usually bold).
`<CODE>...</CODE>`	Code sample (usually Courier).
`<KBD>...</KBD>`	Text to be typed (usually Courier).
`<VAR>...</VAR>`	A variable or placeholder for some other value.
`<SAMP>...</SAMP>`	Sample text (seldom used).
`<DFN>...<DFN>`	A definition of a term.
`<CITE>...</CITE>`	A citation.
`<B>...</B>`	Boldface text.
`<I>...</I>`	Italic text.
`<TT>...</TT>`	Typewriter (monospaced) font.
`<PRE>...</PRE>`	Preformatted text (exact line endings and spacing will be preserved—usually rendered in a monospaced font).
`<BIG>...</BIG>`	Text is slightly larger than normal.
`<SMALL>...</SMALL>`	Text is slightly smaller than normal.
`<SUB>...</SUB>`	Subscript.
`<SUP>...</SUP>`	Superscript.
`<STRIKE>...</STRIKE>`	Puts a strikethrough line in the text.

Other Elements

`<HR>`	A horizontal rule line.

Attributes:

SIZE="..."	The thickness of the rule, in pixels.
WIDTH="..."	The width of the rule, in pixels or as a percentage of the document width.
ALIGN="..."	How the rule line will be aligned on the page. Possible values are LEFT, RIGHT, and CENTER.
NOSHADE	Causes the rule line to be drawn as a solid line instead of a transparent bevel.
COLOR="..." (MS)	Color of the horizontal rule.
 	A line break.

Attributes:

CLEAR="..."	Causes the text to stop flowing around any images. Possible values are RIGHT, LEFT, and ALL.
<NOBR>...</NOBR>	Causes the enclosed text not to wrap at the edge of the page.
<WBR>	Wraps the text at this point only if necessary.
<BLOCKQUOTE>...</BLOCKQUOTE>	Used for long quotes or citations.
<ADDRESS>...</ADDRESS>	Used for signatures or general information about a document's author.
<CENTER>...</CENTER>	Centers text or images.
<BLINK>...</BLINK>	Causes the enclosed text to blink irritatingly.
<FONT>...</FONT>	Changes the size of the font for the enclosed text.

Attributes:

SIZE="..."	The size of the font, from 1 to 7. Default is 3. Can also be specified as a value relative to the current size—for example, +2.
COLOR="..."	Changes the color of the text.
FACE="..."(MS)	Name of font to use if it can be found on the user's system. Multiple font names can be separated by commas, and the first font on the list that can be found will be used.
<BASEFONT>	Sets the default size of the font for the current page.

Attributes:

SIZE="..."	The default size of the font, from 1 to 7. Default is 3.

E

Images, Sounds, and Embedded Media

`<IMG>`	Inserts an inline image into the document.

Attributes:

`ISMAP`	This image is a clickable image map.
`SRC="..."`	The URL of the image.
`ALT="..."`	A text string that will be displayed in browsers that cannot support images.
`ALIGN="..."`	Determines the alignment of the given image. If LEFT or RIGHT (N), the image is aligned to the left or right column, and all following text flows beside that image. All other values such as TOP, MIDDLE, BOTTOM, or the Netscape-only TEXTTOP, ABSMIDDLE, BASELINE, ABSBOTTOM determine the vertical alignment of this image with other items in the same line.
`VSPACE="..."`	The space between the image and the text above or below it.
`HSPACE="..."`	The space between the image and the text to its left or right.
`WIDTH="..."`	The width, in pixels, of the image. If WIDTH is not the actual width, the image is scaled to fit.
`HEIGHT="..."`	The height, in pixels, of the image. If HEIGHT is not the actual height, the image is scaled to fit.
`BORDER="..."`	Draws a border of the specified value in pixels around the image. In the case of images that are also links, BORDER changes the size of the default link border.
`LOWSRC="..."`	The path or URL of an image that will be loaded first, before the image specified in SRC. The value of LOWSRC is usually a smaller or lower resolution version of the actual image.
`USEMAP="..."`	The name of an image map specification for client-side image mapping. Used with `<MAP>` and `<AREA>`.
`DYNSRC="..."` (MS)	The address of a video clip or VRML world (dynamic source).
`CONTROLS` (MS)	Used with DYNSRC to display a set of playback controls for inline video.
`LOOP="..."` (MS)	The number of times a video clip will loop. (-1 or INFINITE means to loop indefinitely.)

START="..." (MS)	When a DYNSRC video clip should start playing. Valid options are FILEOPEN (play when page is displayed) or MOUSEOVER (play when mouse cursor passes over the video clip).
<BGSOUND> (MS)	Plays a sound file as soon as the page is displayed.

Attributes:

SRC="..."	The URL of the WAV, AU, or MIDI sound file to embed.
LOOP="..." (MS)	The number of times a video clip will loop. (-1 or INFINITE means to loop indefinitely.)
<OBJECT> (MS)	Inserts an image, video, Java applet, or ActiveX OLE control into a document.

NOTE

> The full syntax for the <OBJECT> tag is not yet finalized. Check http://
> www.w3.org/pub/WWW/TR/WD-object.html and http://
> www.microsoft.com/intdev/author/ for the latest attributes supported
> by the HTML 3.2 standard and implemented in Microsoft Internet
> Explorer.

<EMBED> (Netscape only!)	Embeds a file to be read or displayed by a plug-in application.

NOTE

> In addition to the following standard attributes, you can specify applet-
> specific attributes to be interpreted by the plug-in that displays the
> embedded object.

Attributes:

SRC="..."	The URL of the file to embed.
WIDTH="..."	The width of the embedded object, in pixels.
HEIGHT="..."	The height of the embedded object, in pixels.
ALIGN="..."	Determines the alignment of the media window. Values are the same as for the <IMG> tag.
VSPACE="..."	The space between the media and the text above or below it.
HSPACE="..."	The space between the media and the text to its left or right.

E

BORDER="..."	Draws a border of the specified size in pixels around the media.
<NOEMBED>...</NOEMBED> (N)	Alternate text or images to be shown to users who do not have a plug-in installed.
<OBJECT> (MS)	Inserts an embedded program, control, or other object. (This tag was under revision when this book was printed.)
<MAP>...</MAP>	A client-side image map, referenced by <IMG USEMAP="...">. Includes one or more <AREA> tags.
<AREA>	Defines a clickable link within a client-side image map.

Attributes:

SHAPE="..."	The shape of the clickable area. Currently, only RECT is supported.
COORDS="..."	The left, top, right, and bottom coordinates of the clickable region within an image.
HREF="..."	The URL that should be loaded when the area is clicked.
NOHREF	Indicates that no action should be taken when this area of the image is clicked.

Forms

<FORM>...</FORM>	Indicates an input form.

Attributes:

ACTION="..."	The URL of the script to process this form input.
METHOD="..."	How the form input will be sent to the gateway on the server side. Possible values are GET and POST.
ENCTYPE="..."	Normally has the value application/x-www-form-urlencoded. For file uploads, use multipart/form-data.
NAME="..."	A name by which JavaScript scripts can refer to the form.
<INPUT>	An input element for a form.

Attributes:

TYPE="..."	The type for this input widget. Possible values are CHECKBOX, HIDDEN, RADIO, RESET, SUBMIT, TEXT, SEND FILE, or IMAGE.

NAME="..."	The name of this item, as passed to the gateway script as part of a name/value pair.
VALUE="..."	For a text or hidden widget, the default value; for a checkbox or radio button, the value to be submitted with the form; for Reset or Submit buttons, the label for the button itself.
SRC="..."	The source file for an image.
CHECKED	For checkboxes and radio buttons, indicates that the widget is checked.
SIZE="..."	The size, in characters, of a text widget.
MAXLENGTH="..."	The maximum number of characters that can be entered into a text widget.
ALIGN="..."	For images in forms, determines how the text and image will align (same as with the <IMG> tag).
<TEXTAREA>...</TEXTAREA>	Indicates a multiline text entry form element. Default text can be included.

Attributes:

NAME="..."	The name to be passed to the gateway script as part of the name/value pair.
ROWS="..."	The number of rows this text area displays.
COLS="..."	The number of columns (characters) this text area displays.
WRAP="..." (N)	Control text wrapping. Possible values are OFF, VIRTUAL, and PHYSICAL.
<SELECT>...</SELECT>	Creates a menu or scrolling list of possible items.

Attributes:

NAME="..."	The name that is passed to the gateway script as part of the name/value pair.
SIZE="..."	The number of elements to display. If SIZE is indicated, the selection becomes a scrolling list. If no SIZE is given, the selection is a pop-up menu.
MULTIPLE	Allows multiple selections from the list.
<OPTION>	Indicates a possible item within a <SELECT> element.

Attributes:

SELECTED	With this attribute included, the <OPTION> will be selected by default in the list.
VALUE="..."	The value to submit if this <OPTION> is selected when the form is submitted.

E

Tables

`<TABLE>...</TABLE>`	Creates a table that can contain a caption (`<CAPTION>`) and any number of rows (`<TR>`).

Attributes:

`BORDER="..."`	Indicates whether the table should be drawn with or without a border. In Netscape, `BORDER` can also have a value indicating the width of the border.
`CELLSPACING="..."`	The amount of space between the cells in the table.
`CELLPADDING="..."`	The amount of space between the edges of the cell and its contents.
`WIDTH="..."`	The width of the table on the page, either in exact pixel values or as a percentage of page width.
`ALIGN="..."` (MS)	Alignment (works like `IMG ALIGN`). Values are `LEFT` or `RIGHT`.
`BACKGROUND="..."` (MS)	Background image to tile within all cells in the table that do not contain their own `BACKGROUND` or `BGCOLOR` attribute.
`BGCOLOR="..."` (MS)	Background color of all cells in the table that do not contain their own `BACKGROUND` or `BGCOLOR` attribute.
`BORDERCOLOR="..."` (MS)	Border color (used with `BORDER="..."`).
`BORDERCOLORLIGHT="..."` (MS)	Color for light part of 3D-look borders (used with `BORDER="..."`).
`BORDERCOLORDARK="..."` (MS)	Color for dark part of 3D-look borders (used with `BORDER="..."`).
`VALIGN="..."` (MS)	Alignment of text within the table. Values are `TOP` and `BOTTOM`.
`FRAME="..."` (MS)	Controls which external borders will appear around a table. Values are `"void"` (no frames), `"above"` (top border only), `"below"` (bottom border only), `"hsides"` (top and bottom), `"lhs"` (left hand side), `"rhs"` (right hand side), `"vsides"` (left and right sides), and `"box"` (all sides).
`RULES="..."` (MS)	Controls which internal borders appear in the table. Values are `"none"`, `"basic"` (rules between `THEAD`, `TBODY`, and `TFOOT` only), `"rows"`

	(horizontal borders only), "cols" (vertical borders only), and "all".
`<CAPTION>...</CAPTION>`	The caption for the table.

Attributes:

`ALIGN="..."`	The position of the caption. Possible values are TOP and BOTTOM.
`<TR>...</TR>`	Defines a table row, containing headings and data (`<TR>` and tags).

Attributes:

`ALIGN="..."`	The horizontal alignment of the contents of the cells within this row. Possible values are LEFT, RIGHT, and CENTER.
`VALIGN="..."`	The vertical alignment of the contents of the cells within this row. Possible values are TOP, MIDDLE, BOTTOM, and BASELINE.
`BACKGROUND="..."` (MS)	Background image to tile within all cells in the row that do not contain their own BACKGROUND or BGCOLOR attributes.
`BGCOLOR="..."`	Background color of all cells in the row that do not contain their own BACKGROUND or BGCOLOR attributes.
`BORDERCOLOR="..."` (MS)	Border color (used with BORDER="...").
`BORDERCOLORLIGHT="..."` (MS)	Color for light part of 3D-look borders (used with BORDER="...").
`BORDERCOLORDARK="..."` (MS)	Color for dark part of 3D-look borders (used with BORDER="...").
`...</TH>`	Defines a table heading cell.

Attributes:

`ALIGN="..."`	The horizontal alignment of the contents of the cell. Possible values are LEFT, RIGHT, and CENTER.
`VALIGN="..."`	The vertical alignment of the contents of the cell. Possible values are TOP, MIDDLE, BOTTOM, and BASELINE.
`ROWSPAN="..."`	The number of rows this cell will span.
`COLSPAN="..."`	The number of columns this cell will span.
`NOWRAP`	Does not automatically wrap the contents of this cell.
`WIDTH="..."`	The width of this column of cells, in exact pixel values or as a percentage of the table width.

E

BACKGROUND="..." (MS)	Background image to tile within the cell.
BGCOLOR="..." (MS)	Background color of the cell.
BORDERCOLOR="..." (MS)	Border color (used with BORDER="...").
BORDERCOLORLIGHT="..." (MS)	Color for light part of 3D-look borders (used with BORDER="...").
BORDERCOLORDARK="..." (MS)	Color for dark part of 3D-look borders (used with BORDER="...").
<TD>...</TD>	Defines a table data cell.

Attributes:

ALIGN="..."	The horizontal alignment of the contents of the cell. Possible values are LEFT, RIGHT, and CENTER.
VALIGN="..."	The vertical alignment of the contents of the cell. Possible values are TOP, MIDDLE, BOTTOM, and BASELINE.
ROWSPAN="..."	The number of rows this cell will span.
COLSPAN="..."	The number of columns this cell will span.
NOWRAP	Does not automatically wrap the contents of this cell.
WIDTH="..."	The width of this column of cells, in exact pixel values or as a percentage of the table width.
BACKGROUND="..." (MS)	Background image to tile within the cell.
BGCOLOR="..." (MS)	Background color of the cell.
BORDERCOLOR="..." (MS)	Border color (used with BORDER="...").
BORDERCOLORLIGHT="..." (MS)	Color for light part of 3D-look borders (used with BORDER="...").
<THEAD> (MS)	Begins the header section of a table. The closing </THEAD> tag is optional.
<TBODY> (MS)	Begins the body section of a table. The closing </TBODY> tag is optional.

Attributes:

<TFOOT> (MS)	Begins the footer section of a table. The closing </TFOOT> tag is optional.
<COL>...</COL> (MS)	Sets width and alignment properties for one or more columns.
WIDTH="..."	Width of column(s) in pixels or relative width followed by a * ("2*" columns will be twice as wide as "1*" columns, for example).
ALIGN="..."	Text alignment within the column(s). Valid values are "center", "justify", "left", and "right".

| `SPAN="..."` | Number of columns to which the properties specified in this `<COL>` tag apply. |
| `<COLGROUP>...</COLGROUP>` | Sets properties of a group of columns all at once (should enclose one or more `<COL>` tags). |

Attributes:

| `ALIGN="..."` | Text alignment within the columns. Valid values are `"center"`, `"justify"`, `"left"`, and `"right"`. |
| `VALIGN="..."` | Vertical alignment of text within the columns. Valid values are `"baseline"`, `"bottom"`, `"middle"`, and `"top"`. |

Frames

| `<FRAMESET>...</FRAMESET>` | Divides the main window into a set of frames that can each display a separate document. |

Attributes:

`ROWS="..."`	Splits the window or frameset vertically into a number of rows specified by a number (such as 7), a percentage of the total window width (such as 25%), or as an asterisk (*) indicating that a frame should take up all the remaining space or divide the space evenly between frames (if multiple * frames are specified).
`COLS="..."`	Works similarly to ROWS, except that the window or frameset is split horizontally into columns.
`<FRAME>`	Defines a single frame within a `<FRAMESET>`.

Attributes:

`SRC="..."`	The URL of the document to be displayed in this frame.
`NAME="..."`	A name to be used for targeting this frame with the TARGET attribute in `<A HREF>` links.
`<MARGINWIDTH>`	The amount of space to leave to the left and right side of a document within a frame, in pixels.
`<MARGINHEIGHT>`	The amount of space to leave above and below a document within a frame, in pixels.
`SCROLLING="..."`	Determines whether a frame has scrollbars. Possible values are YES, NO, and AUTO.

E

NORESIZE	Prevents the user from resizing this frame (and possibly adjacent frames) with the mouse.
FRAMEBORDER="..." (MS)	Specifies whether to display a border for a frame. Options are YES and NO.
FRAMESPACING="..." (MS)	Space between frames, in pixels.
</NOFRAME>...</NOFRAMES>	Provides an alternative document body in <FRAMESET> documents for browsers that do not support frames (usually encloses <BODY>... </BODY>).

Scripting and Applets

<APPLET>	Inserts a self-running Java applet.

Attributes:

NOTE   In addition to the following standard attributes, you can specify applet-specific attributes to be interpreted by the Java applet itself.

CLASS="..."	The name of the applet.
SRC="..."	The URL of the directory where the compiled applet can be found (should end in a slash (/) as in "http://mysite/myapplets/"). Do not include the actual applet name, which is specified with the CLASS attribute.
ALIGN="..."	Indicates how the applet should be aligned with any text that follows it. Current values are TOP, MIDDLE, and BOTTOM.
WIDTH="..."	The width of the applet output area, in pixels.
HEIGHT="..."	The height of the applet output area, in pixels.
<SCRIPT>	An interpreted script program.

Attributes:

LANGUAGE="..."	Currently only JAVASCRIPT is supported by Netscape. Both JAVASCRIPT and VBSCRIPT are supported by Microsoft.
SRC="..."	Specifies the URL of a file that includes the script program.

Marquees

`<MARQUEE>...</MARQUEE>` (MS)	Displays text in a scrolling marquee.

Attributes:

`WIDTH="..."`	The width of the embedded object in pixels or percentage of window width.
`HEIGHT="..."`	The height of the embedded object in pixels or percentage of window height.
`ALIGN="..."`	Determines the alignment of the text *outside* the marquee. Values are TOP, MIDDLE, and BOTTOM.
`BORDER="..."`	Draws a border of the specified size in pixels around the media.
`BEHAVIOR="..."`	How the text inside the marquee should behave. Options are SCROLL (continuous scrolling), SLIDE (slide text in and stop), and ALTERNATE (bounce back and forth).
`BGCOLOR="..."`	Background color for the marquee.
`DIRECTION="..."`	Direction for text to scroll (LEFT or RIGHT).
`VSPACE="..."`	Space above and below the marquee, in pixels.
`HSPACE="..."`	Space on each side of the marquee, in pixels.
`SCROLLAMOUNT="..."`	Number of pixels to move each time text in the marquee is redrawn.
`SCROLLDELAY="..."`	Number of milliseconds between each redraw of marquee text.
`LOOP="..."` (MS)	The number of times marquee will loop. (-1 or INFINITE means to loop indefinitely.)

Character Entities

Table E.1 contains the possible numeric and character entities for the ISO-Latin-1 (ISO8859-1) character set. Where possible, the character is shown.

NOTE

Not all browsers can display all characters, and some browsers may even display characters different from those that appear in the table. Newer browsers seem to have a better track record for handling character entities, but be sure to test your HTML files extensively with multiple browsers if you intend to use these entities.

Table E.1. ISO-Latin-1 character set.

Character	Numeric Entity	Character Entity	Description
	&#00;-&#08;		Unused
	&#09;		Horizontal tab
	&#10;		Line feed
	&#11; &#31;		Unused
	&#32;		Space
!	&#33;		Exclamation mark
"	&#34;	&quot;	Quotation mark
#	&#35;		Number sign
$	&#36;		Dollar sign
%	&#37;		Percent sign
&	&#38;	&amp;	Ampersand
'	&#39;		Apostrophe
(	&#40;		Left parenthesis
)	&#41;		Right parenthesis
*	&#42;		Asterisk
+	&#43;		Plus sign
,	&#44;		Comma
-	&#45;		Hyphen
.	&#46;		Period (fullstop)
/	&#47;		Solidus (slash)
0—9	&#48;	&#57;	Digits 0-9
:	&#58;		Colon
;	&#59;		Semicolon
<	&#60;	&lt;	Less than
=	&#61;		Equals sign
>	&#62;	&gt;	Greater than
?	&#63;		Question mark
@	&#64;		Commercial "at"
A—Z	A-Z		Letters A-Z
[	&#91;		Left square bracket
\	&#92;		Reverse solidus (backslash)

]	&#93;		Right square bracket
^	&#94;		Caret
—	&#95;		Horizontal bar
'	&#96;		Grave accent
a – z	a z		Letters a-z
{	&#123;		Left curly brace
¦	&#124		Vertical bar
}	&#125;		Right curly brace
~	&#126;		Tilde
	&#127;		Unused
¡	&#161;	&iexcl;	Inverted exclamation
¢	&#162;	&cent;	Cent sign
£	&#163;	&pound;	Pound sterling
_	&#164;	&curren;	General currency sign
¥	&#165;	&yen;	Yen sign
¦	&#166;	¦ or brkbar;	Broken vertical bar
§	&#167;	&sect;	Section sign
_	&#168;	&uml;	Umlaut (dieresis)
©	&#169;	&copy;	Copyright
ª	&#170;	&ordf;	Feminine ordinal
_	&#171;	&laquo;	Left angle quote, guillemot left
^	&#172;	&not;	Not sign
-	&#173;	&shy;	Soft hyphen
®	&#174;	&reg;	Registered trademark
_	&#175;	&hibar;	Macron accent
°	&#176;	&deg;	Degree sign
±	&#177;	&plusmn;	Plus or minus
k	&#178;	&sup2;	Superscript two
l	&#179;	&sup3;	Superscript three
_	&#180;	&acute;	Acute accent
µ	&#181;	&micro;	Micro sign
¶	&#182;	&para;	Paragraph sign

continues

Table E.1. continued

Character	Numeric Entity	Character Entity	Description
·	&#183;	&middot;	Middle dot
,	&#184;	&cedil;	Cedilla
1	&#185;	&sup1;	Superscript one
º	&#186;	&ordm;	Masculine ordinal
–	&#187;	&raquo;	Right angle quote, guillemot right
1/4	&#188;	&frac14;	Fraction one-fourth
1/2	&#189;	&frac12;	Fraction one-half
3/4	&#190;	&frac34;	Fraction three-fourths
¿	&#191;	&iquest	Inverted question mark
–	&#192;	&Agrave;	Capital A, grave accent
–	&#193;	&Aacute;	Capital A, acute accent
–	&#194;	&Acirc;	Capital A, circumflex accent
–	&#195;	&Atilde;	Capital A, tilde
Ä	&#196;	&Auml;	Capital A, dieresis or umlaut mark
Å	&#197;	&Aring;	Capital A, ring
Æ	&#198;	&AElig;	Capital AE diphthong (ligature)
Ç	&#199;	&Ccedil;	Capital C, cedilla
–	&#200;	&Egrave;	Capital E, grave accent
É	&#201;	&Eacute;	Capital E, acute accent
–	&#202;	&Ecirc;	Capital E, circumflex accent
–	&#203;	&Euml;	Capital E, dieresis or umlaut mark
–	&#204;	&Igrave;	Capital I, grave accent
–	&#205;	&Iacute;	Capital I, acute accent
–	&#206;	&Icirc;	Capital I, circumflex accent
–	&#207;	&Iuml;	Capital I, dieresis or umlaut mark

Ð	&#208;	&ETH;	Capital Eth, Icelandic
Ñ	&#209;	&Ntilde;	Capital N, tilde
Ò	&#210;	&Ograve;	Capital O, grave accent
Ó	&#211;	&Oacute;	Capital O, acute accent
Ô	&#212;	&Ocirc;	Capital O, circumflex accent
Õ	&#213;	&Otilde;	Capital O, tilde
Ö	&#214;	&Ouml;	Capital O, dieresis or umlaut mark
×	&#215;		Multiply sign
Ø	&#216;	&Oslash;	Capital O, slash
Ù	&#217;	&Ugrave;	Capital U, grave accent
Ú	&#218;	&Uacute;	Capital U, acute accent
Û	&#219;	&Ucirc;	Capital U, circumflex accent
Ü	&#220;	&Uuml;	Capital U, dieresis or umlaut mark
Ý	&#221;	&Yacute;	Capital Y, acute accent
Þ	&#222;	&THORN;	Capital THORN, Icelandic
β	&#223;	&szlig;	Small sharp s, German (szligature)
à	&#224;	&agrave;	Small a, grave accent
á	&#225;	&aacute;	Small a, acute accent
â	&#226;	&acirc;	Small a, circumflex accent
ã	&#227;	&atilde;	Small a, tilde
ä	&#228;	&aauml;	Small a, dieresis or umlaut mark
å	&#229;	&aring;	Small a, ring
æ	&#230;	&aelig;	Small ae diphthong (ligature)
ç	&#231;	&ccedil;	Small c, cedilla
è	&#232;	&egrave;	Small e, grave accent
é	&#233;	&eacute;	Small e, acute accent

continues

Table E.1. continued

Character	Numeric Entity	Character Entity	Description
ê	&#234;	&ecirc;	Small e, circumflex accent
ë	&#235;	&euml;	Small e, dieresis or umlaut mark
ì	&#236;	&igrave;	Small i, grave accent
í	&#237;	&iacute;	Small i, acute accent
î	&#238;	&icirc;	Small i, circumflex accent
ï	&#239;	&iuml;	Small i, dieresis or umlaut mark
u	&#240;	&eth;	Small eth, Icelandic
ñ	&#241;	&ntilde;	Small n, tilde
ò	&#242;	&ograve;	Small o, grave accent
ó	&#243;	&oacute;	Small o, acute accent
ô	&#244;	&ocirc;	Small o, circumflex accent
_	&#245;	&otilde;	Small o, tilde
ö	&#246;	&ouml;	Small o, dieresis or umlaut mark
-	&#247;		Division sign
ø	&#248;	&oslash;	Small o, slash
ù	&#249;	&ugrave;	Small u, grave accent
ú	&#250;	&uacute;	Small u, acute accent
û	&#251;	&ucirc;	Small u, circumflex accent
ü	&#252;	&uuml;	Small u, dieresis or umlaut mark
_y	&#253;	&yacute;	Small y, acute accent
w	&#254;	&thorn;	Small thorn, Icelandic
ÿ	&#255;	&yuml;	Small y, dieresis or umlaut mark

Directory of Sites and Resources

Directory of Sites and Resources

The following is a list of Web sites explaining or demonstrating the advanced features of Internet Explorer. A number of sites that don't focus specifically on Internet Explorer are also included. You can type the URL addresses into Internet Explorer's Location box.

ActiveX

http://www.microsoft.com/ie/appdev/controls/default.htm
Download the ActiveX controls and visit Microsoft's ActiveX gallery

http://www.microsoft.com/intdev/sdk/
ActiveX Software Development Kit

http://nihal02.cdc.deakin.edu.au/cdcsoft/emadweb/xtest.htm
ActiveX demo page

http://www.sky.net/~toma/faq.htm
ActiveX FAQ

http://www.outrider.com/showcase/showcase.htm
Outrider ActiveX showcase

Art Museums and Galleries

http://www.art.net/
Art on the Net

http://linex.com/mdhand/artGallery.html
3D Gallery

http://www.initiative.com/virtual.html
Virtual Museum

http://sunsite.unc.edu/wm/
The Web Museum

http://wwar.com/index.html
World Wide Arts Resources

Audio Players

`http://www.buddy.org/softlib.html`
The Buddy Sound Editor Software Library

`http://www.realaudio.com`
RealAudio

`http://www.xingtech.com`
Streamworks Audio

`http://www.vocaltec.com/iwave.htm`
Iwave

`http://www.dspg.com`
TrueSpeech

`http://www.prs.net/midi.html`
MidiGate

Audio Sites

`http://www.music.sony.com/Music/SoundClips/index.html`
Sony Music clips

`http://www.iuma.com`
Internet Underground Music Resource

`http://www.audionet.com`
AudioNet

`http://www.rockweb.com`
RockWeb

`http://www.prs.net/midi.html`
The Classical Music MIDI Archive

Books and Magazines

`http://www.promo.net/pg/`
Project Gutenberg: Electronic versions of classic texts

`http://sunsite.unc.edu/ibic/IBIC-homepage.html`
Internet Book Information Center: An electronic book club

F

`http://www.mcp.com`
Macmillan Publishing: Shop for computer books, cookbooks, and more right here

`http://www.zdnet.com/~pccomp/`
PC Computing: This popular computer magazine is now on the Web

`http://pathfinder.com/`
Pathfinder: Links to many popular magazines, including *Time* and *Sports Illustrated*

Business

`http://www2000.ogsm.vanderbilt.edu/intelligent.agent/index.html`
The Challenges of Electronic Commerce

`http://www.cbot.com`
Chicago Board of Trade

`http://www.ora.com/gnn/bus/ora/survey/index.html`
Defining the Internet Opportunity

`http://www.edgeonline.com/`
Entrepreneurial Edge Online

`http://www.irs.ustreas.gov/`
Internal Revenue Service: Find answers to your tax questions and download tax forms

`http://www.tig.com/cgi-bin/genobject/ibcindex`
The Internet Business Center

`http://www.hoaa.com/`
SoHo Central (Home Office Center): Visit this site to learn more about working out of your home

`http://www.cs.virginia.edu/~cd4v/graph/StockGraph.html`
Stock Trace

`http://update.wsj.com`
The Wall Street Journal

`http://www.net101.com/reasons.html`
20 reasons to put your business on the Web

CGI and Perl

`http://hoohoo.ncsa.uiuc.edu:80/cgi/overview.html`
CGI 1.1 specs

`http://home.mcom.com/newsref/std/server_api.html`
NSAPI specs

`http://www.ics.uci.edu/pub/ietf/http/draft-ietf-http-v10-spec-03.html`
Hypertext Transfer Protocol—HTTP/1.0 specification

`http://www.w3.org/hypertext/WWW/Protocols/HTTP/HTRESP.html`
Status codes

`http://hoohoo.ncsa.uiuc.edu/cgi/interface.html`
CGI 1.1 specification

`http://www.best.com:80/~hedlund/cgi-faq/new/faq.1-basic.html`
CGI FAQ

`http://www.boutell.com/cgic/`
cgic: An ANSI C library for CGI programming

`http://www.city.net/win-httpd/httpddoc/wincgi.htm`
Windows CGI 1.1 description

`http://solo.dc3.com/wsdocs/32demo/windows-cgi.html`
Windows CGI 1.3 (for reference only)

`http://solo.dc3.com/vb4cgi.html`
VB 4.0 (32-bit) CGI examples

`http://www.wolfenet.com/~rniles/cgi.html`
The CGI collection

`http://solo.dc3.com/db-src/index.html`
VB4/Access CGI programming

`http://home.netscape.com/comprod/server_central/config/nsapi.html`
Netscape API functions

`http://home.netscape.com/newsref/std/nsapi_vs_cgi.html`
NSAPI versus the CGI interface

`http://www.netscape.com/assist/support/server/tn/index.html`
Technical notes on CGI: Server-Side Includes (SSI) and NSAPI

`http://hoohoo.ncsa.uiuc.edu/docs/tutorials/includes.html`
Server-Side Includes (SSI)

`http://web.sau.edu/~mkruse/www/info/ssi.html`
Server-Side Includes (SSI) Tutorial

`http://www.yahoo.com/Computers_and_Internet/Languages/Perl/`
YAHOO!—Perl

`http://www.perl.com/perl/faq/`
Perl FAQ

`http://www.ee.pdx.edu/~rseymour/perl/`
Perl resources

`http://info.hip.com/ntperl/man-pages/ntperl5.htm`
Windows NT Perl 5

`http://www.phlab.missouri.edu/perl/perlcourse.html`
Introduction to Perl: Learn Perl in two hours

`http://www.oac.uci.edu/indiv/ehood/perlWWW/`
perlWWW: Earl Hood's extensive Perl collection

`http://www.eecs.nwu.edu/perl/perl.html`
Perl reference materials

Education

`http://www.scri.fsu.edu/~dennisl/CMS.html`
CyberSpace Middle School

`http://www.tc.cornell.edu/cgibin/Kids.on.Campus/top.pl`
Kids on Campus Internet Tour: Spur interest about computers and the Internet in
students from third to fourth grade

`http://curry.edschool.virginia.edu/insite/`
InSITE: A great place for teachers to learn how to use the Internet in their class-
rooms

`http://sln.fi.edu/`
Franklin Institute Virtual Science Museum

`http://quest.arc.nasa.gov/`
NASA's K-12 Initiative

Entertainment and Leisure

http://www.odci.gov/cia/publications/95fact/index.html
CIA World Factbook

http://www.comcentral.com/com-menu.htm
Comedy Central

http://www.unitedmedia.com/comics
The Comic Strip

http://www.twentymule.com/Fortune.acgi
Daily Fortune

http://www.unitedmedia.com/comics/dilbert/
Dilbert Comic Strip

http://www.unitedmedia.com/comics/drfun
Dr. Fun

http://www.exploratorium.edu/
Exploratorium Home Page

http://www.film.com
Film.com

http://hollywood.com/
Hollywood Online

http://www.msstate.edu/Movies/
Internet Movie Database-U.S. mirror site

http://moonmilk.volcano.org/
Moonmilk (How'd they do that??)

http://movieweb.com/movie.html
Movieweb

http://web3.starwave.com/showbiz
Mr. Showbiz

http://www.gsfc.nasa.gov/
NASA Home Page

http://netboy.com
NetBoy

```
http://www.nbc.com/entertainment/shows/seinfeld/index.html
```
NBC's Seinfeld Page

```
http://www.scifi.com
```
Sci-Fi Channel: The Dominion

```
http://www.si.edu/
```
Smithsonian Institution Home Page

```
http://www.cs.curtin.edu.au/~squizz/cryptics.html
```
Squizz's Cryptic Crosswords

```
http://www.netshop.net/Startrek/web/
```
Star Trek

```
http://tvnet.com/
```
TV Net

```
http://www-swiss.ai.mit.edu/webtravel/
```
Web Travel Review

```
http://www.whitehouse.gov/
```
The White House

Games

```
http://www.cs.uregina.ca/~hoyle/Games/
```
Bots and Games

```
http://www.clearlight.com/~vivi/xw/big.html
```
Online crossword puzzles

```
http://www.indirect.com/www/beetle87/rush/index.html
```
Beetle's Punch Rush Limbaugh Page

```
http://www.interplay.com/mudlist/
```
The MUD List

```
http://www.cni-inc.com/slot.html
```
Shockwave Slot Machine

Graphic Sites

`http://netletter.com/`
Dick Oliver's Nonlinear Nonsense Netletter

`http://netletter.com/cameo/hotlist/hotlist.html`
Texture and Background Wonderland

`http://fohnix.metronet.com/~kira/icongifs/`
Kira's icon library

`http://www.cbil.vcu.edu:8080/gifs/bullet.html`
Buttons, Cubes, and Bars

`http://www.vrl.com/Imaging/`
Imaging Machine

`http://fohnix.metronet.com/~kira/colors/`
256-color square

`http://www.netcreations.com/ramper/index.html`
Color Ramper

`http://www.artn.nwu.edu/`
(Art)^n

`http://www.art.net/Welcome.html`
Art on the Net

Graphic Viewers

`http://www.jasc.com`
Paint Shop Pro

`http://www.corel.com/corelcmx/`
Corel's CMX Viewer plug-in

`http://www.adobe.com`
Adobe Acrobat

`http://www.twcorp.com`
Envoy plug-in

F

Interactive Media

http://www.macromedia.com/Tools/Shockwave/index.html
Macromedia's Shockwave Page

http://www.macromedia.com/Tools/Director/index.html
Background on director "movies"

http://www.ncompasslabs.com/
NCompass ActiveX plug-in

Internet Directories

http://www.yahoo.com/
Yahoo!

http://www.nosc.mil/planet_earth/everything.html
Planet Earth Home Page

http://gnn.com/wic/wics/index.html
GNN Select

http://galaxy.einet.net/
TradeWave Galaxy

http://cool.infi.net/
Cool Site of the Day

http://www.ncsa.uiuc.edu/SDG/Software/Mosaic/MetaIndex.html
Internet Resources Meta-Index

http://www.eskimo.com/%7Eirving/web-voyeur/
Web Voyeur (live camera views)

http://www.commerce.net/directories/products/isp/
Internet Service Provider Directory

Internet Explorer Resources

http://www.clubie.com/
ClubIE: Informal group that gathers to discuss Microsoft's Internet products and strategies

http://www.microsoft.com/ie/

Internet Explorer Home Page

`http://www.microsoft.com/ie/addons/default.htm`
Internet Explorer 3.0 add-ons

`http://www.microsoft.com/ie/showcase/default.htm`
Internet Explorer 3.0 Showcase: Pages that demonstrate Internet Explorer 3.0's
newest Web technology

Internet Search Tools

`http://www.lycos.com/`
Lycos Search

`http://www.webcrawler.com/`
WebCrawler Searching

`http://www.cs.colorado.edu/home/mcbryan/WWWW.html`
World Wide Web Worm

`http://web.nexor.co.uk/public/aliweb/search/doc/form.html`
ALIWEB Search

`http://cuiwww.unige.ch/w3catalog`
CUI W3 Catalog

`http://www.infoseek.com/`
InfoSeek

`http://pubweb.nexor.co.uk/public/archie/servers.html`
Nexor's Archie List

`http://www.scs.unr.edu/veronica.html`
Veronica Home Access Page

F

Internet Security

`http://www.genome.wi.mit.edu/WWW/faqs/www-security-faq.html`
World Wide Web Security FAQ

`http://www.c2.org/hacknetscape/`
Hack Netscape

http://www.microsoft.com/IE/security/default.htm
Internet Explorer 3.0 Security

http://asearch.mccmedia.com/www-security.html
World Wide Web Security Messages

http://www.dstc.qut.edu.au/MSU/research_news/web_sec/NETSCAP1.HTM
Netscape's Secure Sockets Layer

Java

http://www.microsoft.com/ie/java/
Internet Explorer 3.0 Java Support

http://java.sun.com/
Center of the Java Universe

http://www.javasoft.com
Java Home Page

http://www.gamelan.com/
Gamelan—Java resource registry

http://www.hotwired.com/java Web site
HotWired's Java Page

http://www.applets.com
Java Applet Library

http://www.phoenixat.com/~warreng/soup.html
Soup's Up E-zine

http://www.earthweb.com
EarthWeb Java Development

Java Applets

http://www.cnet.com
Scrolling Text

http://www-elec.enst.fr/java/n/test.html
Three-Dimensional Cube

http://www.virtual-inn.co.uk/orbital/beta/adSpace
Advertising Space

http://www.acl.lanl.gov/~rdaniel/classesJDK/PickTest2.html
TeleMed

http://storm.atmos.uiuc.edu/java
The Weather Visualizer

http://www.umich.edu/~dov/webPoker
WebPoker

http://www.zorg.com
Zorg

http://www.dimensionx.com/chat/cafe.html
Cafe Chat

http://www.acm.uiuc.edu/webmonkeys/juggling
Learning to Juggle

http://www.sdsu.edu/~boyns/java/mc
Missile Commando

http://www.javasoft.com/JDK-prebeta1/applets/TicTacToe/example1.html
Tic-Tac-Toe

http://tech-www.informatik.uni-hamburg.de/dance/JDance.html
Learning to Dance

JavaScript Information

http://www.sna.com/mmatteo/Java/jscookies.html
Cookies with JavaScript

http://www-genome.wi.mit.edu/WWW/faqs/www-security-faq.html#java
JavaScript security

http://www.inquiry.com/techtips/js_pro/maillist.html
JavaScript mailing list

http://dezines.com/dezines/javalinks.html
DeZines Java/JavaScript directory

http://www.gamelan.com/noframe/Gamelan.javascript.html
Gamelan JavaScript directory

F

MIME File Types

http://www.oac.uci.edu/indiv/ehood/MIME/MIME.html
MIME—RFC 1521 and RFC 1522

http://www.cis.ohio-state.edu/hypertext/faq/usenet/mail/mime-faq/top.html
MIME FAQ

ftp://ftp.isi.edu/in-notes/iana/assignments/media-types/
Registered MIME media types

ftp://ftp.isi.edu/in-notes/iana/assignments/media-types/media-types
Complete listing of current registered MIME types

News, Weather, and Sports

http://nytimesfax.com
TimesFax

http://cnn.com
CNN Interactive

http://www.nando.net/nt/
The Nando Times

http://www.realaudio.com/contentp/abc.html
ABC News Reports

http://www.sjmercury.com/
Mercury Center Subscriptions

http://www.pathfinder.com/
Time Warner's PathFinder

http://www.intellicast.com
NBC Intellicast Weather

http://iwin.nws.noaa.gov/
Interactive Weather Information Network

http://www-geology.ucdavis.edu/eqmandr.html
Earthquake Information

http://cirrus.sprl.umich.edu/wxnet/
WeatherNet

http://ESPNET.SportsZone.com
ESPNET SportsZone

http://www.igolf.com
iGolf

http://www.audionet.com/audio211.htm
AudioNet Sports

http://www.nba.com/Theater/index.html
NBA Theater

http://qtvr1.quicktime.apple.com/duke/duke.html
Duke Basketball

http://www.tns.lcs.mit.edu/cgi-bin/sports
World Wide Web of Sports

Server Setup

http://home.mcom.com/comprod/server_central/test_drive.html
Netscape Server Central

http://www.proper.com/www/servers-chart.html
Web servers comparison

http://www.sgi.com/Products/WebFORCE/WebStone/FAQ-webstone.html
WebStone

http://www.ncsa.uiuc.edu/InformationServers/Performace/V1.4/report.html
Performance of several HTTP demons on an HP 735 workstation

http://home.mcom.com/comprod/server_central/performance_whitepaper.html
Netscape performance benchmark test

http://union.ncsa.uiuc.edu/HyperNews/get/www/log-analyzers.html
HTTPD log analyzers

http://web.sau.edu/~mkruse/mkstats/
MK-Stats: One of the more popular Perl analyzers

http://clubweb.ora.com/software/VBSTAT31A.ZIP
VB-Stats: Visual Basic tool for logfile analysis (binaries)

http://clubweb.ora.com/software/VBS31ASRC.ZIP
VB-Stats: Visual Basic tool for logfile analysis (source code)

F

`http://www.ics.uci.edu/WebSoft/MOMspider/`
MOMspider Web Robot

`http://www.amazing.com/internet/faq.html`
Internet Access Provider FAQ

Shockwave Sites

`http://www.macromedia.com/Gallery/`
The Interactive Gallery

`http://www.mcli.dist.maricopa.edu/director/shockwavelist.html`
Shockwave List o' Sites

`http://www.mcli.dist.maricopa.edu/alan/nojava/`
Alan's NoJava

`http://www.turntable.com:80/shockwave_plug/`
Turntable's Needle Drop

`http://www.toystory.com/toybox/shock.htm`
Toy Story game

`http://www.dmc.missouri.edu/shockwave/plan.html`
SPG Staff Blast

`http://www.mdmi.com/nomis.htm`
Nomis

`http://www.dreamlight.com/dreamlt/gallery/verttice.htm`
DreamLight Verttice

`http://www.mackerel.com/bubble.html`
Virtual Bubble Wrap

`http://www.hyperstand.com/shockwave`
New Media magazine

Software Archives

`http://cwsapps.fibr.net`
Stroud's Consummate Winsock Apps List

`http://www.teleport.com/~alano/coolhelp.html`
Cool Helpers Page

`http://wuarchive.wustl.edu/`
The Washington University Software Archive

`http://www.winsite.com/`
WinSite

`http://coyote.csusm.edu/cwis/winworld/winworld.html`
The CSUSM Windows Shareware Archive

`file://oak.oakland.edu/SimTel/`
SimTel

`ftp://mirrors.aol.com`
AOL Mirrors

`http://ftp.sunet.se/`
SUNET FTP archive

`http://www.shareware.com`
Shareware.com

Video Players

`http://quicktime.apple.com`
QuickTime

`http://www.vdolive.com`
VDOLive

`http://www.xingtech.com`
StreamWorks Video

Video Sites

`http://www.sony.com/Music/VideoStuff/VideoClips/index.html`
Music video clips

`http://www.acm.uiuc.edu/rml/Mpeg/`
Rob's Multimedia Lab

`http://www.best.com/~johnp/film.html`
MPEG Bizarre Film Festival

`http://www.synapse.net/~ob/welcome.htm`
Cartoon animations

F

Virtual Reality Sites

http://www.newtype.com/NewType/vr/index.htm
Virtual Reality Center

http://qtvr.quicktime.apple.com
QuickTime VR Home Page

http://www.netproductions.com/balcony/default.html
The Balcony

http://www.paperinc.com/wrls.html
Paper Software's Cool List of VRML Worlds

http://www.cybertown.com
Cybertown Virtual Freeway

http://www.neuro.sfc.keio.ac.jp/~aly/polygon/vrml/ika/
Interactive Origami

http://www.ocnus.com/models/mall.wrl
VRML Mall

http://www.tcp.ca/gsb/VRML/models/pc-win95sky.wrl
Virtual PC

http://www.hyperreal.com/~mpesce/circle.wrl
Zero Circle

VRML Renderers

http://www.chaco.com/vrscout/
VR Scout

http://www.cts.com/~template/WebSpace/monday.html
WebSpace

http://www.paperinc.com
WebFX plug-in

http://www.intervista.com
WorldView plug-in

http://www.ids-net.com
VRealm plug-in

http://www.dimensionx.com
Liquid Reality plug-in

APPENDIX

G

Quiz Answers

Chapter 1, "Building Your First Web"

1. FrontPage Explorer, the FrontPage Editor, and the FrontPage Personal Web Server.
2. Click on the Show FrontPage Explorer toolbar button.
3. The same way you enter and edit text in today's word processors.

Chapter 2, "Publishing Your Web"

1. It's a security precaution, because there is no ability to screen out CGI-BIN scripts.
2. Yes.
3. The root Web.

Chapter 3, "Web Publishing Basics: Text, Lists, and Links"

1. This is known as HTML, the programming language used to create Web pages.
2. You can create five list types: bulleted list, definition list, directory list, menu list, and numbered list.
3. A hyperlink to another Web page causes the Web browser to display the top of the page. A bookmark to a page causes the Web browser to jump to a certain point in the Web page.

Chapter 4, "Decorating and Expanding Your Web"

1. The different types of clip-art are Animations, Backgrounds, Bullets, Buttons, Icons, Lines, and Logos.
2. It's easier for users to look at an image and understand what it represents than to read text that describes it.
3. It makes it easier for you to keep track of what Web pages you have—and haven't—worked on. Additionally, when you complete a task, the time that the task was completed is used for record-keeping.

Chapter 5, "Adding Graphics to Your Web Page"

1. GIF.
2. Sprites.
3. Image maps.

Chapter 6, "Adding Tables to Your Web Page"

1. To present data in an well-organized manner, and to create unique page layouts with images.
2. HTML offers very little control to Web authors as to where images and text will be placed. Tables offer some control, because the Web author can define the size and shape of the table and its cells.
3. You should use a template when you're working on a large number of Web pages—either because you're a Web author for a company, or because your job is to help others create Web pages.

Chapter 7, "Including Frames in Your Web"

1. Frames enable the display of both the information (data) and the navigation tools (hyperlinks) at once.
2. Add or change the Web page used as an alternate for browsers that don't recognize frames in the Choose Alternate Content sheet.
3. Type the frame's name into the Current FrontPage Web sheet's Target Frame textbox and click on the OK button.

Chapter 8, "Adding Multimedia to Your Web Page"

1. You don't want large background sound files, because you'll slow down the user. The larger the file, the more time the user spends waiting for the file to be retrieved.

2. These applications are typically known as animation viewers. They can come in the form of a plug-in, an ActiveX control, or a Java applet.

3. The three ways a video file can be activated are: On File Open, On Mouse Over, or both.

Chapter 9, "Adding Forms and Other Interactive Elements"

1. Form fields are elements that exist only within a form. Forms themselves aren't shown, but form fields can be.

2. One-line textbox, scrolling textbox, checkbox, radio button, drop-down menu, pushbutton, and image.

3. To be able to process user response to that particular form field.

Chapter 10, "Tying It Together with Scripts"

1. One of the major characteristics with VBScript and JavaScript is that they are both event-driven. Another major characteristic with both scripting languages is the capability of tying HTML elements together.

2. Scripts recognize form elements as an object when an event occurs. Typically, this is when the form input is submitted by the user.

3. You can easily tie script code with form fields.

Chapter 11, "Adding Java Applets and ActiveX Controls"

1. Java applets have the extension of CLASS.

2. One reason for using Microsoft Form 2.0 ActiveX controls, instead of HTML form fields, is security. ActiveX controls include code signing so that users can be sure that the controls they use are safe.

3. ActiveX controls run both as miniprograms and as components. They can be run by themselves as miniprograms when referred to by Web pages. However, ActiveX controls can also refer to other controls, thereby making them components.

Chapter 12, "Managing Your Web"

1. No. Once you delete a Web, it's gone forever.
2. No. You can only export the currently selected file in the Web.
3. Finding words and general spell checking.

Chapter 13, "Connecting Your Web to a Database"

1. One major benefit of using ODBC is that as long as your database scheme does not change, you can use any other database management system that is supported by ODBC.
2. HTML Extension.
3. The Database Connector Wizard helps you manage Internet Database Connector (IDC) files.

Chapter 14, "Using WebBots with an Extended Server"

1. The Confirmation Field and Search WebBots both depend heavily on the Extended Web server. These two WebBots in particular most closely resemble common CGI scripts.
2. There are three WebBots that aren't available through the WebBot selection dialog box.
3. Because these three WebBots aren't interpreted by FrontPage, they behave exactly the same on a non-Extended Server machine.

G

APPENDIX

H

What's on the CD-ROM

On the *Teach Yourself Microsoft FrontPage 97 in a Week* CD-ROM, you will find all the sample files that have been presented in this book, along with a wealth of other applications and utilities.

NOTE

Please refer to the readme.wri file on the CD-ROM for the latest listing of software.

FrontPage Software Developer's Kit

☐ SDK for FrontPage 1.1 and 97

Explorer

☐ Microsoft Internet Explorer v3.01 for Windows 95 and NT 4

HTML Tools

☐ Microsoft Internet Assistants for Access, Excel, PowerPoint, Schedule+, and Word
☐ W3e HTML Editor
☐ CSE 3310 HTML Validator
☐ Hot Dog 32-bit HTML editor demo
☐ HoTMetaL HTML editor demo
☐ HTMLed HTML editor
☐ HTML Assistant for Windows
☐ Spider 1.2 demo
☐ Web Analyzer demo
☐ WebEdit Pro HTML editor demo
☐ Web Weaver HTML editor
☐ ImageGen

Graphics, Video, and Sound Applications

☐ Goldwave sound editor, player, and recorder
☐ MapThis imagemap utility
☐ MPEG2PLY MPEG viewer
☐ MPEGPLAY MPEG viewer
☐ Paint Shop Pro 3.12
☐ SnagIt
☐ ThumbsPlus

H

ActiveX

☐ Microsoft ActiveX Control Pad and HTML Layout Control

Java

☐ Sun's Java Developer's Kit for Windows 95/NT, version 1.0.2

☐ Sample Java Applets

☐ Sample JavaScripts

☐ Trial version of Jamba for Windows 95/NT

☐ Jpad IDE

☐ JPad Pro Java IDE demo

☐ Kawa IDE

☐ Studio J++ demo

☐ Javelin IDE demo

☐ JDesigner Pro database wizard for Java

CGI

☐ CGI*StarDuo and CGI*StarDuo95

☐ CGI PerForm command language interpreter for Common Gateway Interface (CGI) application design

☐ Several sample CGI scripts and libraries

Perl

☐ Perl Version 5

Servers

☐ Microsoft Internet Information Server

☐ EMWAC servers

☐ Apache Web server

☐ CERN Web server

Utilities

- [ ] Microsoft Viewers for Excel, PowerPoint, and Word
- [ ] Adobe Acrobat viewer
- [ ] Microsoft PowerPoint Animation Player & Publisher
- [ ] WinZip for Windows NT/95
- [ ] WinZip Self-Extractor

About This Software

Some of the software on this CD is shareware. Shareware is not free. Please read all documentation associated with a third-party product (usually contained with files named readme.txt or license.txt) and follow all guidelines.

INDEX

A

Microsoft FrontPage 97 Unleashed, Second Edition

William Stanek

FrontPage 97 works directly with the the Microsoft Office 97 suite of products. Its built-in WYSIWYG (What You See Is What You Get) editor is the best and most popular Web authoring tool on the market. Web publishing is now open to the millions of Office 97 registered users, thus increasing market potential. New and experienced FrontPage users need this book to show them how to use the new version's power to add multimedia, sound, animation, and Office 97 documents to a Web site. CD-ROM contains all the examples, built-in templates, Web publishing resources, and more. Covers FrontPage 97.

$49.99 USA/$70.95 CDN
ISBN: 1-57521-226-9

User Level: Accomplished - Expert
1,000 pp.

Teach Yourself Microsoft Office 97 in 24 Hours

Greg Perry

An estimated 22 million people use Microsoft Office, and with the new features of Office 97, much of that market will want the upgrade. To address that need, Sams has published a mass-market version of its best-selling *Teach Yourself* series. *Teach Yourself Microsoft Office 97 in 24 Hours* shows readers how to use the most widely requested features of Office. This entry-level title includes many illustrations, screen shots, and a step-by-step plan to learning Office 97. Teaches how to use each Office product and how to use all of them together. Readers learn how to create documents in Word that include hypertext links to files created with one of the other Office products.

$19.99 USA/$28.95 CDN
ISBN: 0-672-31009-0

User Level: New - Casual - Accomplished
450 pp.

Microsoft Office 97 Unleashed

Paul McFedries and Sue Charlesworth

Microsoft has brought the Web to its Office suite of products. Hyperlinking, Office Assistants, and Active Document Support enable users to publish documents to the Web or an intranet site. They also completely integrate with Microsoft FrontPage, making it possible to point-and-click a Web page into existence. This book details each of the Office products—Excel, Access, PowerPoint, Word, and Outlook—and shows the estimated 22 million registered users how to create presentations and Web documents. Shows how to extend Office to work on a network. Describes the various Office Solution Kits and how to use them. CD-ROM includes powerful utilities and two best-selling books in HTML format.

$35.00 USA/$49.95 CDN
ISBN: 0-672-31010-4

User Level: Accomplished - Expert
1,200 pp.

Teach Yourself Access 97 in 14 Days, Fourth Edition

Paul Cassel

Through the examples, workshop sessions, and Q&A sections in this book, users will master the most important features of Access. In just two weeks, they'll be able to develop their own databases and create stunning forms and reports. Updated for Access 97. Covers wizards, tables, data types, validation, forms, queries, artificial fields, macros, and more. Readers learn how to program with Access Basic and Access lingo.

$29.99 USA/$42.95 CDN
ISBN: 0-672-30969-6

User Level: New - Casual
700 pp.

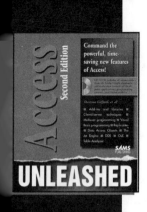

Access 97 Unleashed, Second Edition

Dwayne Gifford, et al.

Access, one of Microsoft's database managers for Windows, has become one of the most accepted standards of database management for personal computers. The *Unleashed* format for this book allows current and new users to find the information they need on the new features quickly and easily. It also serves as a complete reference for database programmers new to Access. Readers learn advanced techniques for working with tables, queries, forms, and data. Shows how to program Access and how to integrate the database with the Internet. CD-ROM includes Access utilities and applications and an electronic Access reference library.

$49.99 USA/$70.95 CDN　　　　*User Level: Accomplished - Expert*
ISBN: 0-672-30983-1　　　　　　*1,100 pp*

Laura Lemay's Web Workshop: Microsoft FrontPage

Laura Lemay & Denise Tyler

This is a hands-on guide to maintaining Web pages with Microsoft's FrontPage. Written in the clear, conversational style of Laura Lemay, it is packed with many interesting, colorful examples that demonstrate specific tasks of interest to the reader. Teaches how to maintain Web pages with FrontPage. Includes all the templates, backgrounds, and materials needed on the CD-ROM!

$39.99 USA/$56.95 CDN　　　　*User Level: Casual - Accomplished*
ISBN: 1-57521-149-1　　　　　　*672 pp.*

Laura Lemay's Web Workshop: Graphics and Web Page Design

Laura Lemay, Jon M. Duff, & James L. Mohler

With the number of Web pages increasing daily, only the well-designed will stand out and grab the attention of those browsing the Web. This book illustrates, in classic Laura Lemay style, how to design attractive Web pages that will be visited over and over again. CD-ROM contains HTML editors, graphics software, and royalty-free graphics and sound files. Teaches beginning and advanced level design principles. Covers the Internet.

$55.00 USA/$77.95 CDN　　　　*User Level: Accomplished*
ISBN: 1-57521-125-4　　　　　　*500 pp.*

The Internet Unleashed, 1997 Edition

Jill Ellsworth, et al.

The Internet Unleashed, 1997 Edition is the definitive bible for Internet users everywhere. This comprehensive guide stakes out new ground as it details the hottest Internet tools and upcoming technologies. Written by the world's top experts in Internet fields, this book provides improved coverage of common tools and takes a futuristic look at the Internet of tomorrow. Includes over 200 pages of an easy-to-use, well-organized listing of the top 1,000 resources on the Internet. Covers the World Wide Web browsers, Internet commerce, and Internet virtual reality. CD-ROM contains all the software needed to get connected to the Internet—regardless of computing platform—Windows 3.1, Windows 95, Macintosh, and UNIX.

$49.99 USA/$70.95 CDN　　　　*User Level: Intermediate - Advanced*
ISBN: 1-57521-185-8　　　　　　*1,200 pp.*

Add to Your Sams.net Library Today
with the Best Books for Internet Technologies

ISBN	Quantity	Description of Item	Unit Cost	Total Cost
1-57521-226-9		Microsoft FrontPage 97 Unleashed, Second Edition (Book/CD-ROM)	$49.99	
0-672-31009-0		Teach Yourself Microsoft Office 97 in 24 Hours	$19.99	
0-672-31010-4		Microsoft Office 97 Unleashed (Book/CD-ROM)	$35.00	
0-672-30969-6		Teach Yourself Access 97 in 14 Days, Fourth Edition	$29.99	
0-672-30983-1		Access 97 Unleashed, Second Edition (Book/CD-ROM)	$49.99	
1-57521-149-1		Laura Lemay's Web Workshop: Microsoft FrontPage (Book/CD-ROM)	$39.99	
1-57521-125-4		Laura Lemay's Web Workshop: Graphics and Web Page Design (Book/CD-ROM)	$55.00	
1-57521-004-5		The Internet Business Guide, Second Edition	$25.00	
1-57521-185-8		The Internet Unleashed, 1997 Edition (Book/CD-ROM)	$49.99	
		Shipping and Handling: See information below.		
		TOTAL		

Shipping and Handling: $4.00 for the first book, and $1.75 for each additional book. If you need to have it NOW, we can ship product to you in 24 hours for an additional charge of approximately $18.00, and you will receive your item overnight or in two days. Overseas shipping and handling adds $2.00. Prices subject to change. Call between 9:00 a.m. and 5:00 p.m. EST for availability and pricing information on latest editions.

201 W. 103rd Street, Indianapolis, Indiana 46290

1-800-428-5331 — Orders   1-800-835-3202 — Fax   1-800-858-7674 — Customer Service

Book ISBN 1-57521-225-0

Its Time Has Come Today.

WEB Publisher
THE INTERNET DESIGN MAGAZINE

You want to make your Web site sizzle, sparkle, pulsate, and rotate. You want to make the world go **WOW!** Last week you couldn't do it, and today you *have* to. Now the tools are here. And *Web Publisher* can help you escape the random chaos that change brings.

Catch the Premiere Issue of *Web Publisher*. It's the first magazine of its kind, with product reviews and shootouts, how-to tips, web publishing strategies, and commentary. Devoted to graphic artists and content creators for enhancing the way you publish on the World Wide Web, it's a dynamic source of information whose time has come.

Each month, *Web Publisher* includes:

- ◆ Features and Commentary
- ◆ Page Design Tips Graphics Tips
- ◆ Creating 3D Graphics and Virtual Worlds
- ◆ Animation
- ◆ Typographical Landscapes
- ◆ Product Reviews and Shootouts
- ◆ And all you need to build hot Web sites without programming

Today's your day!
Start your three-month trial subscription with no cost or obligation.

In the U.S. call 800-884-6367; outside the U.S. call 916-686-6610, or fax 916-686-8497. Please ask for offer SAMS9001. Or, sign up online—visit the *Web Publisher* Test Drive Page at http://www.web-publisher.com.

Evolution/Revolution

Free Three-Month Trial Subscription
Yes! I want to make the world go wow!
Sign me up for a free three-month trial subscription to *Web Publisher*, the Internet Design Magazine.
If I like what I see, I'll renew my subscription for the low price of only $29.95* for 12 issues.
No strings attached and no invoices will be sent.

Name_____

Company_____

Address _____

City/State/Zip_____
(City/Province/Postal Code)

Country_____ E-Mail _____

Phone _____ FAX _____

*International rates: $34.95/year to Canada, $54.95/year to Mexico, $59.95/year to all other countries.   **SAMS9001**
Informant Communications Group ■ 10519 E Stockton Blvd, Ste 100 ■ Elk Grove, CA 95624-9703

A VIACOM SERVICE

The Information SuperLibrary™

Bookstore

Search

What's New

Reference

Software

Newsletter

Company Overviews

Yellow Pages

Internet Starter Kit

HTML Workshop

Win a Free T-Shirt!

Macmillan Computer Publishing

Site Map

Talk to Us

CHECK OUT THE BOOKS IN THIS LIBRARY.

You'll find thousands of shareware files and over 1600 computer books designed for both technowizards and technophobes. You can browse through 700 sample chapters, get the latest news on the Net, and find just about anything using our

We're open 24-hours a day, 365 days a year.

You don't need a card.

We don't charge fines.

And you can be as LOUD as you want.

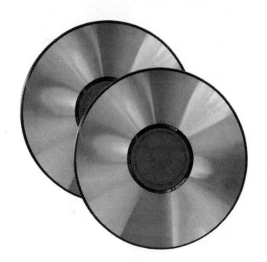

Installing the CD-ROM

The companion CD-ROM contains all the source code and project files developed by the authors, plus an assortment of evaluation versions of third-party products. To install, please follow these steps:

Windows 95/NT 4 Installation Instructions

1. Insert the CD-ROM into your CD-ROM drive.
2. From the Windows 95/NT 4 desktop, double-click on the My Computer icon.
3. Double-click on the icon representing your CD-ROM drive.
4. Double-click on the icon titled setup.exe to run the CD-ROM installation program.

Windows NT 3.51 Installation Instructions

1. Insert the CD-ROM into your CD-ROM drive.
2. From File Manager or Program Manager, choose Run from the File menu.
3. Type `<drive>\setup` and press Enter, where `<drive>` corresponds to the drive letter of your CD-ROM. For example, if your CD-ROM is drive D:, type `D:\SETUP` and press Enter.

Follow the on-screen instructions.

NOTE

> Windows NT 3.51 users will be unable to access the \WIN95NT4 directory because it was left in its original long filename state with a combination of upper- and lowercase. This was done to allow Windows 95 and Windows NT 4 users direct access to those files on the CD-ROM. All other directories were translated in compliance with the Windows NT 3.51 operating system and may be accessed without trouble. (Attempting to access the \WIN95NT4 directory will cause no harm; it simply will not allow you to read the contents.)